The World of the Worker

OTHER BOOKS BY JAMES R. GREEN

The South End: A Boston 200 Neighborhood History (1976)

*Grass-Roots Socialism: Radical Movements
in the Southwest, 1895–1943* (1978)

Boston's Workers: A Labor History (1979)
co-author Hugh Carter Donahue

THE WORLD OF
THE WORKER

Labor in Twentieth-Century America

James R. Green

UNIVERSITY OF ILLINOIS PRESS
Urbana and Chicago

To my parents and my grandparents

First Illinois paperback, 1998
© 1980, 1998 by James R. Green
Reprinted by arrangement with the author
Manufactured in the United States of America

∞This book is printed on acid-free paper.

Library of Congress Cataloging-in-Publication Data

Green, James R., 1914–
The world of the worker : labor in twentieth-century America /
James R. Green
p.   cm.
Originally published: New York : Hill and Wang, 1980 in series:
American century series.
Includes bibliographical references (p.   ) and index.
ISBN 10: 0-252-06734-7 (pbk. : alk. paper)
ISBN 13: 978-0-252-06734-1
1. Working class—United States—History—20th century. 2.
Trade-unions—United States—History. I. Title.
HD8072.G783 1998
331.'0973—dc211   97-47713
CIP

University of Illinois Press
1325 South Oak Street
Champaign, Illinois 61820-6903
www.press.uillinois.edu

Contents

Preface to the 1998 Paperback Edition

In the first few years after *The World of the Worker* appeared in 1980 the trends outlined in its final chapter led to increased pressures on working people and a greater crisis for organized labor. However, in the late 1980s and in the 1990s the union movement rallied strongly, as members became more active and aggressive and officials implemented serious changes.

To some commentators the disappearance of unions in many communities, along with the extinction of the industries those unions supported, brought labor history to an end. To these critics, the labor movement has no future. Like the Industrial Revolution and the Great Depression, worker struggle is part of our past. To others, including workers still in need of protection and representation, and especially to those dedicated to reviving and radicalizing the union movement, labor history has gained new relevance and importance, far more than I believed possible in 1980. Indeed, the critical perspectives on organized labor that initially aroused some controversy seem less objectionable today as union leaders, rank-and-file members, and managers look more critically at past policies and practices and try to understand what went wrong and what worked.

When this book went out of print, trade union students, among many others, requested a new edition that included discussion of developments during the final two decades of this century. Updating *The World of the Worker* is an urgent but demanding task. So, while I struggle with summarizing the dramatic events of recent labor history, the University of Illinois Press has agreed to publish a new paperback edition of the original 1980 text, which, I hope, identifies adequately the issues and challenges working people and their unions have faced in this period.

A revised version of this book would be based on the impressive outpouring of important scholarship since 1980, a fitting answer to the call made by the pioneers of the new labor history such as David Brody, Herbert Gutman, Alice Kessler-Harris, and David Montgomery in the 1960s and 1970s. *The World of the Worker* was an early response to their ideas, an attempted synthesis of the new and the old labor history, one that aimed to integrate social and cultural history with institutional history.

In a new version I would also reconsider some aspects of my interpretation and recompose some aspects of the story based on new research and on the intense interpretive debates that have taken place among labor historians about the role of the law and state power, the effects of management and labor market strategies imposed by employers, and race, class, gender, and ethnic identities.

A revised edition will be challenging and time consuming, but I will probably not alter drastically the perspective and narrative structure of the original work, now available to readers once again thanks to this university press, which stands alone in its effort to make labor history available to the public.

Preface to the 1980 Edition

Traditionally, labor history has centered on notable leaders like Samuel Gompers of the American Federation of Labor and John L. Lewis of the United Mine Workers. These men have a place in this account, but my main emphasis is on the relationship between the leaders and the masses of workers. Debates about labor leadership and misleadership ignore the fact that most of the important breakthroughs in labor history, notably the great industrial union upsurges of the 1910's and the 1930's, originated at the base. By taking a rank-and-file approach, I hope to emphasize the creativity and tenacity of ordinary workers acting together with leaders of their own choosing.

A labor history from the bottom up is now within reach because of new studies produced by social historians which uncover the hidden history of workplaces and working-class communities. The new social history, when combined with older studies of workers' group life, offers the kind of information we need to understand the dynamics and structural bases of labor militancy and organization Of course, a view from below is only one angle of vision. A one-dimensional approach to worker militancy leaves many questions unanswered, notably: why was that militancy invariably repressed, deflected, or channeled into bureaucratic organizations?

To answer this question, we need a dialectical approach which accounts for the challenge of the rank-and-file and response of leadership. The approach must be historical and not static, so that we can explain the specific events that led to the containment or incorporation of militancy. Otherwise, we are left with overdetermined sociological theories like the "iron law of oligarchy" which imply that labor organizations must inevitably be undemocratic.

In addition to adopting this approach, we seek to place labor history in a wider context. The internal dynamics of labor-union development have been decisively affected by depressions and wars, as well as by long-term changes in the labor market, the structure and organization of work, and the social composition of the labor force. Strikes and union struggles must also be seen in their local setting, because community support from families, relatives, and middle-class allies often determined the outcome. Labor policies and strategies developed by government and the state also require close attention, and a dialectical approach. The forces just mentioned created the conditions under which the House of Labor was constructed, but within this framework, workers made their own history.

One theme of special importance, the struggle for control, runs through the book. By control I do not necessarily mean ownership of the means of production, but rather the freedom to determine certain activities in the workplace. If workers were free to take extra time off without punishment, they exercised some control over their time. If employers could arbitrarily lengthen the workday without fear of opposition from the workers, they exercised an important kind of control. By showing that a struggle for control existed throughout the century, I do not mean to imply that workers have always been fighting to seize full control over the means of production. At times, notably during the second decade of the century, revolutionaries did call for the abolition of private property and the creation of a worker-dominated economy. And these ideas won some fleeting support within the labor movement, but this country lacks a revolutionary working-class tradition, like the one created by the Russian soviets or the Italian workers' councils.

Struggles for control have nonetheless taken place throughout the twentieth century, from strikes to win union-dominated hiring halls to attempts to form shop committees with decision-making power. At times, these struggles were largely defensive in nature, like the miners' fight to defend their traditional or customary right to work free of supervision. Often the skilled workers' struggle to preserve craft control was not generalized to others. But when skilled workmen did ally themselves with the unskilled, as in the United Mine Workers, radical questions were usually about the private control of industry. As Carter Goodrich noted in *The Frontier of Control,* workers' struggles that question management authority are of the highest importance in studying the "control problem," and they are inherently political. The fight against being controlled disagreeably has sometimes escalated to a demand that workers be free of any control or that they take a hand in deciding control issues.

In short, my concern is not to establish a revolutionary tradition where one does not exist, but rather to describe conflict over power and authority where it did exist. These conflicts have been continuous throughout the twentieth century and provide us with entry points for studying the hidden history of the workplace. Socialists, Communists, and other radicals have generally failed to politicize the struggle for control, partly because so often they came in as outsiders. But it seems to me that the only solution to the conflict and alienation that still characterize the workplace is the achievement of workers' control and industrial democracy. Radical intellectuals have helped to articulate these ideas and to employ them in making various demands, but the ideas come from the workers. They have been tested in countless workplaces for several generations.

It is important to take an approach that extends beyond the House of Labor to the wider world of the worker, because throughout this century most workers have not enjoyed union protection. Even at their peak strength in the mid-1950's, labor unions only included about one quarter of the paid labor force. We can now take a broader view of this world because of the insights into working-class life recently offered by ethnic and black studies, women's studies, and the new urban and social history. This book attempts to portray workers' lives beyond the union hall, the strike meeting, and the political campaign.

The opening chapter describes two very different early-twentieth-century settings, so that we may see how workers lived on a day-to-day basis. First, the classic company town, dominated by a large corporation. Second, the urban ghetto, the colorful Lower East Side of New York City. We look closely at workers' social and cultural lives, at their workplace and family experiences, and at the influence of their Old World habits and traditions. Finally, we explore the ways in which union organization and political activity differed in these two settings.

This study returns to these issues, but in less detail. It traces two trends of particular importance in social history: the growing participation of women, married and single, in the paid labor force, and the great exodus of black people from the rural South to the industrial cities. Both had great implications for working-class life in this century. We can clearly see that employers used sexism and racism in segregating the labor market and in dividing workers in other ways. But, it is more difficult to provide a comprehensive explanation of how the world of the worker has been affected by changes in family structure and kin relations, or in community structure and race relations. The new social history offers some insight into the effect of these changes, but generalizations are still difficult to make.

I have no doubt that a full social and cultural history of the modern working class will be written. In the meantime, I hope that this book will raise some new questions about the old labor history. I also hope that it makes good use of the new social history to enhance our understanding of the rich and varied world of the worker in the twentieth century.

J.R.G.
Boston, March 3, 1980

Acknowledgments

First, I would like to thank my publisher, Arthur W. Wang, and my editor, Eric Foner, for asking me to write this book, and for sustaining me with patient encouragement and constructive criticism. Many of the interpretations and perspectives in this study have been developed through my work with the *Radical America* editorial collective. When I became an editor in 1972, *RA* had already published many good articles on working people's history from socialist and feminist perspectives. In the past eight years the journal has published many more and I have learned a great deal by working with its contributors. I am particularly indebted to several of the *Radical America* editors, who have helped me to clarify my thinking about working-class history. Frank Brodhead, Margery Davies, Linda Gordon, Allen Hunter, and Ann Withorn have been especially helpful. So have *Radical America* associate editors Staughton Lynd and Stan Weir. Their work as activists, historians, and students of the workplace has been most instructive. There is another *RA* editor who deserves special thanks. Jim O'Brien read the entire manuscript and made many important interpretive and editorial suggestions.

I have also learned from other historians interested in the meaning of twentieth-century workers' history. I have worked with many of them in the Radical Historians' Organization and more recently in the Massachusetts History Workshop. For reading this manuscript and making useful comments, I would like to thank these fellow workers in the labor-history shop: Jeremy Brecher, Sue Benson, Alan Dawley, Melvyn Dubofsky, Paul Faler, Nelson Lichtenstein, David Montgomery, Mark Naison, and Susan Reverby. Thanks also to my friends in Massachusetts labor unions who gave me their views on the book: Jim Bollen, Frank Kashner, and Irene Ryan. I am also indebted to Michele McMills, editor of *1397 Rank & File,* the United Steelworkers of America local newspaper at Homestead, Pennsylvania.

I appreciate the assistance of a number of people at the University of Massachusetts, Boston, especially Paul Rosenkrantz and other members of the Faculty Grants and Development Committee, who provided the support I needed to finish a draft of the manuscript. I am also indebted to my friends at the College of Public and Community Service, notably Marilyn Metro, who typed the manuscript with skill and a good sense of humor, and Ann Doughty, who surveyed some of the recent sociological literature. Arthur MacEwan and Jim Campen of the University of Massachusetts Economics Department and *Dollars and Sense* magazine also offered useful information and advice.

Finally, I want to acknowledge the support of my family. More than anyone else, my wife, Carol McLaughlin-Green, knew how important and how difficult it was for me to do this work. And, more than anyone else, she helped to see me through it. Much of what I have learned about the world of work I have learned from my parents and grandparents, whose working lives spanned the years described here.

The World of the Worker

1

The Company Town and the Urban Ghetto

The world of the worker in 1900 varied enormously. It encompassed stark mining camps on the Rocky Mountain slopes as well as primitive lumber and turpentine camps in the Deep South where blacks toiled like slaves. It included densely packed immigrant ghettos from San Francisco's Chinatown to New York City's multi-ethnic Lower East Side, where men, women, and children worked together in tenements and sweatshops. There were small company towns owned by family firms, and there were large company towns like Lawrence, Massachusetts, and Homestead, Pennsylvania, each controlled by a giant corporation. There were also small, closely knit communities in which skilled workers still exercised some real control over their own life and labor. Despite this variety, the world of the worker was still sharply distinguished from the world of the business class. Nineteenth-century industrialization had created a permanent class of proletarians who lived in a world far removed from those who did not have to sell their labor to survive.

In 1900, 15.9 million people labored in industry and 11.0 million on the farms. Some rural areas of the Northeast and Midwest suffered population loss as country folk migrated to the city. It was a time of explosive growth for the industrial metropolis. Chicago more than tripled in size between 1880 and 1900, when it had a population of more than a million and a half. New York's population leapt to 3½ million in those two decades. Buffalo, Detroit, and Milwaukee more than doubled in size.

The demand for cheap labor grew insatiable as industrial production surged after the terrible depression of the 1890's. By 1900, 4.5 million people worked in manufacturing alone, up from 2.7 million in 1870. In Northern industry the demand for labor had been filled largely by the great migration from Northwestern Europe during the mid-nineteenth century. By 1900, these "old stock" immigrants had established communities around the country. Some had prospered as farmers and businessmen, many remained industrial workers. Indeed, large numbers, like the Boston Irish, still labored in low-paying, unskilled jobs by the turn of the century. In some cases, the foreign-born dominated whole industries, like the British in mining and the Germans in brewing. Old-stock immigrants had also made their mark in many of the skilled trades, where they often outnumbered the native-born Yankees. In 1900, the Germans were the largest foreign-born group in the United States, with over 2 million, followed by the Irish. Then came the Canadians—English- and French-speaking—and the British—from Wales, Scotland, and Ulster, as well as England. The Scandinavian immigrants were close behind the British.

Though workingmen of old immigrant stock dominated many trades and occupations by 1900, their labor had not fully met the employers' demand. The proportion of women in the labor force jumped from 15 percent in 1880 to nearly 25 percent at the turn of the century. Most of the women working for wages in 1900 were single (nearly 6 million), but the number of working wives had grown significantly to 769,000. These women workers did not compete with men. In fact, sex segregation of the labor force had increased by 1900. Women in the textile, clothing, tobacco, and shoe industries worked almost entirely in unskilled occupations. The largest number of women still toiled as domestics. Those in the professions were confined more than ever to two occupations, elementary-school teaching and nursing.

Women earned much less than men in the same industries, and remained dependent on their parents or husbands for support. In fact, nearly half of all women, including the majority of blacks, still lived on farms, where they engaged in the traditional sunup to sundown routine of housekeeping and child rearing, combined with home production and agricultural labor. In the industrial cities, women still put in most of their hours at home, supplementing the family economy by taking in boarders and doing laundry and other forms of homework with their children. Women who worked for wages outside the home also had to maintain the household and manage the family budget.

Domestic ideology emphasized women's primary role as mothers, but housework kept them working "longer and harder than men," as Charlotte Perkins Gilman noted in *Women and Economics* (1898).

In the New South, where industrialization took place largely without immigrant labor, factories attracted poor whites and blacks from farms, on which they toiled in semi-serfdom. Black men were driven from many of the skilled trades and relegated mostly to poor-paid jobs in the Southern extractive and railroad industries. By exploiting the poor whites' long-standing fear of emancipated blacks, Southern industrialists kept wages low. The Knights of Labor and a few other labor unions brought blacks and whites together to struggle for common goals, but, on the whole, employers segregated workers by race and through skillfully exploited racism. In the textile industry, the owners reserved mill jobs for whites and used the threat of black competition to keep wages down. As a result, growth was based largely on the labor of women and children driven into the mills and shops to supplement the low wages earned by men.

In the North, women and children also worked in the mills and the shops, but rural labor was more difficult to exploit. The growing demand for labor in Northern industry was met largely by the new immigrants from Eastern and Southern Europe. By 1910, the foreign-born population from these countries outnumbered the old immigrant population. Unlike their predecessors, these new immigrants found it difficult to apply their agricultural and artisan skills in the New World. They entered the factories, mills, and mines largely as unskilled laborers. As a result, the Northern labor market in 1900 was nearly as segregated by nationality as the Southern labor market was by race. By 1910, employers had met their demands for cheap labor by hiring immigrants to such an extent that in twenty-one major industries, at least 58 percent of the workers were foreign-born.

The ethnic composition of the working class differed considerably by region and by industry. Race, nationality, and gender corresponded to occupational differences. The percentage of skilled workers in the industrial labor force fell slightly from about 19 percent in 1890 to about 17 percent in 1900, but these jobs remained the province of white men of native-born or old immigrant stock. The black building tradesmen in Southern cities, the skilled women shoe stitchers in New England, the East European garment cutters in New York were the exception. Most blacks, women, and new immigrants toiled in unskilled or semi-skilled jobs. Segregation in society was replicated in the labor market and the workplace. These oppressed groups, therefore, suffered from wage discrimination, and were forced to rely on the whole family as an income-producing unit. It was not surprising, then, that the differential between the earnings of the skilled and unskilled workers widened in the early twentieth century. The wages of the first group advanced 74 percent between 1890 and 1914, the wages of the second group by only 31 percent. As we shall see in Chapter 2, the exclusionary policies of many trade unions helped to preserve these divisions within the working class.

The demand for cheap labor reached new levels after the depression of the mid-1890's ended. Innovations in transportation and communication made it possible for manufacturers to reach vast new markets at home and abroad. The return of prosperity, the growth of cities, and the expansion of the United States as a world power helped create new demands for industrial production. Two forms of production—steel and the clothing industry—affected the world of the worker in different ways.

The steel industry provides a good example of how corporate capitalists attempted to gain control of the labor process. Steel manufacturers used collusive trade agreements and corporate mergers to dominate the market and eliminate smaller competitors. The new corporations they created were threatened by the Sherman Anti-Trust Act, but many of these big capitalists saw government regulation as a way of stabilizing the industry to their advantage. Following the lead of steel magnate Andrew Carnegie, manufacturers employed new technology along with new marketing and management tactics to increase productivity and profitability. They vastly expanded the scale of their operations, constructing huge, multi-plant facilities. In 1870, only a few factories employed over five hundred workers. By 1900, over a thousand employed between five hundred and a thousand. And three mammoth steelmaking facilities in Pennsylvania, including the works Carnegie built at Homestead, employed eight thousand to ten thousand. In order to make full use of new technology and meet new production demands, it was necessary to break the power of the skilled iron- and steelworkers. Again, Carnegie took the lead, defeating the workers' craft union during the Homestead strike of 1892.

The U.S. Steel Corporation, formed by finance capitalist J. P. Morgan, incorporated Carnegie's operations in a giant merger and led the way in transforming the steelworkers' world. A close look at this experience shows how the position of the skilled worker was further eroded by new technology and management tactics, how the social and political organization of the company town helped to control the steelworkers, how new immigrants were employed to add stability, and how the work force was restructured to reduce labor costs.

The steelworkers' experience was not typical but it was a forerunner of developments in production controlled by large corporations. By focusing on the lives of unskilled Slavic workmen, we can see the new ways in which corporate employers manipulated the international labor market. Unlike the old immigrants, the newcomers from Eastern and Southern Europe (often single men) intended to return home. The Slavic steelworkers were, to use Frank Thistlewaite's term, "globe-trotting proletarians" who moved back and forth across the Atlantic on a seasonal and cyclical basis. Like the Afro-Americans and Mexican-Americans who came later to work in the mills, these new immigrants were transients. They were attracted to the United States by the lure of higher wages or pushed out of their homelands by oppressive conditions. But they were systematically recruited by corporate employers anxious to exploit their labor when it was needed and to send them home when production was slack.

The social and political implications of this transiency among the new immigrants are interesting. In general, more settled proletarians with families and community roots were more likely to organize effectively against their employers' demands. The new immigrants were not as docile and tractable even at first as the industrialists expected, but their protests were sporadic and were quickly defeated. When the Slavic immigrants did settle permanently in the Pennsylvania steel towns, they became the backbone of industrial unionism, just as they had been in the coal-mining towns.

New York's Lower East Side was not a typical urban ghetto. It was a mosaic of ethnic neighborhoods made up of the largest, most diverse immigrant groups in the world. Many residents of this district were typical "birds of passage," but not the East European Jews, who came as permanent settlers, refugees from anti-Semitism and Tsarist oppression. They came to stay and they brought with them radical ideas and organizing strategies, and these immigrants helped make the Lower East Side a hotbed of militant unionism and socialism.

The Lower East Side, like the Pennsylvania steel towns, produced a rich literature which illuminates the lives of its working people. The stories of the urban ghetto provide us with a different view from those of a company town like Homestead. Unlike the steelworkers, the immigrant clothing workers of the East Side could take advantage of the competitive conditions in their industry to advance their struggle for control and dignity. Working conditions in the labor-intensive needle trades differed from those in a capital-intensive, large-scale industry like steel, in which capitalists used modern machinery and scientific management to transform the labor process. These conditions had differing effects on family and community life. In the steel town, only the men worked for wages, but in the urban ghetto single and married women as well as children had to supplement the family income. The rich literature of the Lower East Side offers insights into the family economy and how it was orgainzed.

Striking differences existed between life in a company town and in an urban ghetto. Still, workers in both places shared common experiences. Steelworkers and clothing workers alike toiled in a world of wage dependency. They and their families lived in constant fear of wage cuts and layoffs, accidents and poor health. They worked in an autocratic world in which the authority of the boss could only be questioned at great risk. In 1900, few workers in either industry enjoyed union protection. America was a land of democracy, but there was no democracy on the job. The immigrants, whether Slavic furnacemen or Jewish garment workers, also experienced the common pain of adjusting to life in a frightening new land. These newcomers lived between two worlds: the old world of peasant and artisan work habits and a new world of modern machinery and industrial discipline; the old world of village communalism and the new world of urban violence and disorder; the old world of patriarchal familism and the new world of individualism and familial strain. The process of adjustment for the immigrant was painful; it was not a process of assimilation but rather of resistance and adaptation.

Workers had virtually no control over the economic and political institutions that dominated their cities, though they did maintain some community control through their family and kin networks, ethnic lodges, saloons, benefit societies, political and theatrical groups, churches and synagogues. Corporate welfare reformers opposed some of these institutions, like the benefit societies, because they allowed for worker autonomy, while urban social workers opposed others, like saloons, because they bred undisciplined, lawless behavior. The workers, however, maintained these autonomous institutions because they affirmed traditional forms of familism and communalism in a world governed by individualism and privatism, and because they offered some security and sociability in a workaday world with little of either. Their rich group life not only provided a fleeting escape from arduous jobs; it provided a way by which working people could exert some control over the painful process of entering the urban, industrial world.

The United States steel industry in the 1890's and early 1900's offers an excellent example of struggles between workers and managers for control. Like many nineteenth-century craftsmen, the skilled iron puddlers, heaters, rollers, and molders controlled many aspects of their work. They owned the knowledge and "craft secrets" of their trade and they controlled access to the craft through apprenticeship programs. Skilled nineteenth-century steelworkers have been placed among the various "autonomous workmen" who labored without significant supervision. In fact, they worked as semi-independent producers who contracted with the steel master to produce iron and steel for a certain price per ton, usually with gangs of laborers they hired. The craftsmen in steel and iron were even powerful enough to establish a sliding scale which gave them a certain share of the profit if the price rose. They also established a minimum floor for earnings, to protect their incomes in slack times. Craftsmen were not, of course, free from the effects of depressions, layoffs, and work-related injuries, but they did enjoy a degree of protection unavailable to the common laborer.

From the manufacturer's point of view, the skilled steelworker stood in the way of increased efficiency and productivity because he insisted on working a certain "stint" each day in order to reach an established quota. Thus, the workers had a surprising degree of control over the use of their time, but owners driving to meet market demands and competitive conditions were infuriated. Skilled workers enforced their own discipline on the job and dealt harshly with "rate busters" who exceeded the quota. "Rationally restricted output," writes labor historian David Montgomery in *Workers Control in America,* reflected the craftsmen's "functional autonomy" as well as their mutualistic ethos of "unselfish brotherhood." To enforce this collective code, the skilled worker was expected to assume a "manly posture" toward the boss. "Manliness," a popular term among nineteenth-century workers, meant, of course, patriarchal male supremacy, according to Montgomery. It also signified "dignity, respectability," and a kind of defiant egalitarianism which put the producer-craftsmen on the same plane as the capitalist-manufacturer.

Craft control was formalized in various union mills through work rules which overtly limited production by quota and called for the expulsion of workers who undermined their brothers by trying to advance themselves as individuals. The Amalgamated Association of Iron, Steel and Tin Workers, one of the strongest craft unions of the time, protected its members with an extensive set of work rules. Complaining about the union's 1889 contract, a Carnegie Company official said of the Homestead plant near Pittsburgh: "The method of apportioning the work, of regulating the turns, of altering machinery, in short, every detail of the great plant, was subject to the interference of some busybody representing the Amalgamated Association.'' Productivity, the engine of profit, could not be fully controlled by the steel masters. As Carnegie production chief H. C. Frick put it: ''The mills have never been able to turn out the product they should owing to being held back by the Amalgamated men.''

Craft unionists in towns like Homestead were even able to gain political control over their communities, and this became crucial during strikes, when local officials often sided with the workers. In 1892, Frick decided to break the union at Homestead. He notified the workers of a wage cut and then declared a lockout. Unable to rely on town law officers, he hired a force of three hundred private Pinkerton guards to keep the mills running with scab labor. But the union had taken control of the town and defeated the Pinkertons in a historic gun battle. The militia arrived shortly, however, and the mills were reopened. This was the pattern in many late-nineteenth-century labor struggles: workers and their allies controlled the terrain at a local level. But employers were able to use private guards, state militia, or even federal troops to turn the tide. Given the degree of control exercised by skilled workers such as miners, steelworkers, and railroad men, employers had to rely upon armed force in many conflicts. As a result, ninety-two people died in strikes between 1890 and 1897.

After defeating the Amalgamated at Homestead, Andrew Carnegie's men moved to cut labor costs by rationalizing the work process and restructuring the work force. Carnegie's steel company had already cut production costs by using high-energy fuel and technological innovations like the Bessemer converter. Carnegie also seized upon the new marketing possibilities afforded by great improvements in transportation and communication. Along with a few other steel barons, he expanded his operations and drove small firms out of business. A series of corporate mergers then took place at the end of the century as huge trusts were created to further reduce competition. The size and scale of steel manufacturing increased: by 1900, the average iron and steel plant employed 333 workers, as compared to only 65 forty years before. The Homestead Works employed upwards of six thousand men.

Carnegie and the other successful steel masters were not content to reduce production costs and set prices artificially high; they also wanted to cut the high labor costs exacted by skilled workers. Carnegie's Homestead operations became the proving ground for new kinds of corporate control. The company was organized hierarchically in a ''highly militarized'' system of superintendents, department managers, and foremen. These officers still had to depend on some non-commissioned officers—the "top skilled Americans, who are part bosses, part workmen," according to one description. Having lost their union, these skilled workers could be enlisted in the company's drive for productivity. "All together," one observer wrote, "this administrative group, almost one third of the force, has real military efficiency." The shape of the modern corporate enterprise emerged clearly at Carnegie's works by 1900. The managerial officer corps obviously had been expanded and strengthened over the rank-and-file of enlisted men.

When prosperity returned in the late 1890's, the steel mills exploded with activity. The officers in Carnegie's new production army drove the men hard. They extended the work week to seven days, despite worker protests, and forced most laborers to put in a twelve-hour day, despite the protests of clergymen who appealed to Christian capitalists for the sanctity of Sunday. Using these methods, Carnegie gobbled up an increasing share of the iron and steel market. But at the end of the century, when the steel baron retired to his castle in Scotland, competition still frustrated the big capitalists who wanted to control the trade. In 1901, Carnegie's firm became part of the giant new U.S. Steel Corporation engineered by finance capitalist J. P. Morgan. In the same year, the corporation forced a confrontation with the remaining lodges of the Amalgamated Association and, after a bitter strike, established open shops in all its plants. U.S. Steel, with its unprecedented financial resources and far-flung facilities, could transfer struck work to non-union plants and hold out for a long period. It could also mobilize private police as well as state and local authorities, and it could even use its political contacts to dissuade other unions from supporting the Amalgamated with sympathy strikes. The defeat of the 1901 strike not only gave U.S. Steel a freer hand in controlling its workers, it discouraged the leaders of other craft unions from risking head-on confrontations with the new corporate giants.

During the early 1900's, U.S. Steel, which employed 168,000 workers, used Carnegie's men to take advantage of the new technology imposed on the non-union plants. Once the managers and foremen had taken control of the work routine from the craftsmen, science and technology could be fully exploited to increase productivity and profitability. Management could eliminate skilled workers (thousands were fired during the 1901 strike) and replace them with semi-skilled machine tenders, and immigrant laborers who worked under the close supervision of foremen.

In breaking the union, the corporation destroyed the old sliding scale that had allowed workers to profit from increased productivity. Gone, too, was the floor on wage rates, which were now strictly the product of management's calculation of supply and demand. As David Brody explains in *Steelworkers in America,* the non-union era introduced a market determination of wages. Labor was clearly "a commodity like anything else," which meant that steel masters treated workers not as fellow producers who shared profit and loss but as proletarian subjects whose labor power could be bought and sold at a market price just like coal and ore.

U.S. Steel also attacked the old wage structure—another means of reducing overall labor costs. The corporation slashed the rates paid to skilled craftsmen (reducing the rollers' rates, for example, to $3 per ton in 1900—half the 1880 rate) and it slightly increased the rates for the new force of semi-skilled operatives. So, as Brody explains, the steelmakers enjoyed the best of both worlds: rising output and falling labor costs. "In the two decades after 1890 the furnace workers' productivity tripled in exchange for an income rise of one-half; the steelworkers' output doubled in exchange for an increase of one-fifth." This "accomplishment," on which increased corporate profits rested, depended on "a labor force powerless to oppose the decisions of the steel men."

Gone were the days, wrote John Fitch in *The Steelworkers* in 1911, when "the men ran the mill and the foremen had little authority." As part of the drive toward vertical integration, corporations like Carnegie's developed a new system of control based on the expanding army of foremen, who gained extensive power over their gangs, including the power to hire and fire, promote or demote, set rates and make rewards, to establish the "stints" and to drive the men to more production.

Much of the stability and productivity U.S. Steel achieved came from the importation of unskilled European immigrants to work as semi-skilled machine tenders and unskilled laborers. The new immigrants provided the steel masters with a transient supply of cheap labor to meet the needs of a reorganized production process and an expanded market. By 1907, Slavic immigrants filled 11,694 of the 14,359 common-laborer jobs in the Carnegie plants of Allegheny County. These Poles, Slovaks, Croats, Serbs, and Hungarians (all labeled "Hunkies") were largely young single men and were willing to work the long "man-killing" shifts, and to provide the employers with a stable and docile work force. Many Slavs came to the mill towns only to earn enough money to return home: thousands did go back. Working in the mills became a temporary prospect for many of these "birds of passage."

The transient newcomers had few illusions about the land in which "one had to do the work of three horses." The shock of entering the demonic mill was unforgettable. As one immigrant told the social investigator David Saposs:

> The man put me in a section where there was terrible noises, shooting, thundering and lightning. I wanted to run away but there was a big train in front of me. I looked up and big train carrying a big vessel with fire was making towards me. I stood numb, afraid to move, until a man came and led me out of the mill.

The environment in the company towns was only a little less awful. "There in Pittsburgh, people say, the dear sun never shines brightly, the air is saturated with stench and gas," Galatian parents told their children. One immigrant warned a prospective steelworker not to complain when he found that "in America there are neither Sundays or holidays." The mills never stopped; it was uneconomical to shut them down. And the immigrants provided their grist.

They were murdered and maimed at an appalling rate. At U.S. Steel's South Works in Gary, Indiana, immigrants suffered twice the accident rate of English-speaking employees who could understand safety instructions and warnings. Crystal Eastman's path-breaking study of work accidents revealed that in 1910 nearly one quarter of the new steelworkers were killed or injured each year. In just one year, 157 Slavs died in the steel mills in Allegheny County. As a result, immigrants depended even more than English-speaking workers on their benevolent societies. These associations offered a measure of protection and a touch of Old World communalism, but they could not cope with the devastating effects of steel-mill slaughter. When the immigrants came to America, they could not easily reestablish Old World self-help networks. As one Polish worker wrote to his wife about the hard lot of an immigrant:

> As long as he is well then he always works like a mule, and therefore he has something, but if he comes home sick then it is a trouble, because everybody is looking only for money to get some of it, and during the sickness the most will be spent.

The immigrants at first concerned themselves mainly with survival, as Thomas Bell showed in his evocative novel about Homestead steelworkers, *Out of This Furnace*. They were willing to work the "man-killing days'' to send wages back to the old country, but in case of sickness or accident, the world came crashing down on them. The newcomers were not helpless, however. As soon as a number of countrymen had gathered in a mill town, they formed a benevolent society for self-help and protection. These mutual-aid associations usually affiliated with national ethnic organizations to provide insurance and death benefits at cheap rates. The Polish National Alliance claimed thirty locals in Pittsburgh by 1908. In Homestead, the Greek Catholic Union, the National Slavonic Society, the First Catholic Slovak Union, and the National Croatian Society each had more than one hundred members. Since the English-speaking skilled workers had their own benevolent societies, and since there was no union to bring the men together, the immigrants' experience with industrial capitalism was mediated by nationality and religion from the very start.

To enhance the loyalty of the skilled worker, the corporations developed a number of welfare schemes and reforms in the early 1900's. George Perkins, who represented the controlling financial interests of banker J. P. Morgan, also wanted to use welfare work to enhance U.S. Steel's image as a ''good trust.'' Judge Elbert Gary, the corporate lawyer who actually managed the firm, shared Perkins's concern to avoid prosecution under the Sherman Anti-Trust Act. As production chief, he was even more concerned with increasing the loyalty and efficiency of his skilled men. U.S. Steel pioneered with a stock option plan in 1902 and followed with a pension plan to reward its loyal workers.

When muckraking reformers began to expose the loss of life and limb, the corporations, worried about rising hostility to the ''trusts,'' created safety programs. U.S. Steel led the way in 1908 with a program aimed at reducing accident rates; it resulted in favorable publicity and increased efficiency on the shop floor. The corporation's workmen's compensation plan in 1910 enabled the employers to avoid costly individual damage suits; it also enabled management to maintain private control over compensation at a time when states were enacting public workmen's compensation plans. Like other aspects of welfare capitalism, these benefit and insurance plans aimed to increase employee loyalty to the corporation by reducing the importance of the immigrant mutual-aid societies. The corporation's workmen's compensation scheme would serve as a ''rebuke and rebuttal'' to the union view that ''workmen get nothing except by . . . struggle.''

Gary and corporate officials were especially concerned with labor turnover, because the skilled workers could still ply their trade with rival firms during boom times. The management, therefore, encouraged skilled workingmen to become homeowners and helped them out in various ways. By 1908, one fourth of all steelworkers owned their own houses and were thus more closely tied to the corporation and the company town. Homeownership increased dependency, and it surely expanded the social distance between the skilled-worker resident and the immigrants in the crowded boardinghouses.

But life in the company town was hardly comfortable for the skilled worker and his family. Men were usually the only wage earners in the steel towns, so families were especially dependent on the corporation. Though few women worked for wages in these towns, housewives took in boarders, sewing, and laundry to augment the family income, and to reduce, even slightly, its dependency on wage earnings. Many women in the steel and coal towns of Pennsylvania also tended gardens and raised chickens, rabbits, and sometimes pigs and goats, to help feed the family and reduce dependence on the company store. The women not only maintained the household and raised the children, they also brought in additional money that could be used to pay a mortgage or buy clothes for the children. The working day of mill-town women extended far beyond the "man-killing" shift the husbands worked. For widows, who were numerous in industrial communities, the choice sometimes came down to a life of prostitution or a bare survival eked out through washing clothes and doing other menial tasks.

The daily lives of company-town housewives were limited not just by dependency on the husband's wage. They were also governed by the technology and ecology of the mill towns. Working-class women in the Pittsburgh area lived a world apart from middle-class women. The difference can be seen in the daily problem of getting water. In Pittsburgh, privately owned services were available on a "pay-as-you go" basis, and wealthier women could enjoy the freedom of having running water. Poor women on the South Side had to rise at five in the morning to haul water up the hills before the supply was drained by the mills on the river's edge below. Besides getting water, other burdens of home life in the steel town fell more heavily on the shoulders of working-class women: the lack of indoor plumbing, sewage disposal, clean-burning gas heat, and home appliances. These services had begun to dispel some of the time and drudgery of housework in the lives of wealthier women.

Social life in the mill towns was sex-segregated, as the men congregated in Homestead's fifty saloons, where they enjoyed a bit of freedom from the tyranny of millwork and developed male bonds of companionship. The corporations tried to regulate the saloons in some towns because drinking caused absenteeism. Workers' wives also feared the effects of alcoholism, and tried to plan other activities to keep the men away from the barrooms. Among the English-speaking workers, the benevolent societies alone provided a social life for men and women. Controlled by the workers, these self-help groups offered some sociability and a measure of collective security (through insurance schemes and other forms of self-help).

Socially and culturally, the immigrants seemed to live in a world of their own, but they could not be ignored. Immigrants took their citizenship seriously, and when they became naturalized and registered to vote, they could become a threat. Republican political bosses therefore sought to control the immigrant vote with some forms of patronage. On a more brutal level, the straw boss in the mill and the bigoted steel-town police kept the immigrant workingman in line. America was the land of the free, but the European soon learned there was little democracy or freedom in the company town.

A few corporate welfare reforms were aimed at the immigrants. Workmen's compensation programs might reduce the importance of the autonomous benevolent societies, and increase dependency on the company. Prohibition reforms struck at the saloon, where Slavic men congregated. Management in the company town also put pressure on immigrant-owned small businesses which reduced workers' dependence on the company store. Corporate welfare schemes often missed the mark with immigrant workers, however. YMCA's and plant libraries did not transform the Slavs into loyal, industrious American workmen. The steel masters could rely on foremen and bonus incentives to "drive" the men, but they found the Slavs resistant to the military discipline modern managers demanded. Work habits and cultural traditions brought from the Old World often clashed with factory discipline and the requirements of the seventy-hour work week. A Polish wedding celebration, for example, might last three or four days. A drinking bout following a funeral could extend through Sunday night and prevent workmen from showing up on "blue Monday." As Herbert Gutman explains in *Work, Culture and Society in Industrializing America,* "peasant parades and rituals, religious and national holidays, and food riots had no place in modern industrial America." But these cultural forms persisted because they provided immigrant workers with "natural and effective forms of self-assertion and self-protection."

In sum, the immigrant steelworker, though not easily disciplined, could be controlled through various forms of dependency and repression. At bottom, though, "stability in the unskilled ranks" rested upon "mobility," according to Brody. Newcomers were kept on the move between the Old and the New World or between one mill and another. In a non-union era, the most common response to industrial tyranny was quitting. But vertical mobility could also be encouraged, and after the first decade or so, corporations made much of the few Slavs who had been allowed to work their way up through the ranks to become skilled workers or foremen. Like the Irish proletariat of the nineteenth century, these new immigrants were immediately exposed to the Horatio Alger mobility myth. In fact, one of the steel companies' most effective tactics was to encourage workingmen to compete with each other for promotion along "strictly demarcated job ladders" that linked "each job to the one above and below it in status and pay." As Katherine Stone shows in "The Origin of Job Structures in the Steel Industry," these ladders gave workers a "sense of vertical mobility" and an incentive to work harder. Employers gained more leverage over the work force through a system which "pitted each worker against all others in rivalry for advancement," thus undercutting feelings "of unity which might develop among them." Instead of gaining an increased consciousness of their common condition, Stone remarks, workers "had to learn to curry favor with their foremen and supervisors and to play by the rules in order to get ahead."

It is unlikely, however, that many immigrants believed strongly in the possibility of climbing up the job ladder. After all, the whole structure of the work force was based on reserving skilled jobs primarily for English-speaking workers. When asked about the concentration of immigrants in dangerous blast-furnace jobs, an American worker replied that "only Hunkies work on those jobs; they are too damn dirty and too damn hot for a 'white man.' " In any case, as John Bodnar shows in his study of Steelton, Pennsylvania, the immigrants were far more concerned with job security than with occupational mobility. And as families began to settle in the mill towns, informal networks were formed to provide jobs for family and kin so that newcomers would not be completely victimized by the labor market. (One recent study shows that black migrants coming from the South also relied on relatives to obtain jobs, but these newcomers were more widely dispersed than the Slavs, who created important occupational beachheads in many company towns.) By the second decade of the century, the Slavs were not as transient as they had been and were not so easily manipulated.

Initially, when the immigrants resisted industrial discipline, they relied upon Old World cultural traditions and habits. They did not assimilate as iron ore did in a giant melting pot, but they did have to adjust. They did have to learn the new ways of industrial America in order to survive. Their employers tried to teach them obedience, punctuality, industriousness, patriotism, and the like. But education was too closely tied to coercion. The immigrant workers' most important teachers were their British, Irish, and American fellow workers. Like the experienced coal miners, the skilled steelworkers passed along the practices and traditions that governed their work. The destruction of the craft union had not eliminated the craftsmen's ability to control the job to some extent. In 1904 the Amalgamated, now reduced to a few lodges, was forced to sacrifice the last contractual restrictions on output in order to maintain its weak presence in the industry. But as Commissioner of Labor Carroll D. Wright observed of the foundrymen: "The customs of the trade did not always vanish when the employer ceased to recognize the standard day's work" in a contract. Workers still found ways of limiting output informally, and they passed these ways on to the immigrants who worked beside them. One gang leader at U.S. Steel's Fort Wayne rolling mills made this observation about the Rumanian stokers: "As soon as the night boss turns his back . . . they just drop down and sleep while the company pays them wages and gets nothing in return." The newcomers, whose main fear was of being laid off in slack times, soon learned from older workers that "slowing down" or "soldiering" spread out the work.

Responding to the immigrants' fear of unemployment, Judge Gary promised that employment would stabilize because the major corporations had agreed to rationalize the industry through cooperation. The old era of destructive competition was over, he said in 1904. In the ruthless competitive period, steel masters had been forced to deal harshly with labor in order to cut their costs, but now that oligopoly had been created, "the relations of capital and labor" could, according to Gary, "settle themselves on sensible and mutually satisfactory lines." But before the new era of corporate liberalism had really begun, the panic of 1907 destroyed trade cooperation and led to wage cuts and mass layoffs. The firings in 1907 and 1908 shook the unskilled immigrants and shattered their loyalty, such as it was, to their employer.

When demand for steel increased again in 1909, demand for unskilled labor also grew. The immigrants then learned that the labor market that victimized them could sometimes give them an advantage. In the fall of 1909, a series of mass strikes beginning at McKees Rocks, Pennsylvania, transformed the image of the Slav from docility to militancy. Like their Slavic brothers in the anthracite coalfields, the steelworkers struck on a family and community basis. They came as

single men without families, as ''birds of passage'' who planned to return to the Old World. But by 1909 they had settled in the steel towns
with their families and relatives and were investing their hard-earned
savings in little homes. They reconstituted their families, churches,
and mutual-aid societies as best they could, and prepared to make their
way in the new world of the company town. The fragmentation of the
early days was replaced by new forms of solidarity that combined Old
World communalism with the discipline necessary for survival in the
New World. This solidarity was reflected in many strikes, from
McKees Rocks in 1909 to the great national steel strike a decade later.
As David Brody explains:

> The principles of collective industrial activity had not suddenly dawned
> on the immigrant. Rather, his ability as a striker sprang from his Euro-
> pean background. The peasant looked upon himself primarily as a
> member of a family and a village. He could not conceive of differing
> with group decisions, unanimously reached. Moreover, nothing mattered
> more than communal approval. Immigration weakened, but did not de-
> stroy, group consciousness. When, therefore, immigrant workers were
> driven to strike, they were likely to persist until the general sentiment
> turned. They were effective strikers because they were peasants.

The McKees Rocks strike, and the Bethlehem strike that followed in
1910, also revealed a convergence of the native skilled workers and
the foreign-born laborers. It was becoming clear that they shared much
in common. The immigrants were ''distinguishable ethnically and socially perhaps,'' Brody observes, but they moved in the ''same orbit
of dependency and repression'' that governed the skilled steelworkers'
world.

Like the East European Catholics who came to the steel towns, the
East European Jews who came to the big cities entered a new world of
intensive labor, wage dependency, and hostile cultural values. The
Jewish immigrants who settled in New York City's Lower East Side
were part of the great migration from 1880 to 1920 which brought
nearly 24 million people to this country. At the start of the 1920's,
when immigration restriction officially began, immigrants and their
children accounted for 58 percent of the population in cities over
100,000. They comprised an even larger percentage in major industrial
cities like Chicago, Pittsburgh, Philadelphia, and New York, where
the city's Lower East Side contained over 500,000 people in various
ethnic neighborhoods.

At first, immigrants in the urban ghetto were preoccupied with survival and concentrated on personal adjustment. Some individuals

adapted quickly, even in a confusing urban setting like New York City. Others adjusted more cautiously to this new world. They were reluctant to compete in the marketplace. Refusing to accept the rationality of capitalist competition, they retained the collective values of family and community. The Jewish writer Marcus Ravage says:

> The immigrant is almost invariably disappointed in America . . . The alien who comes here from Europe brings with him a deep rooted tradition, a system of culture, tastes and habits—a point of view which is as ancient as his national experience . . .

These national experiences, when combined with village and familial loyalties, make the immigrant experience varied and complex. And yet there were patterns of adjustment common to industrial work and city life among the various nationalities.

The immigrant experience in New York City's Lower East Side represented, on a grand scale, the confrontation of Old World people with urban America. This throbbing tenement district, stretching north along the East River from the Brooklyn Bridge, contained a variety of ethnic neighborhoods and housed roughly 135,000 Jews from the five major East European countries, "a seething human sea, fed by streams, streamlets, and rills of immigration from all the Yiddish-speaking centers of Europe."

Along with the Italians, Hungarians, and others, the Jews shared conditions of tenement-house life. As one social worker wrote:

> [Tenements] are great prison-like structures of brick, with narrow doors and windows, cramped passages and steep rickety stairs. They are built through from one street to the other with a somewhat narrower building connecting them . . . The narrow court-yard . . . in the middle is a damp foul-smelling place, supposed to do duty as an airshaft; had the foul fiend designed these great barracks they could not have been more villainously arranged to avoid any chance of ventilation . . . In case of fire they would be perfect death-traps, for it would be impossible for the occupants of the crowded rooms to escape by the narrow stairways, and the flimsy fire-escapes which the owners of the tenements were compelled to put up a few years ago are so laden with broken furniture, bales and boxes that they would be worse than useless. In the hot summer months . . . these fire-escape balconies are used as sleeping-rooms by the poor wretches who are fortunate enough to have windows opening upon them.

Jacob Riis in *How the Other Half Lives* (1890) offered a disturbing view of city life. Riis depicted an urban jungle of exploitation, family disintegration, crime, and human degradation. Hoping to stimulate reforms, he wrote about deplorable tenement living conditions, alcoholism, orphans, and "street Arabs" from broken immigrant homes, and a criminal type that preyed on the poor but also threatened the rich. His camera focused on depressing city scenes: a robber's hideaway on Mulberry Street, young waifs asleep in alleyways, drunks with glazed eyes in basement dives, women sleeping on jail-cell floors, and mug shots of squinting roughnecks and petty criminals.

He focused on the underworld, revealing city life in which people preyed on one another. Many refused to work for wages; others failed to keep a steady job, and still others could not work because they were old or crippled. Unemployment receded after the great depression of the 1890's, but the unemployed still accounted for 12 percent of the work force in 1900 and remained over 10 percent for the next five years. Many were transients who constantly moved from city to city in search of work. These industrial refugees rode the rails in such numbers that 24,000 "trespassers" died on the railroads in the first five years of the century; they lived on the move, surviving in rail yards, jungle camps, and city flophouses.

Though preoccupied with this underworld, Jacob Riis also looked into workers in the city's garment industry, which more than doubled in size between 1880 and 1910, when it employed at least 214,428 persons. He saw degradation here, too. "Before you have travelled the length of a single block in any of these East Side streets," he wrote, you heard "the whir of a thousand sewing machines, worked at high pressure from the earliest dawn till mind and muscle give out all together. Every member of the family from the youngest to the oldest, bears a hand, shut in qualmy rooms, where meals are cooked and clothing dried besides . . ."

The Jewish immigrants were shocked and amazed by much of what they experienced in the city, and especially in the "gray stone world of tenements, where," as one Yiddish writer put it, "even on the loveliest spring day there was not a single blade of grass." But the greatest disruption of all to the traditional Jewish way of life was, according to the educator Morris Raphael Cohen, the "intensity and hurry" of the workaday world, reflected for him in the way his father raced with his uncle to press jackets in their clothing establishment, a place animated by a "tremendous drive"—"nothing like the leisurely air in Minsk where my Uncle Abraham had worked and where the men would sing occasionally."

Unlike many East European immigrants, Jewish craftsmen brought skills along with the traditional habit of alternating between "bouts of intense labor and of idleness." It was a characteristic pattern, observes E. P. Thompson, "wherever men were in control of their working lives.'' In the garment shops of the Lower East Side, Jewish workers, skilled and unskilled, lost much of this control, as contractors and bosses developed piece-rate and task systems which forced the workers to become their own drivers.

Though immigrant men often found it difficult to use Old World skills in America, many did obtain jobs as cutters in the garment industry. These skilled jobs, like others, were closed to women. The clothing industry was rigidly sex-segregated. Young immigrant women had learned hand-sewing skills as children, but they were relegated to unskilled machine-tending jobs. Women held most of the unskilled jobs in the needle trades and were paid much less than men. A cutter might earn $16 a week, but the average female needleworker earned only $6 or $7.

Sadie Frowne, a young clothing worker, speaking her piece in *The Independent* in 1905, explained how the task system was used to extract production from women workers.

> At seven o'clock we all sit down to our machines and the boss brings to each one the pile of work that he or she is to finish during the day, what they call in English their "stint." Sometimes the work is not all finished by six o'clock, and then the one who is behind must work overtime.
>
> The machines go like mad all day, because the faster you work the more money you get. Sometimes in my haste I get my finger caught and the needle goes right through it. It goes so quick, tho, that it does not hurt much. I bind the finger up with a piece of cotton and go on working.
>
> All the time we are working the boss walks about examining the finished garments and making us do them over again if they are not just right. So we have to be careful as well as swift.

Under the task system, which in slack times forced workers to speed up and produce more garments to prevent loss of earnings, the clock and the sewing machine were extensions of the bosses' authority. The pressures of work under a system in which time equaled money contrasted painfully with the irregular rhythms of work in the old-country shtetl. Morris Rosenfeld, a presser of men's clothing who wrote Yiddish poetry, reflected on the new meaning of time in the world of industrial capitalism:

> *The clock in the workshop—it rests not a moment;*
> *It points on, and ticks on; eternity—time;*
> *Once someone told me the clock had a meaning,—*
> *In pointing and ticking had a reason and rhyme . . .*
> *At times, when I listen, I hear the clock plainly;—*
> *The reason of old—the old meaning—is gone!*
> *The maddening pendulum urges me forward*

To labor and still labor on.
The tick of the clock is the boss in his anger.
The face of the clock has the eyes of the foe.
The clock—I shudder—Dost hear how it draws me?
It calls me "Machine" and it cries [to] me "Sew"!

If, as Rosenfeld said, the clock and daytime lost its meaning in the humming garment shops, then the traditional calendar and the marking of traditional religious observances suffered as well. Many Jews worked in shops owned by co-religionists, closed on the Sabbath. Others, however, had to sacrifice religious observances in order to work for non-Jews. Children who had to work on the Sabbath brought "endless unhappiness to Jewish homes on the East Side," wrote one observer, and especially to the patriarchs who wanted the family together for certain observances like the Day of Atonement.

Many Jewish immigrants initially preferred homework to the "Boston" factory system, with its disciplined routine imposed by the boss and the clock. Homework in the garment industry was very exploitative, as Moses Rischin indicates in *The Promised City,* because the contractors introduced the task system under which a team did section work just as they did in factories. "The ten or twenty workers, members of the family, relatives, *lasleit* [neighbors from the old country], or boarders," Rischin writes, "were assigned a work quota: individual workmen were no longer paid individually by the piece." This "infernal cooperative system," wrote a contemporary critic, "by which the contractor shares his misery with his dependent workmen," was "the most ingenious and effective engine of overexertion known to modern industry." Many immigrants preferred it, however, not only because they hated the factory system but because they could work as a family, or kin group, to enhance the family economy.

Jacob Riis's photos exposed the homework system to public view in 1890, and two years later the New York Tenement House Act outlawed homework, but the Act was not strongly enforced. Homework contributed greatly to the family economy and employed most of the sixty thousand New York children working in the garment industry at the turn of the century. In the 1910's, Lewis Hine took up Riis's crusade against child labor, nationally, which occupied over 240,000 young people in the mines, mills, shops, and streets. Hine's photos showed young faces lined with adult determination: the sooty faces of the breaker boys sorting coal between their legs; the beautiful faces of the doffer girls in Carolina textile mills; the tough faces of immigrant "newsies" in the Boston streets; the intent faces of Jewish and Italian immigrant girls sewing garments, making suspenders, and assembling artificial flowers in New York City tenements. Riis's photographs of the Lower East Side showed immigrant families as victims in the urban jungle, Hine's photos show these people as actors in their own right, as workers. The pictures were taken by an indignant reformer who defined his task as "showing the world of consumers exactly what the world of the makers was like," and this, writes Alan Trachtenberg, meant "ripping aside the veil that disguised and mystified a brutal system of production." The same brutality that Riis saw in 1890 is there, but the passivity is gone. "Hine's people are alive and tough," Trachtenberg notes. Even the children "have savvy—savoir-faire, a worldly air. They have not succumbed. Their spirit is at odds with their surroundings."

The young women who toiled in the clothing shops and lofts contributed their earnings to the family, as the working children did, and they usually lived at home. Though Jewish and Italian women worked largely at home, their daughters comprised the largest part of the clothing-industry proletariat. Many immigrant patriarchs were disturbed by the effect of work on their daughters, as Anzia Yezierska shows in her East Side novel of 1925, *Bread Givers,* which centers on the conflict between a Jewish "working girl" and her tyrannical father. Commenting on this novel, Alice Kessler-Harris notes that wage earning allowed a few Jewish women to escape the prearranged pattern of early marriage and, in some cases, to pursue successful careers as socialists, feminists, and trade unionists:

> At least in theory the ideology of success offered opportunities for women to make the most of their capacities. Here women could choose their husbands—could marry for love. And if, in Yezierska's words, "they don't get a husband, they don't think the world is over, they turn their mind to something else."

Of course, factory work did not liberate most young women from the patriarchal family. For an average sixty-hour week, "factory girls" earned roughly half what a male factory worker earned, and they had to contribute most of their earnings to the family. Furthermore, patriarchal authority was reinforced on the job, where, as Mary Bularzik shows, sexual harassment served "to control women's access to certain jobs; to limit job success and mobility; and to compensate men for powerlessness in their own lives."

Instead of becoming "factory girls," many young women entered domestic service, though they complained bitterly about this work. House servants objected to the long hours, hard work, close supervision, and subservience that went with the job. Still, domestic service provided the most job openings in 1900 and remained the major category for female employment. By far, most servants were native-born white women (529,210), followed by 322,062 foreign-born women, mainly Scandinavian, Irish, and German. Few Italians or East European immigrants worked in service. These women preferred homework or factory work, and their men objected to wives and daughters working in another man's house. In Anzia Yezierska's story "America and I," a young Jewish woman quit working as a servant for an "American" family, "where there had been no end to my day," and "turned back to the Ghetto" and the sweatshop, "where I worked on a hard bench with my own kind on either side of me." In this Delancey Street basement, she knew her hours and wages and she "could walk in boldly" into a regular factory "and say I could work at something, even if it was only sewing buttons".

Almost as many black women (319,079) worked in service as did immigrant women, and their number increased dramatically, until black women constituted 40 percent of all domestics by 1920. In the 1910's, native white women, and even a few immigrants, found jobs in clerical and sales work; black women were barred from these jobs. They did not prefer to work as domestics and laundresses; they simply had no choice. They did the same work in Northern urban ghettos that they had done in the South. A black woman in a Southern city explained that "more than two-thirds of the negro women . . . whether married or single" were "compelled to work for a living" usually as "menial servants." In domestic service they enjoyed "nominal freedoms" but were literally "slaves." Black women still suffered from the kind of sexual abuse and exploitation that had prevailed before emancipation.

That black women had no choice is clear from the fact that 90 percent of those who worked in New York City were in service. These women often came to the city alone and had to support themselves. The life expectancy of black males was very low: in 1890, about 10 percent of all black women were widows. In some communities, they could do housework with an extended family, but in the urban ghetto they often had to live alone. As a result, more widows than wives worked regularly for pay in 1890. Married women who entered the labor market often did so because their husbands were paid poorly and worked irregularly. According to a 1901 Bureau of Labor Statistics study of 25,000 working-class families, half the principal breadwinners were unemployed for an average of two months each year. And unemployment among black males was especially high, so married black women worked for wages much more often than white women. Nationally, 26 percent of black women worked, and in New York 32 percent earned wages (a proportion that ranged from four to fifteen times more than various groups of white married women). Though black females were usually forced to leave the home to work, many took in laundry so that they could work and care for their children at the same time. Women had to become wage earners because their marriages often came to an abrupt end. The 1905 New York City census showed that households with the husband absent (dead, disappeared, or separated) were four times as prevalent in the black neighborhood of San Juan Hill as in the Italian neighborhood of Greenwich Village.

The effects of a race-segregated labor market could be seen clearly in the structure of black family life. Sociologists seeking the causes of black poverty have exaggerated the effects of slavery and "black matriarchy" on the family structure. Studies of Boston working-class families show that poor Irish families were more likely to be headed by females than were black families. Afro-Americans had to make special adjustments to survive in the urban ghetto. More women worked and depended on the support networks of kinfolk and friends in their ghetto than in the white ghettos, where men could usually remain the primary breadwinners while women could remain the "bread givers." Still, common patterns of adjustment existed among all the ethnic groups in the urban ghetto. Few could depend solely on the income of a working father, and so the family income was invariably supplemented by relatives and sometimes by friends and neighbors. Turn-of-the-century studies of New York showed that the income of one wage earner could not sustain a family of four. Blacks as well as white immigrants relied heavily on boarders as a source of additional income. Everyone in these augmented households had to work—from the black grandmothers who washed clothes and minded children to the Jewish kids who helped their mothers make suspenders. They had to work in order to survive. Even with a collective family income, millions of city dwellers lived in poverty. In a country of 82 million, Robert Hunter noted in *Poverty* (1904), 10 million did not earn a subsistence income. Most of the poor were the transients depicted in Jacob Riis's underworld, but the "laboring poor" comprised at least 2 million; they were the honest, hardworking families who lived mainly to work, but still lived in poverty.

Married immigrant women rarely attempted to earn wages outside the home. Most employers favored "single girls," and many immigrant husbands refused to accept the idea of a wage-earning wife. One 1909 survey of Russian Jews showed that only one percent of the wives worked for wages. Many Jewish women added to the family income in other ways, especially by taking in boarders (as did 56 percent of the Russian Jews), as well as laundry and various forms of homework supplied by contractors in the garment trade. And these Jewish mothers maintained the boarders and other members of the family who worked for wages by cooking, cleaning, child rearing, healing, and counseling. They not only brought in income and maintained the family, they made the family budget, collected the income, and disbursed it. Against great odds, housewives in the urban ghetto managed to keep their husbands and children in fairly good health. The Jewish people of the Lower East Side had one of the lowest mortality rates in New York City. "These mothers of the slums lugged pails of water up stairways several times a day, slaved in primitive kitchens to get a frugal meal on a crowded table, and devoted a day each week to washing and ironing," according to Mary P. Ryan. "Since such amenities as sewerage and running water had to be purchased by private property owners, few slum landlords provided tenants with this service," she notes in *Womanhood in America*. Working-class women had to devote more time and energy to housework than middle-class women. They also gave birth to more children. The fertility rate for immigrant women was much higher than for native-born middle-class women. Poor women usually gave birth at home with the assistance of a midwife; infant mortality rates were high. Two noted feminists who worked as midwives—Emma Goldman, the anarchist, and Margaret Sanger, the birth-control crusader—described the fear and dread that often accompanied childbirth in the tenements. "Most of them lived in continual dread of conception," Goldman wrote. "The great mass of the women" she met "submitted helplessly, and when they found themselves pregnant, their alarm and worry would result in the determination to get rid of their expected offspring."

The mother, then, was the heart of the working-class immigrant family. "Upon her interest, skill and order the family economy depends," stated settlement-house worker Mary K. Simkhovitch in *The City Worker's World in America*. "Around her the whole machinery of the family revolves. Without her everything falls to pieces." And since the family stood at the center of neighborhood life, the Jewish mothers of the Lower East Side were also at the heart of communal life. They organized child care, home religious observances, as well as food riots and rent strikes.

Men and women participated in different forms of group life within the ghetto: the men in their coffeehouses, clubs, and benevolent societies; the women in their kaffeklatsches, stairway kibitz groups and child-care networks; the young men in the street-corner gangs and baseball teams; the young women in their candy-store and shop-floor sororities. Among Jews and other immigrant groups, religious activity was also sex-segregated. Factory work groups reflected the sexual division of labor. The participation of so many immigrant women in the East Side economy did, however, create the possibility of collective action involving men and women in the work place.

Immigrant working-class associations divided along ethnic lines, and within nationalities people split into local and regional groups. Among most nationalities workers organized benevolent societies of their fellow townsmen. By 1914, over five hundred of these mutual-aid societies (with fifty to five hundred members) had sprung up in New York, each providing job opportunities (through employers from their village), insurance benefits, aid to the sick, interest-free loans, and cemetery rights. Old World Jewish traditions of communal help eased the immigrant's adaptation to the New World. These benevolent groups performed many of the functions the ward machine had performed for the Irish. In 1902, when Charles F. Murphy became chief of New York's Democratic Party organization, Tammany Hall appealed to the new immigrant vote by offering some of the services the benevolent society offered: jobs, recreation in the American form of picnics, holiday gift baskets, and even relief for the unemployed. As one East Side settlement-house reformer said: "The impending threat of beggary or the poor house which hangs over the independent laborer is the power which drives so many into the arms of the political boss, who undertakes to provide an assurance of steady employment, with out-of-work benefits for the laborer's family." Like the Italians, who distrusted the Irish Democratic leaders, some East Side Jews sided with the Republicans, especially after Theodore Roosevelt protested the persecution of Jews in Russia. Many East Side Jews supported the Socialist Party, which was founded in 1901 and grew strong enough to send a comrade, Meyer London, to Congress from the Lower East Side in 1914. The socialists, like the Republican reformers, opposed the Democratic patronage machines as corrupt, parasitic organizations that controlled the immigrant vote through bribery. In *The Rise of David Levinsky,* socialist editor Abraham Cahan has his hero observe that these political parties were "competing business companies whose specialty it was to make millions by ruling some big city, levying tribute on fallen women, thieves, and liquor dealers, doing favors to friends and meting out punishment to foes."

Jewish socialists in New York enjoyed greater success than most of their comrades in breaking the hold of the old-party patronage machine over the immigrant vote. They worried as much about the deeper hold of mutual-aid societies on workers. Socialists and other class-conscious labor-union organizers saw the localistic benevolent societies as paternalistic groups linking laborers to bosses from the same towns and inhibiting collective forms of proletarian organization. In 1901, Jewish socialists formed their own fraternal society, the Workmen's Circle, to promote self-help among workers from different towns and regions.

During the early 1900's, however, socialist and labor organizers on the East Side failed to unite immigrants in new class-conscious organizations. The benevolent societies and the patronage machines remained influential: and, more important, craft unions, which predominated in the needle trades, turned their backs on the "unskilled greenhorns." Even though homework gradually gave way to factory work, the shops remained small. Workers were still indebted to the boss for work, and unemployment was a constant threat. A Jewish proletariat clearly emerged at this time, but many an individual immigrant hoped to gain high wages as a skilled worker or to become a contractor or manufacturer and leave the shop. "The great trouble in the cap trade," said one worker, "and I will say in all trades controlled by my co-religionists, is that the Hebrew wage earner is only in the trade temporarily, hoping and praying that one day he will become a boss."

Paradoxically, Jewish unionism began to show new signs of life in the midst of an anti-union, open-shop drive in 1903 and 1904. The United Hebrew Trades (UHT) refused to restrict themselves to the skilled worker and continued to organize for the union shop in many trades, no matter how lowly. One of the UHT's militant affiliates, the United Cloth Hat and Capmakers' Union, used this strategy effectively. The skilled hatters, who had, as artisans, controlled their own shops, reorganized their union in 1901 and in a 1903 strike opened their ranks to newcomers, including young women. A year later, open-shop employers locked the union out, but the Hat and Capmakers held out and won a fairly good settlement, thanks partly to the community support they mobilized. Like the great strikes that swept the East Side beginning in 1909, this conflict united skilled and unskilled workers from various nationalities against the employers who wanted to maintain total control over production through the open shop. In fighting for the union shop, the workers began actively to assert their collective rights against bosses.

After the Russian Revolution in 1905, a number of exiled revolutionaries who belonged to the Bund movement arrived in the Lower East Side. Among them were experienced socialist and labor organizers who would mobilize the labor movement and the Socialist Party and contribute to the making of a self-conscious Jewish proletariat. These Bundists combined militant unionism with socialist internationalism and Yiddish cultural radicalism. Unlike the older cosmopolitan Marxists who advocated assimilation, the Russian revolutionaries built on a developing Yiddish cultural pride that transcended Old World parochialism. The Yiddish theater performers expressed this pride most clearly, according to Hutchins Hapgood. By the turn of the century, an estimated 2 million persons saw eleven hundred performances that reflected the "world of the ghetto" and events in the larger world from the Homestead strike to the Kishinev pogrom in Russia. Theater guilds were formed by unions and newspapers, anarchists and socialists, to stage these performances; they were, to Hapgood, "a striking indication of the growing sense of corporate interests among Lower East Side workers" and "an expression of the socialistic spirit" which pervaded the ghetto. The Bundists drew on the inclusive industrial unionism of the United Hebrew Trades, the appeal of a universalistic socialist message, and the collectivist spirit of Yiddish cultural radicalism. They mobilized a militant workers' movement that grew as the parochial paternalism of the benevolent societies receded. While the orthodox Jews and Zionists stressed religious or nationalistic identity instead of class identity, the Bundists blended the new collectivist sense of class and culture emerging on the Lower East Side. Unlike many other new immigrants who wished to return home (as 40 percent did between 1908 and 1914), the Jews harbored no illusions about returning to their oppressive homelands; they were in America to stay and the Bundists knew it. They also knew that the "rags to riches" illusions had faded as Jews began to accept their permanent status as proletarians and to see the common oppression under the "task system." As Irving Howe tells in *World of Our Fathers,* these revolutionaries "brought to the socialist and labor movements . . . not merely their elan, combativeness, and sophisticated conviction" but also a special "Jewish dimension" to the class struggle:

> They grasped, better than anyone else, that the problems of the immigrant Jewish working-class were not merely problems of organization but, still more, of morale. They grasped that it was necessary to forge a Jewish working-class that would have a sense of its own worth. Too many Jewish workers still lived under the sign of fear, too many still bore the stigma of *shtetl* passivity, too many still thought of self-exploitation as a

strategy for escaping exploitation. The Bundists understood that they had to confront a major problem in collective self-regard.

Compared to the steelworkers in Pennsylvania's company towns, the garment workers in New York's ethnic ghettos enjoyed certain advantages. The first fought on terrain dominated by a large corporation attempting to extend its control from the workplace to the community. The second group struggled against much smaller manufacturers who could not bring order to their own industry, let alone to the communities in which the workers lived. Jews who emigrated to New York brought radical political ideas and cultural traditions, as well as organizational strategies forged in their struggle against religious and economic oppression. As a result, the Lower East Side emerged in the 1910's as a center of militant industrial unionism and socialism, while corporate capitalism remained dominant in the Pennsylvania steel towns. Both areas felt the shock of mass strikes in 1909 and 1910, but in New York the immigrants' struggle for industrial unionism actually gave workers more control over their world.

2

Rebuilding the House of Labor

The labor movement had sustained major defeats in the late nineteenth century. After the sensational Haymarket riot and the loss of the great eight-hour-day strikes in 1886, the Knights of Labor declined rapidly. The Knights had made the greatest and most effective effort to bring all workers, regardless of skill, race, nationality, or gender, into one big House of Labor. With the decline of the Knights, the American Federation of Labor, founded in 1886, emerged as a unifying force. Unlike the Noble Order, the AFL brought workers together by craft or trade rather than in a mixed assembly based on a city or region. Led at first by Marxists like Samuel Gompers and Peter J. McGuire of New York's Lower East Side, the AFL hoped to build a stronger structure based on the power of skilled workers in certain trades. They also hoped to unionize the unskilled workers in those trades, but they were militantly opposed to the introduction of new workers, or "greenhorns," from Asia, Europe, or the American South, who could be used by employers to undermine the trades. The skilled craftsmen's influence and the emphasis placed on excluding "greenhorns" led the AFL to adopt exclusionary practices and restrictionist policies.

The young Federation suffered when one of its strongest craft unions, the Amalgamated Association of Iron and Steel Workers, sustained a major defeat in the 1892 Homestead strike. Other affiliates were also battered by the great depression of the 1890's, but the AFL survived. It was the first national labor organization to maintain itself through a major depression. In 1897, President Gompers reported

264,000 members in AFL unions, mostly skilled workers in craft unions. Upon this foundation the House of Labor could rebuild. With the return of prosperity, the emergence of progressivism, and widespread labor militancy, the unions multiplied their membership at the turn of the century. Their new strength, which seemed actually to threaten the owners' control in some industries, provoked a violent reaction with the open-shop movement in 1903.

The destruction of the Amalgamated Association in the Homestead strike and the 1901 strike against U.S. Steel indicated that even the strongest craft union could not survive the onslaught of large corporations bent on using new technology to gain increased control. The percentage of skilled workers declined slightly in the 1890's to about one sixth of the industrial work force by 1900. Most craft unions that survived the depression did not have to face huge corporations like U.S. Steel, nor did they operate in hostile company towns like Homestead. Instead, these organizations grew where they could exert some control over the flow of labor and materials, where small companies and employers still required their handicraft skills, and where they could mobilize the support of other unionists and sympathizers at a local level.

Thus, a measure of job control went hand in hand with community influence. To take one example, in the glassmaking town of Muncie, Indiana, made famous by Robert and Helen Lynd in their 1929 study *Middletown,* we find a turn-of-the-century trade-union movement firmly established in the local political economy. Native-born skilled workers regarded themselves as honorable producers, equal in standing to farmers and manufacturers, and morally superior to non-producers like bankers and merchants. Journeymen controlled access to the trades through an apprentice system and protected themselves by organizing thirty AFL locals, with 3,766 members. According to the Lynds, "the unions brought tangible pressure for a weekly pay law, standardized wage scales, factory inspection, safety devices . . . and helped in sickness or death . . ." They also held crowded mass meetings in the opera house, collected large sums of money for striking workers in Homestead and elsewhere, and supported "a special Workingmen's Library and Reading Room, with a paid librarian and a wide assortment of books." One of the "best organized cities in the United States" during the 1890's, Muncie developed a labor movement that gained widespread community support and, as the Lynds put it, "formed one of the most active coordinating centers in the lives" of thousands of Muncie's working-class families, affecting not only their working lives but also their educational, political, and recreational lives. Labor unions sponsored balls, concerts, lectures, baseball games, and speeches, including one by Samuel Gompers, who was dined at the mayor's house before addressing a great opera-house crowd in 1897. Through the craft control exercised by unions like the glassblowers, skilled workers extended their economic power through apprentice systems, alliances with other unions, boycotts, and sympathy strikes. As a result, organized workers in Muncie became "powerful and class-conscious."

Samuel Gompers of the AFL argued that "collective bargaining in industry" did not imply that wage earners wanted to "assume control of industry." But as we have seen in the case of the skilled steel and iron workers, many craft unions influenced and even controlled many aspects of industry directly affecting their jobs. To take another example, in the printing industry the International Typographical Union (ITU) exercised what labor historian Milton Derber called "unilateral control over much of shop life including hiring, apprenticeship, discharge and discipline, the distribution of overtime, the employment of substitutes to fill temporary vacancies, and the exclusion of non-unionists from the composing room floor during work hours." The ITU maintained this remarkable degree of job control by enrolling foremen in their union and by establishing certain national work laws not subject to negotiation or arbitration. At a time when most cities and even smaller towns had several daily newspapers, the demand for skilled typographers was so great that their craft union could literally dictate terms to employers on most questions of job control.

Unions like the Typographers were quite democratic during the late nineteenth century. In 1896, the ITU convention voted to outlaw secret societies and caucuses; it also agreed to a system of direct government by referendum in order to prevent a minority of members from gaining control of the union machinery. Two years later, the membership voted to do away with the cumbersome referendum form of government and to return to national convention proceedings. Like many craft unions, the ITU moved toward a more centralized national union structure as contracts and work rules needed to be enforced across city and state lines. And so, while the Typographers retained a high degree of union democracy on a national level with the formation of a two-party system, most members experienced a loss of democracy as local autonomy gave way to more centralized control. In trades like carpentry, pressure for centralization grew to meet several challenges: the emergence of large intercity companies employing new technologies, the creation of new specialty crafts which caused jurisdictional disputes among unions, and the development of a new group of professional union officials anxious to promote more businesslike methods. The United Brotherhood of Carpenters and Joiners, and their leader Peter J. McGuire, show the growing tension between the old craft union's local autonomy and democracy and the newer pressure for national unions with a centralized bureaucracy.

Like the glassblowers of Muncie, the journeymen carpenters of the later nineteenth century were proud of their craft. Photos show them standing on completed buildings wearing ties and stiff collars under their overalls. After work, many took off their overalls and walked away in white shirts, suit coats, derbies or bowlers, with watch chains in their vests; they were the equal of their bosses. The carpenters maintained their pride and independence by controlling entry to their trade through apprenticeships and by striking against non-union contractors with the support of allied building tradesmen.

The introduction of machinery to the woodworking industry cost the carpenters many jobs; mills sprang up and hired poorly paid "green hands" to manufacture everything from doors to floorboards at a fraction of the old cost. The use of ready-made materials also brought "green hands" to the construction sites to assemble and install windows, flooring, and do other things traditionally done by skilled hands. The "green hands" usually worked for non-union subcontractors who paid them piece rates. The result was speedups and shoddy work.

As leader of the United Brotherhood of Carpenters and Joiners, Peter J. McGuire directed the anger of his members, not against the "green hands," but against the "middlemen" who hired them and profited from their "botched" work. McGuire distinguished these capitalistic middlemen from the "genuine contractors" (often former craftsmen) who supplied jobs and material to union men and refused to pay by piece rates. He was thus a leading figure in the radical, producer-oriented unionism of the late nineteenth century, which expressed the toilers' hostility toward the idlers and capitalists who stood in the way of a producers' cooperative commonwealth.

Born of Irish immigrant parents on New York's Lower East Side, McGuire became a carpenter in 1867 and learned socialist ideas by listening to the German carpenters on the job and by attending free lectures at Cooper Union, school to many self-taught labor radicals. Many early-nineteenth-century artisans, craftsmen of McGuire's generation, were self-educated men who adopted the labor theory of value and saw themselves as producers entitled to the full value of their labor, not as hirelings reduced to wage slavery. Like Adolph Strasser and Samuel Gompers, who built a national union of cigarmakers,

McGuire was a Marxist who left the Socialist Labor Party to create a stronger union movement; they all believed that partisan radical politics deflected workers from the main task of building class-conscious trade unions. Using the experience they gained in organizing their own unions, Gompers, Strasser, and McGuire joined with other trade unionists in 1886 to found the American Federation of Labor. And in 1893 they rallied their forces against the political socialists, narrowly defeating their program, which called for the "collective ownership by the people of all means of production and distribution." Unlike the "pure and simple" unionists he allied with, McGuire did not give up his vision of a socialist society in favor of pragmatic trade unionism, but he refused to commit the unions to a premature political course of action when they were still so weak. Convinced that the grandiose political activities of the Knights of Labor had caused the Order's precipitous decline in 1886, he believed that workers could take control of industry through their trade unions and then establish a producer-controlled society.

AFL leaders like Strasser and Gompers ruthlessly fought the rival assemblies of the Knights in order to build their own trade unions. McGuire also adopted the strategy of organizing by trade, but in addition he believed in the principle of labor solidarity and saw the value of the Knights' mixed assemblies, which organized the workers without a trade and provided a center of community-based political activity; therefore, he sought to make a treaty with the Knights in 1886 to prevent jurisdictional fighting. He even supported the organizing efforts of a rival AFL union, the Machine Woodworkers, who wanted to unionize the "green hands" in the planing mills. Unlike many in the building trades, McGuire never intended for the craft union to be the sole preserve of the skilled workers; if the unskilled were part of the trade, they should be organized too, if not by one trade union, then by another. Though he was out of tune with many leaders in his own Brotherhood, P.J. refused to build one union at the expense of another; the important thing was to foster the labor movement as a whole, and this is why he traveled and spoke ceaselessly for the AFL as well as for his own organization.

McGuire inspired immense loyalty among the rank-and-file, and was responsible for the organizing of many local unions, but opposed strengthening the center at the expense of the locals. The tendency of the labor movement, he stated, should be toward "simplicity of organization, autonomy of function, and federation of interests." Workers would lose control over organizations with "complicated machinery." "The simpler it is the better [it is] understood." Like many old socialists, McGuire feared that trade unionism would become institutionalized—an end in itself, rather than the means to the end of establishing a cooperative socialist society.

In the 1890's, a new group of professional unionists arose in the Brotherhood to challenge these radical views; they did not reject local autonomy and internal democracy, but they put a new emphasis on centralized efficiency and responsible bureaucracy. Several developments weakened McGuire's position. In 1890, he led the Carpenters in many major cities on aggressive strikes for the eight-hour day; the building trades played a leading role in an international May Day demonstration of labor solidarity orchestrated by the new Socialist Second International. Friedrich Engels was so inspired by these eight-hour-day demonstrations that he wished Marx had lived to see "the proletariat of Europe and America" holding this "review of its forces." The Brotherhood won the eight-hour day for 46,197 workers in 137 cities and formed 132 new locals, but it was defeated in other cities by the coordinated efforts of a national employers' association. The union next had to contend with much larger firms that operated in many cities, constructing larger and larger buildings through the new use of ironwork and reinforced concrete. Furthermore, the Brotherhood, despite its growth, had failed to halt the proliferation of piece work, which led to speedup and sweating through subcontracted work. While the large firms spread the use of semi-skilled piece workers, they also created a more elaborate division of labor; they hired specialty carpenters and numerous other tradesmen who, when they formed their own unions, entered into jurisdictional disputes with the Carpenters.

In response to these developments, local leaders from city-wide district councils banded together to fight for a stronger national union administration. Their struggle with McGuire continued for ten years. McGuire won the support of the rank-and-file in his campaign for local autonomy versus centralized bureaucracy, but in 1900 the new professional organizers, largely business agents from the various councils, defeated P.J., and the Carpenters followed the pattern of bureaucratic business unionism already well established in other crafts.

The business agents who rose up to challenge McGuire often began as "walking delegates"—full-time organizers who could move from one building site to another without fear of the blacklist. As these delegates assumed more tasks for the locals, they became business agents empowered to "collect dues and et cetera." Since most locals could not afford to hire a "special agent," they were employed by the city-wide district council, which became the Brotherhood's major administrative unit in the 1890's. As Robert Christie explains in his fine history of the Carpenters, *Empire in Wood,* the business agent not only usurped many of the functions of the elected local officers, he replaced the "old speculator contractor and his piece working carpenters." According to Christie, the business agent

> . . . promised to deliver to the employer a certain number of carpenters possessed of a certain guaranteed degree of skill at a stated time for a stated wage. With the employers or their agents, he annually signed a written contract clearly stipulating these promises. In return, he received the right to control fully the trade in a given community, to bargain for the wages and working conditions received by the men he supplied . . .

The business agents in the Carpenters and other building trade unions had no use for the radicalism of old-timers like McGuire. The agent became a businessman in his own right as well as "a career man in the trade union field, a professional organizer, a union executive, a member of the union bureaucracy." In the name of the workers, he exercised a remarkable degree of local control. The union gave him an opportunity to rise in the world, "to associate with and ape the boss." And so, when he obtained a high position, he had a "vested interest" in keeping business running as usual.

After blocking the "growth of an administrative hierarchy which would have linked the district councils (and the business agents) closely with the national office," McGuire was displaced by these professional unionists in 1900. In his view, the goal of the trade unions was "to educate our class, to prepare it for the great changes to come, to establish a cooperative industry in place of the wage system, to emancipate the workers from subjugation to the capitalists . . ." His successor, William Huber, was a practical business unionist who saw unions as an end in themselves. He had no use for socialists, who "contaminated" the local unions with their "irresponsible" visionary schemes. Huber and the business agents who replaced McGuire even looked different. As Robert Christie remarks:

> McGuire was unkempt, with a long, drooping mustache and deep-set burning eyes. He was given to riding freights and to fiery radical oratory, while Harry Lloyd, leader of the Boston District Council, was described as a "good speaker and fair and conservative in all he had to say. He dressed well in dark clothes, wore a heavy gold chain and charm and might have been mistaken for a young lawyer."

Once the business agents had replaced the local officers as the real powers in the Brotherhood, Huber and the new leaders developed a system of proportional representation in which local delegates could attend national conventions with train fare paid by the national office. Thus, a new form of representational democracy arose, while the business agents, district councils, and national officers assumed the real power.

In some cases, business unionists abused their power. In the competitive building industry, a short strike could seriously hurt a small contractor, and so some builders who failed to defeat the unions attempted to buy labor peace by bribing the business agents. Some agents also went into business for themselves, extorting money from employers who were willing to pay for labor peace on their own site or to pay someone to cause trouble on a competitor's site. This kind of graft helped to support the lavish way of life of some turn-of-the-century union bosses who believed they had to put up a good show— diamond stickpins and all—when they bargained with well-heeled businessmen. A degree of apathy among union members permitted these abuses by a few notorious gangsters, like New York City's Sam Parks, who had organized the iron trade by brute force. Workers sometimes took the attitude that the union leader, like the ward heeler, was entitled to his graft as long as it came out of the rich man's hide. "Once a workman in the iron trade got $1.50 a day," said such a worker. "Parks arose, became our Moses, and led us to the promised land of $5.00 a day. Suppose Sam Parks grafted more or less, and made a bunch of money. He didn't get it out of us." The small number of union officials who enriched themselves through corruption did get it from their own members, however. Some blatantly stole money from their own treasuries or raised their own salaries. Others accepted money from employers to draw up "sweetheart contracts" or to turn their backs on certain contract violations. Union labels could also be sold to employers at handsome prices.

After 1900, the widespread use of binding no-strike contracts, or "trade agreements," and union labels which distinguished work produced by the organized crafts, created opportunities for graft and also helped trade unions grow significantly, especially in the building trades and other local industries where small competitive firms predominated. The Carpenters, for example, increased their membership spectacularly, adding over 100,000 members in the four years after McGuire was replaced by the professional unionists. These gains came at a price, of course. The building trades sacrificed much of their nineteenth-century militancy, abandoning the sympathy strike—one of their strongest weapons—in order to obtain trade agreements. The new centralized organizations created by the business agents contributed to bureaucratic efficiency, but their growth reduced local autonomy and rank-and-file democracy.

The vast majority of the business agents did not enrich themselves at their brothers' expense or take advantage of their new powers to trample on the rights of the membership from whose ranks they were not far removed. A minority, however, fell to the temptations of business unionism. Many craft-union leaders, especially in the building trades, aspired to be bosses themselves, and they were part of a commercial economy in which business values were revered; so it was easy enough for them to adopt business methods. Once in power, the grafters usually held on tenaciously in order to maintain the spoils system. Membership rights naturally suffered when they came into conflict with private careers. Some of the worst grafters even imported thugs to beat dissenters into submission, giving gangsters a foothold in some unions.

Many militant trade unionists, including socialists, favored more centralized, more businesslike methods as essential to survival and growth. There has been a tendency throughout this century for union leaders to consolidate power during hard times. The business agents in the Carpenters union sought to meet the various threats to their trade by advancing toward financial stability, centralized authority, and bureaucratic efficiency. These threats also forced the union to expand and include more "greenhorns" in the less skilled trades. By contrast, the typographers' union could maintain its status as a craft union and its remarkable internal democracy because its skilled members remained extremely powerful in their industry.

The fate of the shoe workers' unions offers another example. During the nineteenth century the Massachusetts shoe-manufacturing towns spawned many militant, democratic unions: first the Knights and Daughters of St. Crispin and then the Knights of Labor and the independent unions of women stitchers and male lasters. These unions enjoyed strong community support in towns like Lynn, Haverhill, Marlboro, and Brockton, and maintained their autonomy. In 1898, the Boot and Shoe Workers Union (B&SWU), a new affiliate of the AFL, lost a critical strike in Marlboro. In the early months of the conflict, the workers received widespread community support from merchants and others who had traditionally viewed the industrialists with suspicion. As the strike dragged on into the winter months of 1899, community support dwindled as small businesses failed and manufacturers threatened to pull up stakes and move. The failure of the Marlboro strike convinced the leaders of the Boot and Shoe Workers, including the socialists, to establish a stronger centralized union with higher dues. No-strike contracts would be sought with manufacturers. Instead of resorting to costly strikes, the union would adopt a businesslike approach of going to arbitration or withdrawing the union label from offending shoe companies. The B&SWU died in Marlboro but it prospered in many shoe towns, including Brockton and Haverhill, where the women shoe stitchers paved the way with a strike victory in 1895. The B&SWU appealed especially to skilled workers threatened with mechanization. The union's socialist leaders also promoted a demand for government ownership of industry to end ruinous competition and to enhance job control and security for workers. In 1898, the new Social Democratic movement, led by Eugene V. Debs, achieved its first success in Haverhill, where a socialist was elected mayor with union support and the votes of Irish Catholic shoe workers. A year later, the socialists elected a city government in Brockton, again with strong union backing.

Within a few years, however, as the Boot and Shoe Workers continued to move toward business unionism in response to employer attacks, unionism and socialism declined in the Massachusetts shoe towns. By 1903, the B&SWU abandoned plans for government ownership and became a conservative craft union whose leaders concentrated mainly on centralizing power and winning union-label contracts with cooperative shoe manufacturers. These policies precipitated a revolt against the union in the largest shoe city, Lynn, where the workers had been especially militant for decades. The skilled shoe cutters maintained two Knights of Labor locals there. In 1903, these locals struck two plants in a jurisdictional fight with the B&SWU. When the AFL union insisted on maintaining its contract with the shoe companies and ordered its members to cross the Knights of Labor picket lines, the whole community rallied around the local cutters and abandoned the Boot and Shoe, which then became known as the "manufacturers' union." It bears that label today.

Reacting against the centralization of power in the AFL business union, Lynn workers organized a new union in 1909 called the United Shoe Workers. The USW, unlike the Boot and Shoe, was an industrial union which included all workers, not just skilled craftsmen. It also rejected accommodation and endorsed the militant tradition that had been carried on since the great shoe strike of 1860. The new union called for the use of the strike instead of union-label contracts and compulsory arbitration to settle disputes. The USW also supported internal democracy and local autonomy as against bureaucratic centralism. The kind of opposition to business unionism that surfaced in Lynn was not an isolated phenomenon in the early 1900's. Other rank-

and-file revolts took place, embracing the causes of industrial unionism and union democracy. There did seem to be a kind of "iron law of oligarchy" in the development of many labor organizations, but the decline of democracy was not inevitable or irreversible. As the shrewd labor economist Robert F. Hoxie noted in *Trade Unionism in the United States,* business unions were "prone to develop strong leadership and to become somewhat autocratic in government," but, he added, when the union bosses trod too heavily on membership rights or failed "to deliver the goods," they were "likely to be swept aside by a democratic rising of the rank and file." And so, while union autocracy and bureaucracy grew, often in response to coordinated attacks by employers, rank-and-file members reasserted their right to democracy and autonomy with surprising frequency.

The Carpenters and other business unions may have gained members and economic strength with their new tactics, but, according to David Brody, the national craft unions also restricted their own growth. Their development as permanent institutions devoted to collective bargaining restricted their own growth "once a stable membership was built up, internal order created, and vested interests formed." After becoming established, craft unions mounted organizing efforts only when their "sheltered" spots in the economy were directly threatened. For example, once McGuire left, the Carpenters "fought relentlessly to secure jurisdiction over the entire wood industry, destroying the vigorous Amalgamated Wood Workers in the process." The Brotherhood waged this jurisdictional war to protect skilled jobs in the event that more work shifted to the mills, and also to "control the suppliers of unionized construction markets." Gone was McGuire's principle of labor solidarity. Jurisdictional warfare raged in the building trades, and even led to what the socialist humorist Oscar Ameringer called "Union Scabbing." If one craft union— say, the "Undivided Sons of Varnish Spreaders"—struck, another— say, the "Benevolent Compilation of Wood Work Gluers"—might keep working.

The craft-union strategy not only promoted disunity within the building trades; it encouraged exclusionary practices. Craft control was based on limiting access to the trade through apprenticeship programs and other controls on hiring. In fact, the growth of national trade unions like the Cigarmakers and the Carpenters resulted largely from the pressure of unskilled "green hands." AFL leaders like McGuire and Gompers urged the organization of the unskilled into special locals, but it was much easier for the various trade unions to exclude them altogether. Prejudice made it even easier to keep out these less skilled workers if they were black, foreign-born, or female.

The American Federation of Labor included some women in its affiliates. Many belonged to separate female locals. In 1892, as the new Federation struggled to gain status, Gompers appointed a woman organizer, Mary E. Kenney, though she was denied full status as an executive board member. Kenney was born in Hannibal, Missouri, in 1864, of Irish working-class parents. After the fourth grade, she was apprenticed for two years without pay to a dressmaker, and then, when her father died, she started working in a book bindery to support her invalid mother. In the 1880's, she moved to Chicago, then a storm center of militant labor activity. She found work in a bindery and joined the Ladies Federal Local Union. These federal locals were set up to include women, blacks, and others barred from craft unions. Kenney then organized other women workers into the Woman's Bookbinding Union No. 1. She lived for a while at Hull-House, the famous progressive settlement, and became acquainted with Jane Addams, the pioneer social worker. She left Chicago to be a full-time AFL organizer, but her job lasted only six months. Kenney returned to Chicago, where she worked briefly on a state women's-suffrage campaign with Florence Kelley, the newly appointed factory inspector of Illinois. She must have been discouraged, not only by her own short tenure as a women's organizer, but by the fact that Gompers's request to hire more women was voted down by the executive council in 1894. The secretary of the Boston Central Labor Union expressed a prevalent view when he stated in the *American Federationist* in 1897: "The invasion of the crafts by women has been developing for years amid injury and irritation to the workman. The right of the woman to win honest bread is accorded on all sides, but with a craftsman it is an open question whether this . . . is . . . a healthy social growth or not. Is it a pleasing indication of progress to see the father, the brother and the son displaced as the breadwinner by the mother, sister and daughter?" The AFL convention of 1898 answered this rhetorical question with a resolution against women's entry into wage-earning jobs.

Actually, few women entered the male-dominated crafts. The largest numbers still worked as domestic servants, farm laborers, cooks, elementary-school teachers, and laundresses. The number of women working for wages doubled from 4 to 8 million between 1870 and 1910 (an increase from 13 to 23 percent of the total labor force). Sex stratification remained pervasive. New occupations like clerical work were being completely feminized, and even when women worked with men in the same place, they performed different jobs and received lower wages. E. W. Bloomingdale boasted in 1895 that not one woman in his department store performed the same work as a man. It was difficult for women to organize or to obtain the support of male unionists. However, when women controlled a skilled trade, like shoe stitching, they developed strong unions which won the support of male craft unionists. During the great Lynn shoemakers' strike of 1860, women stitchers struck with male cutters and lasters. And in the 1895 Haverhill, Massachusetts, strike, the Ladies Stitchers Union won with the support of middle-class women allies, like Frances Willard, the temperance reformer, as well as male craft-union allies.

Women union organizers received as much support from female allies outside the House of Labor as from the men within. Therefore, when the Women's Trade Union League was formed to support unionization in 1903, middle-class allies, including prominent social workers, joined union organizers like Mary Kenney, who had moved to Boston and worked in the Denison Settlement House. At the League's founding meeting in Boston's Faneuil Hall, a philanthropist from that city, Mary Kehew, was elected president, and Jane Addams of Chicago vice-president. Mary Kenney O'Sullivan, whose husband Jack, the Boston labor editor, had died a year earlier, became secretary, and a shoe worker, Mary Donovan, became treasurer. The League's constitution called for a board with a majority of worker members, but this did not come about until 1907. The working-class women and their middle-class allies worked together effectively for common goals, though there were some class tensions. The socialist and feminist aims of women in both groups were reflected in the WTUL principles adopted in 1907. The goals include the following:

> To provide a common meeting ground for women of all groups who endorse the principles of democracy and wish to see them applied to industry.

> To encourage self-government in the workshop.

> To secure for girls and women equal opportunity with boys and men in trades and technical training and pay on the basis of occupation and not on the basis of sex.

Women played an active part in the surge of unionism after the 1890's depression. Between 1895 and 1905 they were involved in 1,262 strikes, including eighty-three in which they struck alone. This record, coupled with pressure applied by the WTUL, prompted the

American Federationist to note in 1905 that the organization of women workers was "possible and practicable."

The enthusiasm of the early 1900's faded quickly as employer opposition and layoffs hit women's unions hard. In Chicago, for example, 31,000 women belonged to such unions because they could run their own local affairs and not have to take a back seat to men. By 1908, however, the ranks of female unionists in Chicago had been reduced to 10,000 by the open-shop drives and the rise in unemployment. "Organizations composed entirely of women" had vanished from sixteen of the twenty-five industries in which they had been organized. Part of the problem was internal to the labor movement. The president of the predominantly female Shirt, Waist and Laundry Workers' Union wrote to Gompers: "A major handicap of our already exceedingly difficult task arises from the fact that in many localities the Central Labor bodies composed almost exclusively of men refuse to recognize our locals and the women delegates duly elected by them." Others complained that trade-union doors simply remained closed. By 1907, many members of the Women's Trade Union League had become disillusioned with the AFL and its affiliates.

As a result, the WTUL turned its energy toward securing minimum-wage laws and protective legislation for women factory workers. In this work the League enjoyed the support of progressives and settlement-house workers, who had labored for tenement-house reform and the prohibition of child labor and homework. Progressive attorney Louis D. Brandeis filed the landmark brief before the Supreme Court in the case of *Muller v. Oregon* (1908), in which he argued that protective legislation limiting the hours of female factory workers should be sustained because the "two sexes differ in structure of body, in the function to be performed by each, in the amount of physical strength [and] in the capacity for long continued labor." The Court sustained the law on the grounds that women would always be dependent on men for "protection." Protective legislation helped to eliminate some of the awful conditions imposed on women factory workers (it did not apply to domestics or the growing number of office workers); but it also reinforced the status of women as secondary wage earners whose primary role was in the home. Reforms enacted in the Progressive Era to protect women factory workers did not stop employers from hiring women. They did, however, help to stratify occupations according to sex and to maintain a separate female labor market. Unions supported protective legislation for women, but not for men, who could supposedly count on their trade unions to fight low wages, long hours, and dangerous working conditions. Instead of encouraging women to join with men to fight for the same goals, the protectionist strategy encouraged them to depend on the state, even though the history of factory legislation showed enforcement to be lax.

White supremacy could be used even more blatantly than male supremacy to rationalize exclusionary craft unionism. In 1900, only 30,000 Afro-Americans belonged to unions, and of these only a third belonged to craft unions. Thirty-nine of the eighty-two AFL affiliates contained no black members, and many of them included charters officially barring nonwhites. Several consequences followed from these exclusionary policies. Blacks seeking better-paying jobs were often forced to enter the trades and shops as strikebreakers. Indeed, Booker T. Washington actually advocated strikebreaking, because blacks were "engaged in a struggle to maintain their right to labor as free men." Some trade-union leaders, like AFL president Gompers, argued that blacks should be unionized if only to prevent their use as strikebreakers, but most retained the traditional exclusionary view that blacks, like "coolies," were compliant tools of the bosses, incapable of exercising the rights and duties of trade unionists. Exaggeration about black strikebreaking became part of a vicious circle which ended in condoning the exclusionary practices of AFL unions. White unions opposed the hiring of blacks even if they were not breaking a strike. And employers took full advantage of the situation by playing one group off against another. White workers in the South made less than their Northern counterparts, but they accepted this difference as long as they made more than Southern black workers at the same jobs. Exclusionary practices resulted, of course, in the overall depression of wage rates in segregated trades and industries. As the editor of the Atlanta *Journal of Labor* told the U.S. Industrial Commission in 1900:

> My observation of colored labor in the South, so far as it relates to the trades where skilled labor is required is that it is held over the head of white labor to the extent of holding down wages . . . In the building trades, for instance . . . the wages paid to white labor are based primarily on the wages paid to colored labor; and in every instance in which an increased wage scale has been secured, with one or two exceptions, it has been reached only after the colored man was organized and the combined effort of the two was made.

In 1905, AFL president Gompers told a union gathering in Minneapolis that "caucasians" were "not going to let their standard of living be destroyed by negroes, Chinamen, Japs, or any others." In referring to these "others," Gompers meant to include the new immigrants from Eastern and Southern Europe, who came in large numbers to work in a variety of jobs from the mills of Homestead to the garment shops of New York. The racist ideology of the period extended to include these groups as inferior and not entitled to the full benefits of citizenship—or union membership.

Since only about 20 percent of the new European immigrants arrived in the United States with skills, labor leaders treated them as "green hands," like the Chinese, and attempted to keep them out of the trades and out of the craft unions. AFL affiliates discriminated against the foreign-born worker through a number of special requirements: naturalization papers, high initiation fees, and either membership in a European union or apprenticeship program or success on a test. "It was difficult for an immigrant to get into the building trades," one foreigner recalled. "The smallest initiation fee was $25.00; in some cases it was as high as $100. Second, even when an immigrant could pay this sum, he was not sure that he could pass the required examination." An Italian immigrant echoed the complaint of many blacks when he told the New York labor council in 1909:

> The Italians have been reviled as scabs time without number. But there is a reason for this. Your delegates of unions and central labor bodies have never taken enough interest in the Italian to help him organize. These men . . . are workingmen like the rest of you, and they are willing to fight for recognition as organized workmen.

The immigrants did show a willingness to organize, not only in heavy industries like mining, but in cities like New York and Boston. Italians formed their own Hod Carriers' and Building Laborers' Union, just as black construction workers organized in the South. Jews organized their own United Hebrew Trades unions. The AFL correspondence, however, records situations in which the national headquarters actually refused charters to immigrant locals. For example, in 1903, Japanese agricultural workers joined with their Mexican fellow workers in a strike against sugar-beet growers in Ventura County, California. After winning the strike, they organized a local and applied to the AFL for a charter. President Gompers himself wrote back to J. M. Larraras, the local secretary, explaining that Federation policy prohibited issuance of charters to locals with Asian members. Larraras replied that the Mexicans would "stand by" their "Japanese brothers," because the Asian immigrants also stood by them "in the long, hard fight which ended in victory over the enemy." Displaying far more class-consciousness than Gompers, Larraras continued: "We would be false to them and to ourselves and to the cause of unionism if we now accepted privileges for ourselves which are not accorded to them."

Ironically, it was Sam Gompers, a Jewish immigrant and described by an anti-union writer as "wholly un-American in appearance," who assumed the task of administering exclusionary policy at the Federation level and, more importantly, attempting to justify it. Born of Dutch Jewish parents in London's East End ghetto, young Sam arrived in New York in 1863, becoming a cigarmaker and immersing himself in Lower East Side radical politics. Gompers worked in a shop where German Marxist cigarmakers hired people to read political literature to them while they worked. He actually learned German to be able to read the first volume of *Das Kapital* by Karl Marx, whose writings, Gompers said, not only constituted a "terrific indictment" of capitalist society but also showed that the workers' own exploitation could be the basis of liberation.

Unlike his fellow East Sider, P. J. McGuire, the ambitious cigarmaker rapidly shed his socialist views, as he rose in his union. Like Adolph Strasser, the effective German activist who built the Cigarmakers International Union into a national organization, Gompers adopted "pure and simple unionism" as his philosophy. Trade unionism was not the means to an end but an end in itself. Gompers brought this philosophy to the AFL when he became president in 1886, and he defended it militantly. His ruthless maneuvering to defeat the socialist political program in 1893 cost him the presidency for one term but saved the Federation from being taken off its true course of "pure and simple" trade-union organization. Gompers tried to keep the Federation out of partisan politics. He not only opposed the socialist "politicals" and their "impossible dreams" of a worker-controlled society. He opposed reform politicians who demanded labor legislation from the state. Firmly convinced of the business orientation of the state and the judiciary in particular, Gompers propounded a philosophy of "voluntarism," stating that unions should never seek "at the hands of government what they could accomplish by their own initiative and activities." This philosophy did not prevent Gompers from demanding that the state legislature restrict the manufacture of cheap cigars in tenements. Voluntarism might have been an inconsistent philosophy, but it reflected the old trade unions' desire to keep workers dependent on the unions, rather than the government, for the regulation of wages and hours, the provision of social insurance, and so on. Of course, unorganized workers, especially those barred from unions, had only the government to turn to if their communal and familial resources failed. These working people were of little concern to Gompers, who became the main defender of the large international craft unions and their exclusionary policies.

Gompers's economic determinism reinforced his belief in "pure and simple" craft unionism. He rejected the political approach of the Knights in which producers would unite to create a harmonious social order. Instead, he embraced the British model of trade unionism based on permanent economic conflict in the marketplace. Economic determinism also convinced the AFL president that corporate concentration (which had allowed 185 firms to control 40 percent of all manufacturing by 1904) was not only inevitable but irreversible. Thus, the cooperative alternatives of the Knights seemed impractical and the socialists' vision of a worker-controlled cooperative society appeared downright utopian. Gompers even opposed the progressive reformers' trust-busting suits; he preferred instead to deal directly with the large corporations through the National Civic Federation.

The destruction of the skilled steelworkers' union by the corporations did not lead Gompers to reject the craft-union model. Rather, it indicated to him that trade unionism might have to be restricted to those sectors of the market economy where craft control remained strong. Exclusionary craft-union strategy and the business unionists' urge for respectability led Gompers to seek accommodation with the corporations rather than take on the arduous task of organizing the unorganized mass of steelworkers. When those workers rebelled in 1909 and 1910, Gompers reluctantly endorsed efforts of the militants who attempted to organize across craft lines. Unlike these industrial unionists, he considered labor to be a beleaguered minority in a capitalist world increasingly dominated by huge corporations. However, the employers' open-shop drive and the hostility of the courts forced Gompers to endorse political action and even to question private-property rights. Still, he pursued a timid lobbying strategy rather than open the door to Socialist or Labor Party advocates who assumed a working-class majority could take control. A short man with a gnome-like face and matted hair, Gompers dressed and acted the part of a prosperous business unionist. At the turn of the century, he cut a dapper figure. Wearing a business suit, with a diamond stickpin, and smoking an expensive cigar, he talked and acted the equal of the most important businessmen and politicians of his era. His widening girth, the result of plentiful food and liquor, showed that he enjoyed the fruits of the good life. But Sam Gompers was no slouch; he worked endless hours for the Federation and saw its membership triple between 1899 and 1904. He and Strasser had perfected the model of centralized, national trade unions, and the model worked well in various trades around the country. Gompers saw the AFL through the depression of the 1890's and he used its meager resources to rebuild the

House of Labor. He was the architect of this century's labor organization. He built well, but the exclusionary strategy of the craft unions had closed doors to thousands of workers anxious to be organized.

Within the House of Labor, however, other unions rejected the craft-union strategy and organized workers on an industry-wide basis without regard to skill. After a dozen years of bitter struggle, the United Mine Workers of America (UMWA) emerged as the strongest industrial union of the early twentieth century. By 1904, it claimed 260,300 members in the hard- and soft-coal fields, making it the largest AFL affiliate. The origins and development of the UMWA are instructive.

The pit-face miner, like other nineteenth-century craftsmen, enjoyed a great deal of job control, working by the piece and subcontracting to hire his own helpers. "In most respects, having to do with the conduct of his work, the miner was his own boss," recalled John Brophy of his early days in the Pennsylvania mines. "His judgement was at work as well as his own muscles, and he made his own decisions—how deeply to undercut the face, how much powder to use, how to pace himself in loading the car and many other things." The underground workers, who were only visited by the pit boss once or twice a week, enforced their own discipline against fellow miners. One Ohio observer of the 1870's noted that the local miners "have worked in these mines since they were boys and feel they have an actual property right to their places." They also held a "good position in society" and enjoyed some political control in their towns. When absentee owners cut wages during the depression of the 1870's, they found it difficult to impose their will on these communities in which small businessmen and professionals supported the miners in strikes and lockouts. The coal companies defeated many of these strikes by using state militia, private police, and by importing strikebreakers, often from great distances. The miners also discovered that their strikes to enforce work rules and to control the piece-rate payment system required an inclusive form of organizing.

The skilled miners, however, did not control the flow of coal cars or the weighing of coal. Therefore, they could not rely solely on craft-union organizing strategy. In response to the growth of larger interstate coal companies, often owned by large railroads, the miners formed their own national union and adopted an inclusive union strategy that would ally underground workers with other employees. As a result, when mineowners began introducing mechanized methods in the 1890's, the UMW organized the machine miners, and when the owners imported strikebreakers, the union attempted to recruit them.

Using this inclusive organizing strategy, the UMW struck the small and medium-size soft-coal operators of the Midwestern Central Competitive Field in 1897. Taking advantage of the solidarity in its own ranks, the union won recognition and its first interstate contract agreement. The mineowners were anxious to stabilize labor costs and reduce them as a competitive factor. In addition to recognizing the UMW, the operators conceded the eight-hour day and allowed for a checkoff of union dues at the pay office. In return, the owners gained conciliation machinery designed to regulate competition over wages (a very large percentage of the cost for coal companies) and to provide arbitration in wage disputes. John Mitchell, the popular new president of the UMW, recognized that industrial unionism helped the miners win an important closed-shop victory and maintain some control over their labor in a chaotic industry. Mitchell rejected craft unionism but shared the business-union approach advocated by Gompers, whom he joined on the National Civic Federation. In order to build the UMW as an institution, Mitchell believed that the union had to collaborate with industry. The interstate agreement would bring stability by equalizing the ''cost of production'' for the operators from district to district, he told the U.S. Industrial Commission, ''regardless of whether or not the earnings of the miners are equal.''

After winning a closed shop in the Midwest, the UMW used skilled British, Irish, and black organizers to move into the soft-coal fields of the South. In heavily industrialized Birmingham, Alabama, where segregation prevailed and where white crafts struck against the employment of blacks, the UMW, led by black Executive Board member Richard Davis, unionized 65 percent of the work force by 1902—including native-born miners of both races as well as new immigrants from Southern Europe. In the same year, W. E. B. Du Bois estimated that half the 40,000 black AFL members in the country belonged to the UMW. In segregated Birmingham, the UMW provided one of the few institutions that included both blacks and whites. In 1901, the UMW refused to hold its district convention there because members were refused a hall in which to hold their integrated meetings. The district leader informed the merchants who owned the hall that ''the Negro could not be eliminated. He is a member of our organization and when we are told that we cannot use a hall because of this fact then we are insulted as an organization.''

The industrial-union strategy also produced results in the Pennsylvania anthracite fields, where Slavs and other East Europeans worked in large numbers. Since the miners' wives were at the center of social life in these close-knit communities, they played a leading role in strikes. In 1897, for instance, Slavic and Italian miners near Hazleton, Pennsylvania, struck against the posting of new work rules. They also demanded the removal of a foreman for his "tyrannical methods of ruling." When the strike extended to other coalfields, hysteria spread as the miners marched from one colliery to another. In Lattimer, sheriff's deputies shot at the marchers, killing nineteen Slavs. Troops were soon called in to break the strike, and women took a more active role. A boardinghouse keeper and community leader, Mary Septek, led women in attacking scabs with clubs, rolling pins, and pokers. Military officers were in a "quandary" over how to cope with "the foreign women raids." On September 17, 1897, a Wilkes-Barre newspaper editorial declared: "Those who have made themselves so conspicuous . . . in the Hazelton region were the wives, mothers, and sisters of the Hungarian, Polish and Italian strikers, and it is assumed that they had the sanction of their husbands, sons, and brothers in their ill-advised and unwomanly demonstrations." As Victor Greene indicates in *The Slavic Community on Strike,* the mine wars involved everyone—men, women, and children—in a communal struggle against employers.

Old World solidarity and loyalty were combined in these strikes with a new sense of democratic rights. The immigrant miners' parades often included the American flag. In a mass march on Hazelton at the height of the 1897 struggle, a parade stopped on the edge of town with the warning that the police awaited them. According to one account, the Italian leader paused and considered the issue. "He slowly raised his head and with a voice as steady as the earth on which he stood, exclaimed: 'I gotta the right! I am a American citizen. I have my papers. They cannot stoppa us. Forward!' He pulled his naturalization papers from his pocket and waved them aloft." The "army" revived and marched triumphantly through the city and closed down a mine on the other side.

Immigrants learned quickly to demand their democratic rights as part of the struggle for dignity. They also learned from settled workers to demand their customary rights on the job as part of the struggle for control. The older English-speaking coal miners were highly concious of their "customary rights." They were "autonomous workmen" who required little supervision, worked by the piece, and carried on the British tradition of the "independent collier" who did his own work with his own helpers. In *The Miners' Freedom,* Carter Goodrich notes that the techniques of coal mining made it difficult for owners to discipline workers. There were more than structural reasons for the miners' freedom from control. There was a "vigorous human tradition'' which was taught at the workplace itself by fathers to sons and by British and American miners to Slavic and Italian miners. One anthracite miner, for example, told Goodrich how ''he had given a lesson in the ways of the mines to the newly-landed 'hunky' who was working as his laborer: 'Come here, Frank, says I. Here's the boss. Don't work. Always sit down when the boss is around.' ''

The UMW depended greatly on this new sense of solidarity among ethnic groups when it launched a crucial strike against the Pennsylvania anthracite-coal operators in 1902. The bituminous-mine owners accepted the union to bring order to their competitive industry, but the anthracite-mine owners, who were often the most powerful railroad and steel corporations of the day, intended to keep the UMW out. G. F. Baer of the Pennsylvania and Reading Coal and Iron Company spoke for the owners when he declared: ''The rights and interests of the laboring men will be protected and cared for . . . by the Christian men to whom God in his infinite wisdom has given control of the property interests of this country.'' Baer, like the steel masters, had no intention of sacrificing any control or property rights to a union.

The great 1902 strike, which began on May 12, carried on into the summer as the miners and their families held out by using food from their own gardens and little farms, obtaining credit from sympathetic merchants, and relying on immigrants' cooperatives. A bloody riot erupted at Shenandoah when Slavic miners confronted a group of scabs and a sheriff's posse, but the immigrants showed great forbearance, and once again, the Slavic community became the center of resistance, displaying unanimity in its support of the strike.

Mitchell used his popularity with the miners to keep the strike peaceful and to contain it. In May, he worked with Gompers to prevent the soft-coal miners from striking in sympathy with the anthracite miners; in doing so, he responded to the intervention of National Civic Federation president Marcus A. Hanna, a coal operator and Republican politician, who viewed the potential sympathy strike with ''alarm.'' The Civic Federation was founded in 1900 by Ralph M. Easley, a Chicago reformer who hoped to create better relations between labor and capital. Finance capitalists and major industrialists joined with Republican politicians and AFL leaders like Gompers to promote conciliation between conservative trade unionism and welfare capitalism. The NCF leaders could accept a certain kind of unionism, but they opposed strikes and favored compulsory arbitration. Federation chief Hanna told Mitchell that a wider coal strike in 1902 would cost the UMW its public support; it would also violate an NCF principle of opposition to sympathy strikes. At a special convention of the bituminous miners in July, Mitchell defended the "sanctity" of the no-strike contract their union had signed with the soft-coal operators, and persuaded them to set up a defense fund instead of launching a general sympathy strike. "The hardest fight of a conservative labor leader is always within the union," wrote journalist Lincoln Steffens a month later in contrasting Mitchell with the "old fashioned labor leaders." The young president represented the modern type whose policy of pursuing binding trade agreements, Steffens wrote, was understood better by the employers than by the employees.

John Mitchell was the leading business unionist of his era. He not only looked the part of a prosperous young business executive; he also displayed a remarkable business acumen, investing in the stock of various companies, without regard to conflict of interest. He profited directly, at the expense of his own members, by selling under his name insurance policies, property, and a range of products from miner's soap to the "John Mitchell Cigar." It was not surprising, then, that he saw no "fundamental antagonism between the laborer and the capitalist."

Mitchell was a Catholic and a conservative who shared with other NCF members a concern about the rising tide of socialism. During the 1902 coal strike, members of the Socialist Party of America, founded only one year before, gained support for their demand to nationalize the mines. By midsummer, the Pennsylvania socialists were forming three or four locals a week in the mine region, attracting hundreds of new members. Mitchell, who shared Gompers's nonpartisan approach to politics, wrote that the socialists were holding "immense meetings in every mining town" and that "there is a growing independent political sentiment in the coalfields."

Mark Hanna also worried about the "spread of a spirit of socialism" and joined various citizens, including many progressives, in pressuring President Theodore Roosevelt to intervene in the strike. The leading "progressive" of the time, Roosevelt courted the votes of middle-class consumers, who feared the coal shortage but also worried about violent conflict between labor and capital. Journalist Jacob Riis wrote to the President: "A remedy must be found or the arrogance of money power will bring revolution." Roosevelt had been in office only a short time, and had just begun his "trust-busting" campaign, after consulting with George Perkins of the Morgan interests and the NCF. The Northern Securities case of 1902 prevented the formation of a holding company but did not alter the ownership of the railroads involved, and it did not mean, as the President assured J. P. Morgan, that he intended to break up the steel trust.

Theodore Roosevelt assumed the Presidency in 1901 after President William McKinley was assassinated by an anarchist. An advocate of reform at home and expansion abroad, the young President wanted to attract more of the growing labor vote to the Republican Party. He hoped to do this by threatening to bust the trusts and by acting as an arbitrator in the 1902 coal strike. Roosevelt and his party could count on traditional loyalties for some support. Protestant workingmen, black and white, often voted for the party of Lincoln because of their traditional opposition to the Democrats' pro-Catholic, pro-Southern policies. GOP slogans denouncing "Rum, Romanism and Rebellion" could still attract votes from Protestant workmen after 1900. Many of these voters also favored state intervention of various kinds like temperance and compulsory public education. Catholic voters opposed both reforms. The Republicans also used the issue of protective tariffs to win votes from workers in steel towns like Homestead and in other manufacturing centers. The GOP could claim to represent both bosses and workers by supporting high tarriffs on foreign-made goods. Finally, Republican patronage machines in company towns, and in cities like Philadelphia and Chicago, maintained party loyalty through jobs and favors. The Democrats retained the loyalty of the Irish and most other Catholic immigrants, as well as most white workingmen in the South. During the depression of the 1890's, conservative Democratic "politicos" had to move to the left to maintain their restive working-class constituents. In the North, where Coxey's "army" of the unemployed symbolized great unrest, the Democratic Party's leaders began actively to support labor reforms. As President Grover Cleveland and the old-line forces failed in the mid-1890's, Irish and other ethnic politicians took over the party in many cities. In Boston, the Democrats transformed themselves briefly into a surrogate labor party and retained the loyalty of their massive Irish constituency. In the South, the People's Party pushed many Democrats into adopting sweeping reforms. Elections in 1894 and 1896 divided candidates on class issues, but after the depression ended, the two old parties resumed politics as usual, appealing to working-class voters largely on racial, religious, or cultural grounds. Roosevelt played this game better than most Republicans. Advocating reform, he attempted to recruit newer urban immigrants like the Jews, Italians, and blacks who felt shut out by the Irish urban Democrats. Roosevelt was also aware that the socialists were having increasing success in many of the immigrant districts, in the urban ghettos as well as the strike-ridden Pennsylvania mining towns.

In October of 1902, Roosevelt intervened in the anthracite strike, not by sending in the U.S. army as the owners demanded, but by appointing an arbitration commission, including representatives of labor and capital. Arbitration was important to Roosevelt and Civic Federation leaders, who hoped to reduce class warfare and stop the growth of socialism by creating bureaucratic machinery to solve disputes. To do this, the progressives were willing to recognize unions led by reasonable men like John Mitchell. Reactionary open-shop employers like George Baer opposed any form of recognition, but the reformers argued that unions could become responsible partners of business. As Attorney Louis D. Brandeis of the Civic Federation explained, stable trade unionism would allow labor leaders to gain valuable business experience, which "almost invariably makes the leaders responsible and conservative."

Roosevelt's arbitration commission brought the five-month anthracite strike to an end without serious violence. Its settlement awarded the miners a wage increase and a nine-hour day, but in place of union recognition, it created a six-member conciliation board to adjudicate all disputes between labor and management. Mitchell and Gompers joined the Civic Federation in praising the settlement, but many miners, notably the socialists, complained about a sellout. A remarkable figure named Mother Jones, who had already developed a reputation as the "miner's angel" for her bravery in numerous mine strikes, became disillusioned with the UMW's popular "boy president" when miners were asked to help contribute to the purchase of a house for Mitchell. "If John Mitchell can't buy a house to suit him . . . out of his salary, then I would suggest he get a job that will give him a salary to buy a $10,000 house," she said, not knowing of the wealth Mitchell would amass.

Born in Cork, Ireland, Mary Harris came to America in the 1840's. She taught school in Michigan and made dresses in Chicago before marrying George Jones, an iron molder, in 1861. Her husband and her children all died in a yellow-fever epidemic six years later. After, she returned to Chicago and set up a thriving dressmaking business, which burned to the ground in the fire of 1871. In the depressed seventies, she began attending lectures by the Knights of Labor. She became a radical agitator in the 1890's and remained a thorn in the side of the ruling classes for the next three decades. She supported populism and became a socialist by selling subscriptions to the Kansas-based *Appeal to Reason,* the most popular radical newspaper in United States history. During the late 1890's, she agitated in the Pennsylvania coalfields and, from then on, gave her heart and soul to the coal miners.

From Lattimer, where she led miners' wives on the picket line, to Ludlow, where she was imprisoned, Mother Jones, dressed deceptively in the matronly fashions of the age, put herself on the line. The UMW's president, at first, inspired her loyalty, but after the 1902 strike, she became an outspoken critic of well-heeled business unionists like Mitchell. As she wrote in her *Autobiography:*

> Many of our modern leaders of labor have wandered far from the thorny path of the early crusaders. Never in the early days of the labor struggle would you find leaders dining and wining with the aristocracy . . . In those days labor representatives did not sit on velvet chairs in conference with labor's oppressors; they did not dine in fashionable hotels with the representatives of top capitalists such as the Civic Federation.

If John Mitchell brought the moderating effects of the business approach to industrial unionism among the Eastern coal miners, William D. Haywood expressed the radical approach to the industrial unionism of the Western hard-rock metal miners. After the formation of the Western Federation of Miners in 1893, these workers fought violent battles with the gold, silver, and copper barons of the Rockies, culminating in the Coeur d'Alene strike of 1899 in which federal troops marched into Idaho and 1,500 miners were imprisoned in a "bull-pen." It was in this year that Bill Haywood joined the WFM executive board and began a twenty-year career as the country's leading revolutionary labor leader.

Haywood was born thirty years before in Salt Lake City, Utah, where his father worked as a Pony Express rider. At fifteen he entered the Nevada mines as a hauler and then learned the skills of a miner. He read extensively and wanted to be his own boss. He tried prospecting and homesteading for a while after he married Nevada Jane Minor. After "booming" around the West, Haywood returned to the mines, specifically to a large, absentee-owned, mechanized lead mine in Utah, where he became radicalized. In 1894, he left home and, failing to get work as a skilled miner, took a job as a driver in a Silver City, Idaho, mine. Haywood had lost his eye in a childhood accident, and when he mangled his hands he retired from mining to union work. He built up the Silver City local of the WFM in the years when the Federation's members were being radicalized by their brutal conflicts with the mineowners. Haywood moved to the left with them, learning to despise the craft unionism of the AFL and its leader Samuel Gompers, who incensed the WFM by refusing to respond to an appeal for funds during the 1896 Leadville strike. Haywood not only rejected craft unionism, but like many in the WFM, he rejected "pure and simple" unionism. After the intervention of federal troops at Coeur d'Alene in 1899, other Western miners who recognized the ultimate need for workers' control over the state became socialists.

After the turn of the century, Haywood helped lead the WFM in a series of violent strikes for the eight-hour day and recognition of union control of working conditions. The confrontation between the union and employers exploded into a protracted war at Cripple Creek, Colorado, where thirty men died in numerous gun battles and dynamitings. With the WFM officers in prison, Haywood assumed leadership of the strike, which carried on into 1905, when the WFM, already hostile to the AFL, angrily attacked Mitchell and Gompers for calling off a sympathy strike of UMW coal miners in Colorado.

The Mine Owners Association, using armed citizens' groups, the militia, censorship, and deportation, defeated the WFM at Cripple Creek and other Colorado towns, but the Federation continued to grow in the West by using its industrial-union strategy. By 1907, it claimed 44,000 members, including 8,000 in the giant Butte, Montana, local. The WFM lost out at Cripple Creek to superior forces mobilized by the mining companies and the state government. In places like Butte, though, the radical union struggled successfully against the "copper barons" and other big capitalists. Unlike the steelworkers in the East, the hard-rock metal miners in the West maintained considerable job control, despite mechanization. They also eschewed craft unionism in favor of industrial unionism open to all who worked in and around the mines, including smeltermen, regardless of race, creed, color, or nationality. In fact, the leaders made a special effort to recruit European and Mexican immigrants by publishing literature in foreign languages: they rejected the craft-union view that immigrants tended to be scabs and argued that, on the contrary, they were often the militants in strikes.

Though the vast majority of women in the Western mining towns were economically dependent on male wage earners, wives formed auxiliaries and participated actively in the WFM: as historian Elizabeth Jameson indicates, the miners' union helped to relieve some of the pain that accompanied industrial work for all families. "Enormous human loss accompanied corporate mining in the forms of sickness, injury, and death." And women, "whose security depended upon their men, were all too aware of the human costs of mining, costs for which the mining corporations took scant responsibility." Women in the Western Federation were very active in the consumer boycotts and union-label campaigns in the mining towns that were used to enforce worker demands. During strikes, "when class action became imperative, women left their homes and violated prescribed roles." Emma Langdon, who wrote the history of the Cripple Creek strike, believed that "women's natural sphere should be in the home and not in public life," but when unified action was required, she took on the job of telling the strikers' story, while maintaining her household duties. "I have compiled the work, set the type, read the proofs, and made the pictures from which many of the illustrations are made, folded the pages and while getting out the work have taken care of my work as usual, doing my own sewing, baking, washing and ironing and the other work that falls to the lot of women . . ." In addition to attending the trials of her "union brothers," she worked as a local secretary and an organizer for both the WFM and the Socialist Party. Militants like Langdon and Mother Jones could enter the public sphere, especially during strikes, when unified class action was needed, but unlike the feminists of the time, they did so without challenging the traditional sexual division of labor. Women activists like Langdon would fulfill their traditional role and also join in the struggle of their "union brothers," but this required uncommon energy as well as a deep commitment to a movement that continued to treat women as auxiliaries to the struggle. Industrial unionism could help some working women overcome their subordinate position, as in the case of the garment workers, but only after these women had already entered the men's sphere of factory labor.

Out of the crucible of violent class war in the Rockies, the Western Federation created a form of industrial unionism premised on class struggle. It leaders and its members were highly class-conscious and showed a strong interest in populism and socialism. It was not surprising, then, to see WFM leader Big Bill Haywood presiding at Brand's Hall in January of 1905 when labor radicals gathered to found the Industrial Workers of the World. A tall, heavyset man wearing a black slouch hat, with a booming voice and a mean glare (though he had only one good eye), Haywood spoke for the radical industrial unionists who created their unions out of violent class struggle and saw in them the institutions that would eventually control the economy. Banging the convention to order with a two-by-four, Big Bill declared the opening of the first "continental congress of the working-class." He denounced the AFL for not representing the working class as a whole. "What we want to establish at this time is a labor organization that will open wide its doors to every man that earns his living by his brain or his muscle."

According to the IWW manifesto, AFL craft unionism had made

"industrial solidarity impossible" at a time when the concentration of wealth and the centralization of management increased the power of the employing class. "Craft division hinders the growth of class-consciousness of the workers, fosters the idea of a harmony of interests between employing exploiter and employed slave," the document continued. "They permit the association of misleaders of the workers with the capitalists in the National Civic Federation, where plans are made for the perpetuation of capitalism, and the permanent enslavement of workers through the wage system." Like the Western Federation, the IWW repudiated the binding trade agreement, because labor contracts negotiated between parties of unequal strength could easily be violated by employers. Workers had to retain their freedom to strike or slow down. The only rights and standards workers could count upon were those they could secure and defend through direct action, which, of course, required an industrial union strong enough to "control the work." Radically distinguishing themselves from the business unionists who sought labor peace, the IWW founders declared: "The working-class and the employing class have nothing in common. There can be no peace so long as hunger and want are found among millions of working people and the few, who make up the employing class, have all the good things of life."

The Industrial Workers of the World presented no immediate threat to the AFL; its membership was composed largely of the Western Federation of Miners, still locked in a bloody struggle in Colorado and occupied also with the trial of Bill Haywood and WFM president W. D. Moyer on charges of assassinating an anti-union former governor of Idaho. The famous labor lawyer Clarence Darrow won an acquittal in this case after a national defense campaign in 1907.

As the effects of the Panic of 1907 set in, all unions suffered. The IWW failed to grow significantly. The hard times and violent employer resistance hurt, but so did factionalism. One faction, headed by Socialist Labor Party chief Daniel De Leon, favored industrial unionism combined with Marxist political action and party building. De-Leon's "politicals" were expelled at the 1908 Chicago convention by a direct-action faction whose leaders wanted the IWW to be free of partisan influence. Unlike the Socialist Party supporters, most IWW's believed that political action could only supplement economic power organized on the job. Leading the attack on De Leon at the 1908 convention was "an overalls brigade" of Wobblies from the West who rode the rails cross-country to reaffirm the primacy of industrial action.

This brigade of transient Western workers expressed the essential spirit of the Wobblies. They filled the jails in Spokane, Washington, and the other cities where the Wobs mounted their "soapboxes" to fight for free speech, and they wrote the bawdy songs satirizing the Salvation Army and the AFL "aristocracy of labor." They were openly contemptuous of all forms of bourgeois respectability, whether it came from "longhaired preachers" or AFL "labor fakirs." Poor but defiant, the Western "hobo" workers blamed the system for throwing them out of work and joyously made the best of life "on the bum." Rejecting the Protestant work ethic, they made a unique contribution to proletarian culture by celebrating the humanity of the unemployed worker. In the midst of the Spokane free-speech fight in 1908, the Wobblies who filled the city jail borrowed a Gospel tune and added their own words to a song they called "Hallelujah, I'm a Bum." Unlike the craftsmen, who enjoyed some control and a measure of respect on the job, the casual laborers of the West gained little respect from their work as "harvest stiffs," lumberjacks, sailors, and so on. These men had abandoned job consciousness for revolutionary class consciousness.

Though the IWW did not actually raid AFL locals, it was widely condemned as a rival or "dual" union. Its contempt for craft unionism and skilled workers generally alienated some socialists. Eugene Debs, who had helped to found the One Big Union, let his membership lapse in 1908. Like other party comrades, Debs was busy "boring from within" the AFL. And his strategy was beginning to gain results, and AFL members and their leaders were taking a much more militant stance on many issues.

Union membership had more than doubled between 1897 and 1901, when it reached well over a million. By 1904, it had climbed to just over 2 million—a 400 percent increase in just eight years. Craft unions, like the Carpenters and Typographers, as well as strong industrial unions of miners, brewers, and shoemakers, demanded more and more job control in the form of union "rules." Even huge railroad and mining companies had been forced to come to terms with unions. Smaller employers in more competitive markets were hurt by rising labor costs. They also believed that unions actually threatened their rights as property owners. How could they be free to run their businesses if unions kept defending so-called "customary rights" and then demanded new standards and work rules the employer was bound to honor?

In 1903, these smaller industrialists formed the National Association of Manufacturers (NAM) and launched an open-shop drive to stamp out unionism. NAM's campaign involved opening strikebreaking employment agencies in several major cities, employing large numbers of spies and private guards through Pinkerton's and other "detective agencies," and forming anti-boycott associations to prevent unions in one trade from supporting walkouts in others. NAM's strategy ran counter to the Civic Federation's more conciliatory scheme. The NCF's effort to prevent strikes and increase productivity through the binding trade agreement had already suffered a setback, however. The Murray Hill Agreement of 1900 between the International Association of Machinists and the National Metal Trades Association (NMTA) was based on a national no-strike contract in which machinists won the nine-hour day, a minimum wage, shop committees to handle disputes, and seniority rights, in return for removing work rules which limited productivity and accepting an arbitration board to settle disputes. The Civic Federation praised the agreement as a model, but a year later the NMTA violated the agreement, and a nationwide strike erupted. The Machinists lost the strike, and sentiment grew for amalgamating the various metal trades unions in order to cope with the employers' coordinated national attack.

After the defeats sustained by the steelworkers and machinists in 1901, an open-shop drive and an economic downturn followed, and the unions went on the defensive. The courts also aided the employers' counterattack by issuing injunctions against strikes and deciding key cases that restricted workers' rights. In 1905, Massachusetts courts held that a union-shop contract did not require the discharge of non-union employees; a Chicago court decision prohibited picketing during a violent teamsters' sympathy strike because the use of force constituted a criminal act; and the Federal Circuit Court in Connecticut decided in the Danbury Hatters' case that a union boycott against a manufacturer violated the Sherman Anti-Trust Act, the implication being that boycotted employers could sue union members as well as leaders for "restraining trade."

The open-shop drive, the judicial offensive against labor, and layoffs accompanying the economic slumps of 1904 and 1907 led to serious defeats in the next five years, when AFL unions won only 32 percent of their strikes. Gompers and the leadership responded with a "bill of grievances" in 1906 that took the Federation back into partisan politics, partly to quiet rumblings in the ranks for a labor party and growing support for the Socialist Party, whose 1904 Presidential candidate, Eugene V. Debs, hero of the 1894 Pullman strike, quadrupled his 1900 vote. Suppressing labor-party sentiment in the ranks and abandoning nonpartisanship, the AFL endorsed Democrat William Jennings Bryan in the 1908 election. The Republican "injunction judge" William Howard Taft won, however, and the AFL remained on the defensive. Gompers himself nearly went to prison when the *American Federationist* printed the name of a boycotted firm after the American Anti-Boycott Association had obtained an injunction against the publication of an AFL "We Don't Patronize" list. In 1908, the Supreme Court upheld the Danbury Hatters' case, opening the door to suits against unions engaging in boycotts and sympathy strikes.

As employers aggressively attacked union members' collective bargaining and free-speech rights, the labor leaders responded by defending human rights against property rights. When the courts and other arms of the state aided anti-union businesses, even conservative craft unionists were forced, almost against their will, to question the primacy of property rights. Gompers became distinctly more militant in defending his rights to free speech and the larger rights of unions to strike, boycott, and picket. "Rights?" Gompers asked rhetorically in 1908. "Yes, there is no hesitancy on the part of our courts to grant us certain rights—for instance, the rights to be maimed or killed without any responsibility to the employer; the right to be discharged for belonging to a union; the right to work as long hours for as low pay as the employer can impose . . ."

Members of the AFL affiliates responded to the employers' onslaught in two significant ways: in the building trades, there was terrorism against open-shop employers, and among unskilled and unorganized workers there were new forms of industrial union organizing within the trade unions. In 1905, the International Association of Bridge, Structural and Ornamental Ironworkers struck when their employers declared an open shop. The conflict centered at first on New York City, where the union had been constructing many new skyscrapers and where violence had characterized labor relations in the building trades. As the struggle grew in intensity, the Structural Ironworkers began a "dynamite campaign" against open-shop employers that led to eighty explosions over the next few years, culminating in the 1910 conflagration at the open-shop Los Angeles *Times* building which killed twenty workers. The McNamara brothers of the Ironworkers were arrested and tried for the crime, and after a national defense campaign had been mounted, they stunned the labor movement by confessing. The McNamaras were militant craft unionists skilled in the use of dynamite, but they were also conservative Catholics who had joined the Militia of Christ to battle the influence of socialism. They terrified open-shop employers, who responded with a ruthless anti-union program, but their terrorism primarily hurt the labor movement, which could no longer deny that its ranks included violent men.

A far more constructive response to the open-shop movement came from trade unions who opened their ranks to the unskilled and entered into new alliances to meet the crisis. In Chicago, the Amalgamated Meat Cutters and Butcher Workmen altered their strategy and organized unskilled meat-packers, many of them immigrant women and blacks who had come into Packingtown as strikebreakers in the 1880's. Upton Sinclair's sensational novel *The Jungle* showed the degradation and exploitation workers experienced in Chicago's "back of the yards." In 1904, the Amalgamated Meat Cutters struck, against Gompers's wishes, when the packing companies refused to accept a minimum-wage demand for unskilled workers. Despite the militancy and solidarity displayed by the strikers, they lost to one of the strongest open-shop employer associations in the country. A year later, Chicago Teamsters conducted an equally aggressive strike in sympathy with garment workers struggling against the open shop of the Montgomery Ward Company. An extraordinarily violent strike which resulted in fourteen deaths, the conflict brought about a visit from President Roosevelt, who spoke in the strife-torn city on the dangers of "class hatred." Having won the election in his own right the previous fall, the Chief Executive was less inclined to "truckle" to the labor vote; in fact, he threatened to use federal troops to break the strike, which was eventually defeated by a solid front of open-shop employers.

Roosevelt's more belligerent posture toward organized labor was paralled by the National Civic Federation's acceptance of judicial injunctions against strikers. Earlier enthusiasm for the trade agreement began to wane as industrial relations became more violent. The NCF labor-union representatives were embarrassed when a founding member, the millionaire traction magnate August Belmont, hired scabs to break a strike of his employees on New York's Interborough Rapid Transit Company. Gompers and Mitchell were also under fire from the socialists, whose influence reemerged within the AFL. In his speech at the founding of the IWW in Chicago, socialist leader Eugene Debs branded the labor members of the NCF "lieutenants of capitalism." There was "certainly something wrong," he said, with the "pure and simple" form of unionism when it led to an alliance "with such a capitalist combination as the Civic Federation, whose sole purpose it is to chloroform the working-class while the capitalist class goes through its pockets." As industrial relations became more violent, the NCF turned to promoting various welfare schemes. But conflict between progressives and socialists still had a lively future.

The building trades had abandoned the sympathy strike after the turn of the century, but newer unions with less craft control continued to use the tactic. The most massive strike of the period took place in 1907, when the thirty-six unions of the New Orleans Dock and Cotton Council, an interracial alliance of waterfront workers, struck in support of the United Brewery Workers, a socialist-led industrial union which insisted on including all workers in their "one big union" even though the AFL awarded jurisdiction over the beer drivers to another union. The general strike that followed saw great solidarity between the trades and the races, as had an earlier city-wide strike in 1892; it also led to a greater polarization of craft and industrial unionists. The AFL, in fact, expelled the Brewery Workers Union because it refused to recognize craft distinctions, and then, during the New Orleans strike, it recognized a special local of beer drivers who were breaking the general strike. This was the last straw for Oscar Ameringer, the socialist satirist and editor of the Brewers newspaper in New Orleans, who wrote the biting comment on "union scabs" mentioned earlier.

William Trautman, who edited the Brewers' national, German-language paper, offered a critical summary of a decade of conflict between craft and industrial unionism when he explained in an IWW tract "Why Strikes Are Lost." Trautman, who resigned his post as editor to join the IWW, of which he was elected general organizer in 1908, argued that craft autonomy caused the defeat of many strikes like the 1904 Chicago strike. Fifty-six different unions claimed jurisdiction in the meat-packing industry. "What a horrible example of an army divided against itself in the face of a strong combination of employers." Binding contracts and trade agreements only made matters worse, insisted radical industrial unionists like Trautman. During the early 1900's, the employers, supported by "labor lieutenants" like Mitchell and Gompers, "would harp continually on the sanctity of contracts with some craft unions, while at the same time slaughtering piecemeal other craft unions with whom they were in conflict."

Most craft unionists dismissed the criticisms of Trautman and blamed the IWW for committing the grave sin of forming a "dual union"—but others could see the handwriting on the wall. "On the whole," one craft-union supporter wrote to Gompers, "the skilled craftsmen, being better paid, are apt to be ultra conservative. The unskilled, on the other hand, being poorly paid, are the hardest fighters. But they are also the most troublesome, and I fear that this is the element we will have to cope with if the Socialists behind the industrial union scheme have their way.'' Another like-minded union man told the AFL chief that if the industrial unionists won out, the leadership might be seriously threatened. ''Some fine morning,'' he concluded, ''you will wake up with a revolution on your hands''.

3

The Struggle for Control in the Progressive Era

In 1909, a revolution did begin that shook the House of Labor for the next decade. It was a revolution of the unskilled "machine proletariat" that began with the McKees Rocks steel strike and the great "uprising" of the women shirtwaist makers in the Lower East Side. These unskilled proletarians had been forced by machine industry to work in unison, noted IWW theorist Austin Lewis in *The Militant Proletariat*. Machinery forced workers of various backgrounds into the mold of "industrial organization," and this, Lewis argued in 1911, was the "first step to the self organization" of the industrial proletariat. The uprising of the unskilled led naturally to the industrial form of unionization, and heightened tensions within the House of Labor.

After McKees Rocks, the IWW challenge to the AFL gained real force, and reached a climax with the great victory in the "bread and roses" strike at Lawrence, Massachusetts, in 1912. The Wobblies exposed the exclusionary policies of the Federation by organizing the unorganizable from immigrant textile workers in Lawrence to black and white lumberjacks in Louisiana. Within the Federation, the socialists gained support by attacking business unionism and "class collaboration" as espoused by the Civic Federation. In general, the Debsian socialists attempted to politicize the class-conscious militancy that arose throughout the 1910's. They succeeded in linking party building and union organizing in the Lower East Side of New York and other industrial cities, but in other places the immediate demands created by strikes conflicted with the socialists' longer-range political goals. Indeed, worker militancy could not always be channeled into radical politics. Many combative workers were actually conservative craft unionists hard pressed by employer attacks.

As skilled workmen attempted to defend job control against scientific management and other strategies, they sought alliances with the unskilled and with other craft unions. Exclusionary policies failed in the midst of violent struggles with well-organized employers. A "new unionism" emerged within the AFL during the Progressive era, partly as a result of mass strikes that swept American industry, culminating in the most strife-torn year in United States history, 1919. Even after the radicalism of the IWW and the Socialist Party had been suppressed during World War I, the new unionism thrived as some AFL unions demanded the nationalization of their industries and made other demands that extended the struggle along a new frontier of control.

In 1909, the Pressed Steel Car Company, a subsidiary of U.S. Steel located at McKees Rocks, Pennsylvania, introduced a new piece-rate pay system to increase output. The company kept the piece rates secret and pooled wages, so that a slowup caused by one worker hurt everyone. When forty immigrant workers walked out in protest and were fired, six hundred more laid down their tools, followed by skilled English-speaking workers. Management in its struggle to gain more control had unified a diverse work force. An "Unknown Committee" took leadership of the strike; it was composed largely of immigrants, including three members of the Industrial Workers of the World determined to show that industrial unionism could succeed where craft unionism could not.

U.S. Steel had abandoned all interest in signing trade agreements with skilled workers and said so in its open-shop declaration of June 1, 1909. Some members of the AFL called for a reevaluation of craft-union strategy. "The self-centered, aristocratic Amalgamated Association looked with contempt upon the unskilled workers," one member complained, "and the manufacturers took advantage of the situation." Faced with an open-shop drive, the Amalgamated began a desperate new organizing drive aimed at unskilled immigrant workers, previously dismissed as poor union prospects. When the McKees Rocks strike erupted, however, the Amalgamated found itself displaced by the IWW.

When violence and bloodshed resulted from clashes between strikers, led by immigrant women, and the mounted Pennsylvania constabulary (called Cossacks by the workers), the Amalgamated distanced itself from the struggle. While an AFL spokesman blamed the violence on "ignorant, foreign labor," the Wobblies plunged into the fray, with multi-lingual organizers and newspapers, and tactics which helped the strikers to hold out for forty-five days and, despite thirteen deaths and five hundred injuries, win a victory over the steel trust. The IWW attracted the attention of progressive and socialist "muck-rakers," who wrote extensively about the tyranny of the company and the state police, but the key to victory was provided by a conservative craft union, the Brotherhood of Railway Trainmen, whose members blocked the arrival of strikebreakers by rail.

The McKees Rocks strike was of great importance because it brought adverse national publicity to the "steel trust"; because it showed that unskilled immigrants could organize effectively; and because it gave the IWW an opportunity to import its class-struggle approach to industrial unionism from the West. The uprising at McKees Rocks was no fluke. Other similar mass strikes followed at another U.S. Steel subsidiary in Hammond, Indiana, where the IWW took leadership in a walkout involving workers of many different nationalities, and at the steel plants of McKeesport and South Bethlehem, Pennsylvania, where skilled and unskilled workers combined to protest speedups resulting from the piece-rate system. In these steel strikes, the immigrants again displayed communal solidarity through parades and other old-country rituals. The Slavic workers were no longer "green hands." Only about a third were still single men; most had settled down in the steel towns with their families. Management's attempts to control the labor process and to create networks of dependency in the steel cities had not atomized the immigrant workers.

Sam Gompers was impressed. The steel trust had crushed the old unions and "lulled itself into a fancied security," but the mass strikes of 1909–10 had shown that the corporation did not completely dominate the world of the worker. Stimulated by the IWW's bold move into the East, the Amalgamated Association took more interest in industrial union strategy. As an AFL flyer in one of the 1910 strikes read: "For years thousands of men employed by the Bethlehem Steel Company have suffered under the iron heel of the most crushing institution known to the civilized world . . . AT LAST THEY HAVE REVOLTED . . ."

The rebellion at McKees Rocks had been caused in part by the introduction of piece rates designed to increase output. Piece rates were used more and more frequently, along with other incentive systems, to combat the job control workers exercised informally and formally through union work rules. The use of new management-control strategies in the 1910's significantly escalated the struggle for control at the point of production. As Harry Braverman indicated in *Labor and Monopoly Capital,* the financial power of twentieth-century corporations enabled scientific managers to press science and technology into the service of capital. They also employed the new social-science disciplines like psychology and sociology in their struggle to gain total control over the labor process. The emergence of the modern corporation involved the creation of a professional group of engineers and managers who attempted to increase labor stability, productivity, and efficiency. Scientific managers attempted to divide each step of the production process into small tasks that could be studied and timed. Engineers could then plan each worker's job in advance and provide instructions on exactly how the job should be done. Management could thus "control each step of the labor process," while the workers, deprived of all decision making and planning, would lose control over their own labor.

Frederick Winslow Taylor, the pioneer of scientific management, argued that mechanization and coercion by foremen could not attain maximum productivity. Workers would still find ways of restricting output by operating the machinery at reduced speeds or by influencing the foremen who set the rates. After working in Bethlehem's Midvale steel plant, Taylor stated in *Shop Management* that loafing, or what he called "soldiering," still existed to a shocking degree. Far more disturbing was "systematic soldiering" organized to restrict output; it was, he argued, "almost universal under ordinary schemes of management" because piece-rate schemes with bonus incentives, quite popular in the steel industry, failed to convince workers to perform at peak efficiency. Workers knew that piece rates were rigged so that a doubling of production would not yield a proportionate increase in pay; they also knew that employers cut the rates if workers made too much money. Finally, workers engaged in soldiering because they feared layoffs and wanted to spread the work out. To replace the old piecework incentive schemes, Taylor proposed a differential piece rate establishing special rates of pay for "first-class workmen." These men could earn substantial bonuses if they performed the work as predetermined by the time studies of the engineers, who would remove "brainwork" from the shop floor to the planning department.

Most corporations did not employ Taylor's complete system of scientific management. The machine tool and arms manufacturers, who wanted to reduce the craft control exercised by machinists, found union opposition formidable. Unionized molders, for example, opposed all forms of piece-rate incentive. The *International Molders*

Journal condemned Taylor's attempt to separate "craft knowledge" from "craft skill." After management gathered up "craft knowledge," systematized it, and then doled it out again in the form of minute instructions, "the worker is no longer a craftsman in any sense, but is an animated tool of management."

In 1911, the Iron Molders at the federal arsenal in Watertown, Massachusetts, struck against the use of the stopwatch and the bonus system. Their strike attracted much support among AFL unions and resulted in Congressional hearings on Taylorism. Skilled workers testified that scientific management was little more than a new kind of speedup. Taylor's own arrogant testimony only fueled the fires of opposition. By 1914, Robert Hoxie's survey showed that few firms had adopted the full Taylor system. Nonetheless, the stopwatch and the time-and-motion study had arrived and a new form of management control had been developed which would eventually have profound effects on the workplace.

More important than the strikes involving skilled and unskilled metalworkers was the startling revolt of the women clothing workers in New York and Chicago. The 1909 "uprising of the 20,000" shirtwaist makers in New York City signaled the beginning of the unskilled workers' movement toward industrial unionism and the opening of doors to women's renewed participation in the labor movement. In September of 1909, women employed by the Leiserson Shirtwaist Company walked out, and shortly thereafter employees of the Triangle Shirtwaist Company were locked out in a dispute over sick benefits. Both groups turned for assistance to Local 25 of the International Ladies' Garment Workers' Union. Founded in 1900 on a semi-industrial union basis, the ILGWU had struggled in vain against open-shop employers and in 1909 had only $4 in its treasury. Nonetheless, its leaders called a strike against the Triangle Shirtwaist Company. The company responded by hiring thugs and prostitutes to attack the union pickets. The New York Women's Trade Union League became involved as prominent women allies joined the picket lines, where they soon confronted the police, who arrested League president Mary Drier and caused a publicity flap. Violence spread as scores of young women pickets were beaten and arrested.

On November 22, 1909, thousands of strikers and their allies jammed Cooper Union to consider a general strike call. After two hours of talk dominated by the ILGWU male leaders, a young striker made her way slowly to the platform. Clara Lemlich, a young Jewish immigrant, told how she had been beaten by thugs on the picket line. She galvanized the predominantly Jewish audience by calling for a general strike immediately. When the chairman finally restored order and asked for a second to the motion, the crowd rose as one. A bit shaken, he asked: "Will you take the Jewish oath?" Two thousand women raised their arms, swearing to honor the strike or see their hands wither from the arms they had raised. The "great uprising" of the shirtwaist makers had begun.

Roughly 30,000 workers, or three quarters of the people in the trade, answered the general-strike call. Most of them were young women of Russian or Italian parents, who had had no union-organizing experience, but they maintained their picket lines in spite of police brutality, spread their strike to Philadelphia, and received valuable assistance from the WTUL, the United Hebrew Trades, and the Socialist Party, whose own women's branches had begun to grow substantially. After nearly three cold months on the lines, the women won their strike, and the ILGWU, which suddenly had a large active membership, negotiated contracts in all but nineteen of the 337 shirtwaist companies in New York and Philadelphia. The "unyielding and uncompromising temper of the strikers" showed that "women make the best strikers," as Helen Marot of the WTUL wrote. The uprising also proved again, and in an especially convincing fashion, that women and new immigrants could organize their own unions.

The strike gave birth to the ILGWU as a powerful union; it also saw the emergence of a group of militant young women unionists who worked closely with middle-class allies in the Women's Trade Union League. Clara Lemlich and Pauline Newman emerged from the strike as important ILGWU leaders, though the top offices remained in control of the male cutters. Most of these immigrant women were socialists and "social feminists" who believed the cause of working women's rights could be advanced through unionization and the struggle for women's suffrage. Unlike the radical feminists of the Women's Party who campaigned for an Equal Rights Amendment, the social feminists in the unions and in the WTUL favored protective legislation.

These immigrant women rebelled against limiting women to the home, but accepted women's role as secondary wage earners. Rose Schneiderman, of the Capmakers, an important WTUL leader, said that these women "who wanted to work at the same hours of the day or night and receive the same pay" as men "might be putting their own brothers or sweethearts out of a job." Like many WTUL activists, Schneiderman was a socialist and a woman's suffragist, but she opposed the Women's Party demand for complete equality, fearing it would undermine protective legislation and turn workingmen against the women's movement just as unions were starting to support the female-suffrage movement. She saw women's suffrage as a way for her sisters to gain more political and social power in their struggle for rights as citizens and workers. In agitating for the Women's Suffrage Association, she found that economic argument for suffrage appealed to workingmen. Though social feminists like Schneiderman did not expect suffrage to lead to complete equality, they did see it as a radical demand that would bring women into public life, a sphere hitherto restricted to men.

Born in a small village in Russian Poland to a tailor and his wife, Rose came to the Lower East Side and made an exemplary career for herself in the labor movement. "The only cloud in the picture was Mother's attitude toward my becoming a trade unionist," she later wrote. "She kept saying I'd never get married because I was so busy—a prophecy which came true." The labor movement "molded" Rose's subsequent life and "opened wide many doors that might have remained closed to her." A diminutive, round-faced woman with an erect bearing and a strong voice, Schneiderman became an organizer for the Capmakers at a time when the skilled cutters had decided to ally with the female operators. She used her experience to fight for the eight-hour day, the WTUL, and the larger goals of socialism. Jewish socialists like Schneiderman and Pauline Newman, the ILGWU's first female organizer, were intensely class-conscious and found it difficult at times to work in the WTUL. As one comrade assured her: "You need not chide yourself for not being able to be more active in the Socialist Party. You are doing splendid work." This work with reformist middle-class allies in the WTUL came at a price, however. "Jewish women had been nurtured in the cradle of socialism, and for them, alliances with other women were largely ways of achieving a more just society," Alice Kessler-Harris remarks. Working with wealthier, more educated allies in the WTUL created tensions in the lives of organizers like Schneiderman. But there were even more problems involved in working with union brothers and socialist comrades who held traditional ideas about women. Women activists worked in an isolated, lonely world, but they were the advance guard who built industrial unionism in the needle trades and opened the doors of the House of Labor to their sisters.

The victory of the shirtwaist makers in 1909 checked the momentum of the open-shop drive and popularized the use of the general strike. New York's 50,000 cloakmakers, three quarters of them men, followed the shirtwaist makers' lead and struck the next year against the hated subcontracting system; they also went out for a union shop with a forty-eight-hour week, equal distribution of work in the slow season, and a union representative on the shop floor. This general strike, called the "uprising of the 50,000," accelerated a confrontation between employers and unions that would continue for the next few years. As historian Melvyn Dubofsky writes in *When Workers Organize:*

> The struggle in New York City between capital and labor stemmed from a conflict between the demands of industrial discipline and those of industrial democracy which intensified during the Progressive era. On the one hand, the employer exhibited a justifiable concern for efficiency, economy and the elimination of all waste; to accomplish these ends he insisted upon absolute responsibility for shop organization, strict worker discipline, and selection of employees entirely on the basis of efficiency and productivity. On the other hand, workers were determined that wage regulations and working conditions no longer be treated as matters of *individual* bargaining; they desired to limit the employer's exclusive control of production by interjecting the trade-union.

The 1910 cloakmakers strike was finally settled when Attorney Louis D. Brandeis intervened as mediator and convinced the manufacturers, who opposed the closed shop, to accept a "preferential union shop" that gave union members first chance at jobs if they were qualified. The Protocol of Peace emerged from the settlement as progressives attempted to use the industry-wide collective-bargaining agreement to stabilize and rationalize labor relations in the cloakmaking industry. Unions sacrificed the right to strike during the agreement, while manufacturers promised to bargain in good faith and not lock employees out during disputes. The Protocol also established official groups to inspect factories and to conduct binding arbitration of disputes.

Several months after the Protocol was signed and order began to return to the East Side, an explosion and fire erupted in the Triangle Shirtwaist Company, where the 1909 uprising had begun. On March 25, 1911, 146 women died in the fire or jumped to their deaths. Some doors of the burning building were locked. William G. Shepherd, a reporter who witnessed the fire, said that after seeing countless bodies thudding to the street, his senses became dulled. He went to the rear of the building, where he saw an airshaft and saw a "heap of dead girls." He concluded:

> The floods of water from the firemen's hose that ran into the gutter were actually stained red with blood. I looked upon the heap of dead bodies

and I remembered these girls were the shirtwaist makers. I remembered their great strike of last year in which these same girls demanded more sanitary conditions and more safety precautions in the shops. These dead bodies were the answer.

The spirit of the Protocol had been shattered. At a memorial meeting for the Triangle victims at the Metropolitan Opera House, Rose Schneiderman said:

> I would be a traitor to these poor burned bodies if I came here to talk of good fellowship. We have tried you good people of the public and found you wanting . . .
> This is not the first time girls have been burned alive in the city. Every week I must learn of the untimely death of one of my sister workers. Every year thousands are maimed. The life of men and women is so cheap and property is so sacred.
> I can't talk fellowship to you who are gathered here. Too much blood has been spilled. I know from my experience it is up to the working people to save themselves. The only way they can save themselves is by a strong working-class movement.

Between 1909 and 1916, the immigrant workers of New York built such a movement, using their own militancy and solidarity and taking advantage of the support offered by progressive reformers and mediators. As organizational strikes spread to other garment trades, various protocols were arranged and supervised by a Jewish reform group called the Kehillah, founded by Rabbi Judah P. Magnes in 1909 to bring some order to the chaos in the ghetto. The Kehillah also fought crime and prostitution and supported education reforms that combined religious instruction with lessons in Americanization. And it assumed a classic shtetl role of arbitrating disputes. Enlisting the support of wealthy uptown Jews like banker Jacob Schiff and downtown social workers, Rabbi Magnes created a labor-conciliation service designed to heal the political, cultural, and class conflicts in New York's turbulent Jewish community. Magnes intervened in the furriers' strike of 1912 and in the 1913 strikes of tailors and men's clothing workers.

The protocols survived for several years through the efforts of the Kehillah. Rank-and-file workers, angry at the loss of their right to strike, kept challenging the accords, however, while manufacturers fought to retain old forms of power on the shop floor. By 1915, management attempts to reassert control generated a series of wildcat strikes which moderate leaders of the garment workers' unions found difficult to suppress. Indeed, the militant rank-and-file in the Chicago men's clothing industry conducted a general strike in 1910, and led a revolt against the conservative craft-union leadership of the old United Garment Workers.

During the early 1900's, the Chicago clothing industry doubled in size. Many East European Jews and Italians came to fill the demand for labor. The skilled women workers, largely Scandinavian, had organized their own unions, but in order to gain an AFL charter they had to merge with the male-led United Garment Workers (UGW). The new immigrant women lacked a union, but when piece rates were arbitrarily cut by Hart, Schaffner and Marx in 1910, two young immigrants, Bessie Abramowitz and Anne Shapiro, led a walkout which shut down the company. The UGW was not interested in organizing a group of rebellious, unskilled immigrants who espoused socialist ideas, but when workers in the rest of the men's clothing industry went out, the craft-union leaders had to act. At its height, the Chicago general strike involved roughly 40,000 workers.

They were assisted primarily by the WTUL, the Hull-House social workers, the Socialist Party, and the progressive leaders of the Chicago Federation of Labor. When UGW leaders called an end to the strike, there were cries of a sellout. And when the union bosses tried to pack a convention against the insurgent forces, the rank-and-file rebelled and set up a new industrial union in 1914. The Amalgamated Clothing Workers of America, led by a younger Jewish cutter, Sidney Hillman, combined socialist principles with industrial union tactics. It remained unrecognized by the AFL for a number of years. Though Hillman and other men led the Amalgamated, it was a women's union.

Tension between rank-and-file and leaders had always existed, but in the Progressive Era, as the unskilled displayed unusual militancy and willingness to strike, the tension increased as many union leaders, following the path of business unionists and progressive reformers, sought binding trade agreements with arbitration as a replacement for the strike and the lockout. The socialists, who had become influential in New York, sided with the rank-and-file and opposed the progressives' efforts to rationalize industrial relations through no-strike agreements. Dr. Isaac Hourwich, a socialist intellectual and a leading critic of immigration restriction, represented the unions on the various protocol boards. He defended the rank-and-file's demand for the right to strike and accused the union leadership of ''class collaboration'' with the employers. The socialists believed that the class struggle could not be bridged by trade agreement or by the conciliatory appeals to Old World communalism made by the Kehillah. Abraham Cahan, whose *Jewish Daily Forward* reached a remarkable circulation of 142,000 by 1913, spoke for the socialists when he told Kehillah leaders that no more ground existed "for bridging deep distinctions of class interest, class consciousness and origin" in the New World than in Europe. Indeed, in America these differences had increased because the class struggle had been heightened. Socialism reached a high point in the Lower East Side when its immigrant constituency sent Socialist Party labor lawyer Meyer London to Congress in 1914.

In 1916, the cloak and suit makers walked out, launching a general strike to demonstrate their new control over the work force and to equalize conditions in all shops. Mass strikes followed in other garment trades, as the protocols broke down and the conciliation machinery was jammed by rank-and-file militancy. The 1916 settlement in the cloak and suit industry broke new ground in labor relations. Mobilizing a great deal of support from socialists and reformers, the workers forced John P. Mitchel, the progressive mayor of New York, to intervene. The ILGWU won a much better contract, including the right to strike against discriminatory layoffs and arbitrary shop practices. After depending on the protocols and the services of social workers, lawyers, and other public arbitrators, the "union felt competent to stand on its own feet," writes Melvyn Dubofsky. "By rejecting the Protocol and perpetual industrial peace, the workers regained the option to strike and the will to rely on their own organization rather than upon outside boards and impartial arbitrators." When the needle trade unions began organizing, they accepted "middle-class reform assistance," but when they attained new power through rank-and-file militancy and aggressive leadership from the Bundists and other socialists, they cut themselves free from the machinery created by the industrial relations reformers.

In the decade after 1910, socialism and progressivism contended for political influence within the working class. The AFL endorsement of William Jennings Bryan in 1908 and progressive Democrat Woodrow Wilson in 1912 and 1916 brought the Federation back into partisan politics on the side of reform. As we have seen, the protocols in New York's garment industry brought socialists and progressives into conflict over the question of industrial peace. Many AFL leaders maintained the business-union posture of Gompers and Mitchell and favored the Civic Federation approach of binding arbitration. The New York socialists, unlike the IWW, accepted the idea of contracts, but refused to sacrifice the workers' right to strike or to allow manufacturers to exercise arbitrary control under the protection of the trade agreement.

Socialist criticism of union officials in New York was reflected in the Federation on a national level. In 1911, the socialist faction in the AFL won substantial support for a resolution condemning Gompers's membership in the Civic Federation. In the same year, the left in the United Mine Workers won support for a resolution that made NCF membership grounds for expulsion from the union. As a result, John Mitchell decided to resign as chairman of the NCF Trade Agreements Committee.

By this time, the socialists had gained many supporters in the craft unions. In 1912, Max Hayes of the Typographers, who represented many of the skilled socialist workers, ran against Gompers for the presidency and polled one third of the vote. The socialists even showed strength in the Carpenters union, where McGuire's old followers and the younger supporters of Debs challenged the control of William Huber and the conservative business unionists. Skilled workers who enjoyed some control over their trade saw, perhaps, the possibility of a worker-controlled society. This insight may account for the socialist sentiments among machinists, printers, bakers, painters, carpenters. Generally, though, craft-union consciousness did not fit well in the twentieth century with socialist consciousness.

Most of the socialists' strength was to be found in the industrial unions with noted socialist leaders: the UMW, the Western Federation of Miners, the ILGWU, the Brewers, the Amalgamated Clothing Workers, and, of course, outside the mainstream in the IWW. Nothing in industrial unionism necessarily led to socialism. But to construct one big union in an industry like coal mining or clothing required militant tactics and often deepened anti-capitalist views. Industrial union efforts built solidarity among all workers regardless of skill, race, nationality, and contributed strongly to the development of socialist ideas. As Big Bill Haywood remarked: "Industrial Unionism is socialism with its working clothes on." Socialist strength in the skilled trades and in the industrial unions of the unskilled showed growing working-class discontent with old-party machine politics and with the new progressivism.

The Socialist Party reached its high-water mark in 1912 when Eugene V. Debs polled nearly 900,000 votes in a race with three formidable opponents: Republican incumbent William Howard Taft, progressive insurgent Theodore Roosevelt, and the winner, Democratic reformer Woodrow Wilson, who received the AFL endorsement. Then at the height of his influence, Debs came closer to being a working-class hero than any other radical figure. Born to Alsatian parents in 1855, Debs grew up in Terre Haute, Indiana, and became a railroad man. An articulate youngster who read Victor Hugo at home, he rose rapidly in the Locomotive Fireman's union and became the editor of its journal in the 1880's. The Homestead strike of 1892 helped him see the weakness of craft unionism; the depression of 1893, combined with the rise of Populism, made him a radical and led him to organize the American Railway Union, one of the pioneer industrial organizations. During the national Pullman strike of 1894, Debs became a Robespierre to the business classes. A cartoon of "dictator Debs" showed him sitting atop a drawbridge that blocked the nation's rail traffic. Crushed by the intervention of federal troops, the ARU collapsed, while Debs read radical tracts in his jail cell at Woodstock, Illinois. In the late 1890's, he experimented with various cooperative ventures and joined the Social Democratic organization led by the German-Americans, notably Victor Berger of Milwaukee. He became the Social Democratic Party's Presidential candidate in 1900 and criticized the deflated Populism of Democrat Bryan and People's Party candidate Tom Watson. The Populist moment had passed, and the possibility of a radical producer alliance of farmers, artisans, and workers passed with it. The class struggle of the 1900's demanded a workers' party.

Disgusted with the sectarianism of Daniel De Leon's Socialist Labor Party, Morris Hillquit of the Lower East Side joined with Debs, Berger of Milwaukee, and other Social Democrats to form the Socialist Party of America in 1901. Though he never became deeply involved in the factional disputes that shook the party, Debs was indisputably its spiritual leader and its main attraction to working-class voters. De Leon had formed his own Socialist Trade and Labor Alliance outside the AFL and then joined IWW until he was purged in 1908, but Debs followed his party's strategy of "boring from within" the AFL unions. His disgust with craft unionism led him to the IWW founding convention in 1905, but he rapidly parted company with the Wobblies as industrial unions surged forward within the AFL. Though Elizabeth Gurley Flynn criticized the Socialist Party and remained a loyal IWW member, she loved Debs. No mean orator herself, the "Rebel Girl" admired Debs's ability to hold a crowd:

To hear Eugene V. Debs speak on any occasion was an unforgettable experience. He was a matchless orator. No one who heard Debs came away entirely unaffected. People who came merely from curiosity were held spellbound by his burning eloquence. Debs paced back and forth on the platform, like a lion ready to spring, then leaned far over the edge, his tall gaunt frame bending like a reed, his bony finger pointing—his favorite gesture. His deep blue eyes appeared to look searchingly at each one in the audience . . . Debs' voice was strong and clear and could be heard

in the largest hall and outdoor places. He spoke with imagery and the poetry of expression, drew word pictures of the lives of workers . . . He
was full of loving kindness of those who are heavily laden, and had a
searing contempt for the "gory-beaked" vultures who fatten on their
exploitation.

Debs's 1912 campaign, combined with grass-roots local organizations, helped 1,200 party members win offices, including 79 mayorali-
ties in 300 cities. Robert Hoxie, a political scientist, studied the
hundreds of municipalities that elected socialists in 1911 and 1912,
including mining centers like Butte, Montana, and Coeur d'Alene,
Idaho, and industrial cities like Granite City, Illinois, New Castle,
Pennsylvania, and Schenectady, New York. The party's persistent program of "agitation, education and organization" yielded results at a
time when workers were being radicalized by the struggle for "corporation control" through mechanization and scientific management,
the anti-union onslaught of employers' associations. "General corruption" also played a part. As Hoxie concluded: "It is in the boss-ruled,
corporation-ridden, tax-burdened city with its poorly paved, ill-
lighted, dirty streets, its insufficient water supply . . . its industrial
fire-traps, its graft-protected vice district, its fat politicians, untaxed
wealth, crooked contracts, and wasted resources, that Socialism finds
its best object-lessons and has won some of its most significant if not
its most numerous, successes." The socialist program for "great local
autonomy for direct control of officials; for clean, honest, efficient administration of affairs; for the equalization of tax burdens, the curbing
of corporations, the improvement of housing, education and amuse-
ments of the people" appealed to middle-class as well as working-
class voters, Hoxie reported, though the socialists elected were
"mostly workingmen." Some historians underestimate "gas and
water" socialism, and portray it as another variety of urban re-
formism. In many industrial cities, socialist politics clearly represented
a working-class response to the struggle for control launched by
business-class progressives.

The progressives also opposed bossism and machine control, but
their municipal reforms did not aim to increase workers' control of
city government. On the contrary, in proposing the city-manager or
commission form of government to replace the old ward system, reformers enhanced the power of business and professional men in city
government at the expense of workers. In the nineteenth century,
workers often elected their own representatives to local office, and industrialists often learned during strikes that they had to import private
police or enlist the militia because locally elected officials sided with

the strikers. In the larger cities, ethnic machine politicians patterning themselves after Boss Tweed of Tammany Hall represented a diverse constituency which included gangs, small-shop keepers, liquor dealers, peddlers, and ghetto employers, as well as workers. Machine politicians often considered trade unions to be a threat to the patronage system on which political dependency was based. They were, however, generally responsive to the working-class constituencies. For example, in Boston, Martin Lomasney created the prototypical ward organization by including Jews and Italians as well as Irish voters. John "Honey Fitz" Fitzgerald advocated labor reform during the depression of the 1890's when workers threatened to break with the Democratic Party. He was later elected mayor. Fitzgerald's successor, James Michael Curley, who used politics to rise out of Roxbury's Irish ghetto, created a city-wide patronage machine by reaching an accommodation with labor unions and adopting an anti-business stance during his first term as mayor. Unlike Lomasney and Fitzgerald, Curley rose above the ward bosses and created a city-wide organization. He was a skilled populist politician, of a new urban sort. Abandoning the conservatism of the old ward heelers, Curley tapped the frustration of Boston's large Irish working class, which according to Stephan Thernstrom's study, *The Other Bostonians,* remained immobilized and overwhelmingly proletarian in the 1910's. Curley frustrated the "blue-blood" reformers by winning office in spite of the Republican-inspired reforms that stripped Boston of its ward-based council and its partisan elections. Yankee "good government" forces did, however, use their power to elect some businessmen as mayors and to exert state control over the police and other city agencies, thus depriving "boss-ridden" Boston of home rule.

Business-class reformers often used charges of corruption to unseat politicians like "Honey Fitz" and Curley, though businessmen themselves encouraged graft by bribing public officials to obtain cheap franchises, tax breaks, and other favors. Municipal reformers did not limit their attacks to dishonest politicians. The primary issue was not corruption but control. The gospel of efficiency and honesty in government could be used effectively to help regain some of the power the business and professional classes lost when their electoral influence shifted to the streetcar suburbs. In some cases, the progressive reformers clashed directly with urban socialists organizing for working-class political power. In Oklahoma City, for example, socialists in the country's largest state party organization attempted to introduce the tactics of their Milwaukee comrades: they teamed up with trade unionists in 1910 to defeat a referendum for the commission form of government on the grounds that it would reduce democracy and encourage oligarchy.

Business-oriented reformers often expressed frankly elitist views about the inability of workers, immigrants, and blacks to exercise their democratic rights. "Employment as an ordinary laborer and in the lowest class of mill work would naturally lead to the conclusion that such men did not have sufficient education or business training to act as school directors," said the Voter's League of Pittsburgh in 1911, complaining about the absence of "prominent" businessmen in education. After the state legislature imposed a new charter on the city in the same year, the voters lost the right to elect school-board representatives. Ten of the fifteen members on the new, appointed Pittsburgh school board were businessmen. In his study of municipal reform, Samuel P. Hays concluded that urban progressives effectively used centralized forms of bureaucracy to replace ward-based democracy, and significantly increased the power of the professional and business classes.

In general, businessmen and professionals tended to propose reforms, and the unions responded slowly and reluctantly, hoping in most cases to prevent employers from completely controlling the administration of reform. For example, in mine-safety reform, the United Mine Workers moved ambiguously. In its state organizations, the union pushed hard for safety proposals it could influence. But on a national level, the union was inactive. President Theodore Roosevelt advocated federal regulations to be enforced through a Bureau of Mines. UMW leaders were skeptical about the independent lobbying role played by the American Mining Congress, whose officials wanted mine-safety regulation to be the responsibility of the mining engineers rather than the miners. Following the dreadful disasters at Monongah, West Virginia, in which 361 miners died, and in Jacobs Creek, Pennsylvania, where 239 lost their lives, the pressure for mine-safety reform grew, but, according to William Graebner's study *Coal-Mining Safety in the Progressive Period,* it was "above all, a business reform." If employers could not control labor reforms themselves, as U.S. Steel did through its own safety and insurance programs, they favored uniform regulation through federal bureaucracies, like the Bureau of Mines, created in 1910. Reform-oriented businessmen allied with bureaucratic reformers to create uniform regulations on wages, hours, safety rules, and forms of compensation that would rationalize the workplace and stabilize industrial relations by reducing wage cuts, accident lawsuits, and strikes.

The unions opposed business-dominated reforms like the U.S. Steel workmen's compensation plan. They were also skeptical of federal compensation plans that favored private insurance companies while reducing the possibility of damage suits against employers by workers and their dependents. Organized labor's voluntarist philosophy was still influential. Gompers and other leaders urged workers to organize for their own protection rather than to depend on corporations or the government. Unions had learned throughout the nineteenth century to view the state as an enemy, because its military and judicial might had been used against workers. Very few bills emerged from Congress that favored organized labor. When state legislatures and city governments began to pass labor reforms, though, unions began to abandon their voluntarist position to ally themselves with politicians from working-class districts in support of legislation on minimum wages, maximum hours, child labor, and workmen's compensation. As the slaughter in American industry was exposed by radical "muckrakers" like Crystal Eastman, socialist and progressive politicians increased their support of state-controlled accident insurance. When the courts began to declare many state compensation laws unconstitutional, former President Theodore Roosevelt argued that the strength of the Socialist Party would be "immensely" increased. He made this a major issue in his 1912 Progressive Party Presidential campaign, when Eugene Debs, the Socialist Party candidate, polled his highest vote.

Woodrow Wilson, the victorious Democratic Presidential candidate, opposed the kind of federal intervention proposed by the Progressive and Socialist Parties, but he did favor some labor reforms, and won organized support from AFL unions. Under Wilson's Administration, Congress passed a number of pro-labor laws. Sam Gompers hailed the passage of the Clayton Act in 1914 as "labor's Magna Carta," because it freed the unions from prosecution under the Sherman Anti-Trust Act. The language of the Clayton Act challenged the courts' effort to dehumanize workers, declaring that "the labor of a human being is not a commodity or an article of commerce," but it failed to secure the unions' legal right to collective bargaining or to seriously impede the use of injunctions. Congress also created a Federal Mediation and Conciliation Service to reduce industrial conflict. The Wilson Administration pleased the AFL by creating a Cabinet-level Department of Labor and appointing a commission to investigate the increasingly violent turn in industrial relations. More important, progressive legislators took advantage of the liberal tone of Congress to pass two important bills: Senator Robert La Follette's Seaman's Act of 1915, which secured basic human rights for merchant seamen, and the Adamson Act of 1916, which secured the eight-hour day for railroad workers, the first group of private employees to win the shorter work-day as a legal right.

Organized labor responded differently to progressive reforms. It op-posed workplace reforms based on Taylorism and welfare capitalism. It also opposed municipal reforms that reduced democracy and strengthened business influence, as well as national reforms like Prohi-bition that aimed at increased state control over working-class behav-ior. It did support some progressive reforms like workmen's compen-sation in which increased state control was an alternative to domination by business. Finally, the AFL abandoned voluntarism in order to fight the coercive role of the courts in industrial affairs. Dur-ing the Wilson Administration, the Clayton Act and other measures convinced Gompers and other labor leaders that the federal govern-ment could be influenced to protect union interests. And when Wilson ran for reelection in 1916, Gompers and many union leaders, includ-ing some socialists, officially endorsed the Democrats.

During the 1910's, a new relationship developed between worker militancy and labor reform. Sometimes strikes and other actions stimu-lated progressive lawmakers, who could use the threat of spreading class violence to gain support. In other cases, reformers codified cer-tain workers' rights and provoked employer resistance and employee revolt. For example, when the Massachusetts legislature reduced the maximum work week for women and children from fifty-six to fifty-four hours, employers cut wages for the textile workers in Lawrence, and the workers responded with the most important strike of the Pro-gressive Era.

The giant American Woolen mill dominated Lawrence, employing 40,000 largely foreign-born people, roughly half the city's population. Corporate paternalism characterized the early years of the city, and its prototypes in Waltham and Lowell; it gave way to a kind of cor-porate totalitarianism that effectively checked union organization. Trade unions of weavers and other groups organized against the cor-porations in the 1880's, as did the Knights of Labor. In most company towns, though, the "lords of the loom" prevailed against the unions by exploiting their political influence and their ability to import foreign labor. The Knights also rebelled against paternalism in the smaller Southern textile manufacturing centers. In both areas, however, the economics of the industry helped employers regain control. "In the midst of a pool of surplus labor in an industry that required a mini-mum of skills, the operative, if he made demands, was expendable," concludes Southern labor historian Melton A. McLaurin in *Paternal-ism and Protest*. Like the steel corporations, the textile manufacturers had reduced their dependency on skilled labor and cleverly exploited the labor market to maintain their dominance. They also used the labor of women and children effectively, and in fact incorporated whole families into a paternalistic network. In the North, older English-speaking workers feared the invasion of French Canadians, and in the South the white "lintheads" worried about blacks taking their jobs.

In Lawrence half the work force in the American Woolen mills were young females, aged fourteen to eighteen, whose health was appalling. Given the extreme dependency of the mill operatives, the sex segregation, and ethnic fragmentation of the immigrant work force, the company's executives were confident that they could cut wages when the state forced them to reduce the work week for women and children. However, when a group of young Polish women received "short pay" on January 11, 1912, they organized a walkout that spread throughout the city and shocked employers.

By the next morning, their walkout had spread to the other mills, and the great Lawrence strike was on. The small number of Wobblies and Italian anarchists who organized the strike were soon joined by leading radicals, including Bill Haywood, Joseph Ettor, and Elizabeth Gurley Flynn of the IWW, the anarchist Carlo Tresca, and Arturo Giovannitti of the Italian Socialist Federation. The leader of the AFL's United Textile Workers denounced the strike as "anarchistic" and tried unsuccessfully to take leadership from the IWW. Gompers admitted that this uprising of 23,000 unskilled ethnic workers was a "class-conscious industrial revolution," but he dismissed it as a "passing event."

Many observers who flocked to Lawrence commented on the unified spirit of the strikers; they absorbed a heavy dose of the IWW's multilingual strike literature, which explained that the common oppression of corporate tyranny had welded together workers from more than a dozen different lands. One reporter, Ray Stannard Baker, remarked on the spirit generated by industrial unionism. The strikers seemed to be constantly singing and continually marching under many banners, including the famous slogan: "We Want Bread and Roses Too." "It is the first strike I ever saw which sang," Baker wrote in *The American Magazine*. "I shall not soon forget the curious life, the strange sudden fire of the mingled nationalities at the strike meetings when they broke into the universal language of song"—their favorite being the "Internationale," which begins:

> *Arise, ye prisoners of starvation!*
> *Arise, ye wretched of the earth,*

For justice thunders condemnation—
A better world's in birth.
No more tradition's chains shall bind us,
Arise, ye slaves! No more in thrall!
The earth shall rise on new foundations,
We have been naught, we shall be all.

The multi-lingual strike force at Lawrence held its lines for more than two months. Strikers battled police, militia, and bitter cold, and won a great victory, including significant wage increases. Socialist Party members aided the strike by raising money and opening their homes to the children of Lawrence strikers. Socialist Congressman Victor Berger conducted an investigation, which aided the effort. But on the whole, party leaders kept their distance from the strike, which involved disenfranchised immigrants unlikely to contribute to the party's growth at the polls. Berger actually supported immigration restriction and racial segregation. Like other moderate socialists, he favored boring from within the AFL, rather than risking all to organize the unorganized. In May 1912, the Socialist Party avoided a split over the question of the IWW, and endorsed industrial unionism without reference to the AFL or its radical rival. But the convention also passed a resolution prohibiting membership to anyone advocating sabotage, a tactic frequently preached by the Wobblies. The socialists who supported the resolution were concerned about attracting AFL and middle-class votes in the fall of 1912, and were anxious to disassociate themselves from the lawless IWW.

A situation strangely analogous to the Lawrence strike developed in rural Louisiana during the "lumber war" of 1911 and 1912. An independent industrial union, the Brotherhood of Timber Workers, organized secretly in the piney woods of western Louisiana and east Texas in 1911 and recruited black mill hands and white lumberjacks into separate locals. In 1912, the Brotherhood affiliated with the IWW and became an integrated union with a revolutionary leadership. It fought a bitter and violent battle against the Southern Lumber Operators' open shop. Haywood himself came South from the great victory at Lawrence to urge the Brotherhood to integrate. Along with Southern Wobblies like Covington Hall, Big Bill boldly advocated sabotage in defiance of the Socialist Party's position. Left-wing socialists in Texas, who were organizing tenant farmers, supported the IWW strike, but the right-wing socialists in Louisiana kept their distance from the conflict. Alarmed by the interracial nature and violent character of the strike, they steered Gene Debs away from strife-torn piney woods when he made a campaign trip to New Orleans. Haywood and the Wobblies did not renounce political action, however, and campaigned for Debs, who won a surprisingly large vote from Texas tenants, Oklahoma yeoman farmers, Arkansas coal miners, and those Louisiana timber workers who were not disenfranchised. Debs polled about 80,000 votes from these four predominantly agricultural states, where white tenant farmers were battling capitalist landlords, bankers, and merchants. In fact, the Southwestern socialists polled far more votes from indebted Populist farmers than from industrial proletarians. In other states, like Massachusetts, the socialists pursued AFL and middle-class votes while avoiding the new immigrant workers who had risen at Lawrence. But the party won few of those "respectable" votes. The socialists gained their largest totals in states like New York, Pennsylvania, Ohio, and Illinois, where the party's AFL and middle-class support was extended to include new immigrant voters mobilized through militant unions like the UMW and the Garment Workers.

Though disappointed with the 1912 vote of fewer than one million ballots, the socialists maintained their strategy of boring from within the AFL and competing with the progressives for middle- and working-class votes. The Wilson Administration's reforms, however, brought many socialists, including some prominent union leaders, over to the Democrats, who were creating an entente with the AFL. The IWW tapped the militancy of the new immigrant masses, but it failed to build permanent union locals in cities like McKees Rocks and Lawrence. The Wobblies failed not because of their refusal to sign nostrike trade agreements with employers or because they remained hostile to the AFL. Rather, they lost their struggle to organize industrial workers on terrain thoroughly controlled by the nation's largest corporations. By 1913–14, the American Woolen Company, through espionage and mass layoffs caused by a depression, decimated the IWW local in Lawrence. In Louisiana, the Lumber Operators' blacklist, the state militia, company guards, armed citizen's leagues, and local sheriffs beat the Brotherhood of Timber Workers into submission. In 1913, the IWW suffered a number of other serious setbacks as industrialists and their allies defeated militant strikes by Paterson, New Jersey, silk workers, Akron, Ohio, rubber workers, and auto workers at the Studebaker factory in Detroit. The Wobblies reluctantly decided that, in spite of the victory at Lawrence, spontaneous strikes, no matter how militant, were difficult to win when waged against the "most powerful forces of organized capital." More than one Wobbly suggested that the One Big Union turn back to the West, where it could organize short, quick strikes that did not require vast financial and organizational resources.

The uprising of the unskilled machine proletariat confirmed the Wobblies' view that class-conscious militancy could be mobilized rapidly without the existence of job consciousness or craft-union organization or reformist political activity. But militant action was not confined to IWW strikes during the Progressive Era. In fact, a "new unionism" emerged within old AFL affiliates after 1909, and even in the conservative railroad brotherhoods. The "new unionism," argues labor historian David Montgomery, reflected a "transformation of workers' consciousness" between 1909 and 1922. Old craft unions like the Carpenters, Electricians, and Iron, Steel and Tin Workers adopted a semi-industrial form and began to recruit unskilled workers. They also urged the amalgamation of craft unions in many industries. Some old-line union leaders rejected the progressive remedies offered by the Civic Federation and its Trade Agreement Department, headed by John Mitchell. They were, of course, responding to an anti-union onslaught by employers that began with the open shop and judicial injunctions of 1903–12 and continued during the "age of industrial violence" that followed. Unions also responded to the continuing efforts corporations made to gain control through technological innovation, scientific management, and welfare programs. The "new unionism" did not usually contain the explicit statements about a worker-controlled society advanced by the Wobblies. But in waging their struggle against hard-hitting employers, "pure and simple" trade unionists often militantly defended existing forms of job control. And during the World War I era, they even demanded new forms. In this sense, the "new unionism" resembled European syndicalism. Taking its name from the French word for union (*syndicat*), this movement was premised on the need to win workers' control of society through militant union action at the workplace, including sabotage, violence, and ultimately the revolutionary general strike. The syndicalists, whose main strength lay in France and Spain, became very popular in Britain by 1911, where Tom Mann and Jim Larkin led dockers and others in sympathy strikes that closed down Liverpool and Belfast. The syndicalists rejected trade agreements and all forms of compromise with employers and took a dim view of socialist efforts to advance the workers' struggle through political action. To a degree, the IWW was syndicalist, though its leaders called themselves industrial unionists. Syndicalism in the militant AFL unions was also unstated. But as strikes to defend or extend job control escalated, a kind of American syndicalism emerged.

The shopmen's strike against the Illinois Central Railroad, which began in 1911, epitomized this new kind of struggle and showed a spirit of syndicalism. As early as 1900, craft unions on Western railroads formed system federations to fight the introduction of piece rates and maintain some control over the pace of work. In 1911, the strike against the Illinois Central began with a concern over scientific management. Six craft unions jointly struck the E. H. Harriman system in the Mississippi Valley to force the IC to negotiate with the federation rather than with one craft union at a time. The conflict was a long and bloody one as gunplay continued for four years. The corporation used sweeping court injunctions and federal militia to enforce its new standards of work discipline and to show its determination not to negotiate with allied craft unions.

The Harriman strike overlapped the infamous Ludlow massacre in the southern Colorado coalfields. Armed attacks on strikers by gun thugs and troops resulted in the killing of eleven children and two women seeking refuge in a tent camp. Armed bands of Colorado miners, who had been on strike against the Rockefeller interests, fought troops for ten days. These two episodes were among the most notorious investigated by the U.S. Commission on Industrial Relations in 1915. The investigators, headed by lawyer Frank P. Walsh, concluded that violence naturally followed when working people were "denied their rights," provoked by strikebreakers, and treated with an "incredible" degree of brutality by law-enforcement agencies. Class violence was now of greater concern than ever to the progressives. It could be stopped, said the commissioners, only by reforms to redistribute the wealth through taxation, to restrict industrial and land monopoly, to limit the use of private detectives and armed guards, to protect workers' rights to freedom of speech, union organization, and collective bargaining. These recommendations were far too radical for the Wilson Administration to accept, and it ignored them. Leftists expected this. Indeed, Bill Haywood, who testified before the commission, realized that legislative reforms could not resolve the control struggle or restrict class warfare. "An irreconcilable class struggle" existed between the workers, who had "nothing but their labor power," and the capitalists, who controlled the means of production as well as the "forces of law." The fight for "what the capitalist has control of" would continue in spite of anything the commission would say or do.

The "munitions strikes" that spread through New England in the summer of 1915 reflected a new spirit of aggressiveness. Striking against arms manufacturers hard-pressed to fill Allied war orders, the machinists won recognition in open-shop cities like Bridgeport, Connecticut, a key armament center, and attained the eight-hour day as well as the abolition of premium-pay incentives. The munitions workers had consistently taken the lead in the struggle against scientific management, beginning with the iron molders' successful strike in 1911 against Taylorism at the federal arsenal in Watertown, Massachusetts. The strike wave beginning in 1915 aimed at sweeping other vestiges of scientific management from the shops. According to P. J. Conlin, vice-president of the Machinists, whose members had been at the center of the most explicit control struggles, the introduction of new management strategies had provoked a workers' response in the form of "sabotage, syndicalism [and] passive resistance. We did not hear of any of these things," he told the Industrial Relations Commission, "until we heard of scientific management and new methods of production."

In 1916, the number of strikes and lockouts reached a twentieth-century high of 3,789, more than twice the previous year's total. Unemployment dropped from 15 percent to 9 percent and workers began to take advantage of the new demand for their labor. According to David Montgomery, these strikes, unlike those of the previous few years, did not center primarily on wage demands, but rather on "control" issues like union recognition, sympathy strikes with other workers, retention of old work rules, and the retention of popular foremen. These strikes did not, of course, mean that workers actually intended to seize control of the means of production; rather, the strikers challenged the arbitrary authority of management, demanded the protection of their rights through the union shop, and fought to maintain or extend their control over the pace and length of the work day.

In 1916, Eugene V. Debs chose not to run for President and Wilson formalized his entente with the AFL. These developments, among others, led to the first decline in the socialists' national vote. The party faithful began to see that the Cooperative Commonwealth, which once seemed so inevitable, was receding from their grasp. While Wilson captured many labor votes for his armed-neutrality program, workers in some areas agitated against U.S. war preparations. The labor movement rallied to the defense of Tom Mooney and Warren Billings, two California labor radicals accused of bombing a business-sponsored 1916 Preparedness Day parade in San Francisco. A similar defense movement in 1915 failed to save the life of the famous Wobbly songster Joe Hill. Hill was executed before a Utah firing squad, after a biased murder trial; however, worldwide demonstrations, including one in which Petrograd workers threatened the United States embassy in Russia, helped win a commutation of Mooney's death sentence.

The unpopularity of the United States declaration of war in April 1917 was also reflected in the strong showing of socialist anti-war candidates in the municipal elections that fall. In New York, party leader Morris Hillquit, attacked for being Jewish and "pro-German," still increased the socialist vote fivefold, winning 21.7 percent. More important, the AFL's pledge to refrain from strikes for the duration of the war was violated repeatedly, as rank-and-file workers engaged in a record number of wildcat strikes against employers, federal agencies, and their own union leaders.

In 1917, a record year for strikes and lockouts, the IWW revived itself, returning to the West, where its Agricultural Workers Organization effectively organized the wheat harvest hands on the Great Plains. Wobblies also struck for the eight-hour day in the forests of the Pacific Northwest, a den of IWW "sabcats" (wildcat strikers who practiced sabotage), and led a walkout of 10,000 Montana copper miners when the North Butte Speculator mine exploded, burning 164 workers to death. Like the aggressive "new unionism" in the East, rough-and-tumble industrial unionism in the West took advantage of wartime labor scarcity.

The IWW's Agricultural Workers Organization did develop more efficient, centralized methods of collecting dues and organizing locals. And these methods revived the union's sagging membership. But the IWW still refused to sign contracts or to sacrifice the right to strike at any time. Moreover, it established a union structure that stayed on the job, and not in some union hall or national headquarters. Using its new power in the West, the IWW tied up production in crucial war industries.

The response to the Wobbly revival was vicious. Vigilantes took action first, massacring Wobblies at Everett, Washington, in 1916, lynching organizer Frank Little in Montana, and literally deporting 1,100 IWW copper-mine strikers from Bisbee, Arizona, in 1917. This deportation left hundreds of strikers stranded in the desert in boxcars. Bill Haywood wired President Wilson in Washington, threatening a general strike in the West. This threat, writes Melvyn Dubofsky in *We Shall Be All: A History of the IWW,* "convinced Woodrow Wilson and the Justice Department that 'IWW-ism,' not vigilantism must be repressed." In the fall of 1917, Justice Department officers raided Wobbly offices across the country, confiscated records, and arrested key leaders for conspiring to violate federal sedition laws. The Postmaster General also suspended most IWW and Socialist Party publications, and in 1918 the Justice Department turned its attention to anti-war socialists. Its agents arrested Eugene Debs for a "treasonous" speech made in Canton, Ohio, in which he declared that it had become "extremely dangerous to exercise the right of free speech in a country fighting to make democracy safe in the world." Debs was sentenced to ten years in a federal prison for violating the Sedition Act, and the socialist anti-war movement lost its greatest leader. By this time, the pre-war Socialist Party had been destroyed by vigilante and government repression and by internal divisions. Thousands of East European immigrants, electrified by the Russian Revolution, flooded the Finnish, Lettish, Russian, and South Slav language federations, but except for a few cities in which these groups were concentrated, the Debsian socialists were in retreat. For the next fifteen years, the socialist movement became largely an affair of new immigrants.

In 1918, only 1.4 percent of the work force was unemployed, and factory turnover reached a shocking level as workers moved from town to town looking for higher wages. With the supply of European immigrants cut off, employers desperately recruited women, Southern blacks, and Chicanos. Pushed by the President's Mediation Commission, industrialists granted recognition to many new unions, especially in industries where militant strikers threatened war production. Gompers and other AFL leaders gladly abandoned most of their reservations about state intervention in return for places on the War Industries Board and the War Labor Board established in 1918. For the progressives and for a number of socialist intellectuals who joined the Wilson Administration, the war presented an ideal opportunity to fulfill their ambition of making the state the arbiter between labor and capital.

The war served progressivism in several ways. It allowed reformers to use the federal government to extend protection to more workers. Many unions won new contracts with employers and also won the eight-hour day, a goal since the Civil War. During the First World War, 49 percent of all workers gained a forty-eight-hour work week, partly through the efforts of the War Labor Board. Federal labor policies also created the kind of arbitration system progressives had long favored. Wartime progressivism also had a repressive side, as we have seen. The government aided in crushing revolutionary movements at home and abroad. Many workers also viewed the Eighteenth Amendment for national Prohibition, passed by Congress in 1918, as an attempt to control working-class culture. Union leaders pledged to cooperate with the pro-labor government by opposing strikes, but thousands of workers violated this pledge. Most of the 6,025 strikes recorded during the war were the unofficial, outlaw type. Union leaders supported the progressives' idea of a new corporate state in which labor's interests would be recognized, but thousands of industrial workers refused to hold up their end of the arrangement. They continued to strike, in spite of the existence of high-level no-strike pacts. As the progressive philosopher John Dewey wrote in 1918, the workers might be less enthusiastic than policymakers about the new role of the state advocated by corporate liberals. "The wage-earner is more likely to be interested in using his newly discovered power to increase his own share of control in an industry than he is in transferring control over to the government officials."

In 1919 workers exercised their new power in the greatest strike wave in United States history. Over 4 million workers fought in thousands of strikes and lockouts for a wide range of demands. Several unions gained unprecedented strength. The Machinists' membership jumped from 54,000 in 1910 to 331,450 in 1919. By then, the United Mine Workers had recruited over 400,000 members. The newly unified railroad unions claimed 1.8 million members in sixteen organizations. A majority in their ranks demanded nationalization of their industry in order to maintain wartime gains. During the mass strikes of 1919, various groups of workers united across lines of race, nationality, and gender to battle the nation's biggest corporations and sometimes the state itself. Between July 4 and 9, political strikes occurred demanding freedom for the imprisoned anti-war radical Tom Mooney.

The millions who engaged in the 1919 conflicts represented a remarkable 22 percent of the entire work force and included a variety of working people, from policemen and telephone operators to steelworkers and coal miners. In Boston, the city's Irish police force confronted conservative Governor Calvin Coolidge and the state militia in a desperate battle for recognition, better pay, and shorter hours. Gompers and other AFL leaders discouraged general-strike sentiment that might have allowed the police to win their fight. But the police were defeated and the cause of public employee unionism was set back. In the same city, young Irish telephone workers walked out, and spread their strike throughout New England with the help of male cable splicers and electricians. The strikers held firm and forced concessions from the Postmaster General, who still held wartime powers over the communications system. The textile workers at Lawrence organized another major uprising and extended their strike to other New England mills. The coal miners also conducted a massive nationwide strike. Many miners held out even after their new president, John L. Lewis, condemned them for striking against the government.

The largest strike of the early twentieth century involved 360,000 steelworkers in all the major mill towns. Led by the syndicalist William Z. Foster, the strikers fought for union recognition and an end to autocracy in the company towns. After a bitter struggle, the strike was defeated by the corporations and the police, crushing post-war hopes for a new industrial unionism. Employers exploited ethnic and racial divisions among workers and the anti-radical hysteria stirred up by the government's "red raids" in 1919. Foster also charged that the AFL leaders sabotaged the strike by withholding funds and opposing the organizers' radical politics. The steel strike's outcome showed that corporations could still overcome organized opposition by taking advantage of social and political divisions within the labor movement and by acting with great force and unity of purpose. Nevertheless, the great steel strike revealed the strong sympathy among mill workers for industrial unionism and "industrial democracy." For example, the leaders of the strike in Steelton, Pennsylvania, put out this flyer:

> During the war we fabricated munitions plants, small arm plants . . . We did the work cheerfully, without strikes or trouble of any kind. We were so exhausted after a day's work that we fell asleep at the supper table. We pared to the bone in order to buy Liberty Bonds, to give to the Red Cross and similar organizations. For what? To make the world safe for democracy . . .
>
> The whole industrial world is in chaos and it is up to the Industrial Kings of America to grant their employees industrial democracy.

The year 1919 even took on a quasi-revolutionary character, partly as a result of the worldwide context in which the strikes occurred. The Bolshevik revolution had held power in Russia for two years despite the efforts of reactionary forces inside and outside the country. The Communists gained power in Hungary and posed a serious revolutionary threat in Germany. As a result, Communism enjoyed great prestige among thousands of East European immigrants in the United States, who flocked into the Socialist Party's foreign-language federations. They provided the rank-and-file for a new Communist movement in the United States. In Britain, the Labour Party had announced its post-war socialist policy and had replaced the Liberals as the second party. Thus inspired, radical unionists formed labor parties in Chicago, New York, and other cities. The founding convention for a national labor party was held in Chicago in November. In Italy, metalworkers copied the Soviets and seized factories, while in Britain a militant shop stewards' movement extended the "frontier of control'' on the shop floor. In the United States, workers talked more openly about controlling their industries, and in some cases strikers demanded recognition of shop committees and amalgamated trade unions to represent them. In Seattle, Washington, where a general strike stirred the nation, 110 locals, including AFL craft unions with binding contracts, walked out in sympathy with shipyard workers who, like the New England telephone workers, had struck, in defiance of federal decrees. The committee directing the general strike of 35,000 workers declared:

> Labor will not only SHUT DOWN the industries, but Labor will REOPEN, under the management of the appropriate trades, such activities as are needed to preserve public health and public peace. If the strike continues, Labor may feel led to avoid public suffering by reopening more and more activities
>
> UNDER ITS OWN MANAGEMENT.
>
> And that is why we say that we are starting on a road that leads—
> NO ONE KNOWS WHERE!

In 1920, the leaders of railroad brotherhoods and shop-craft unions polled their members' view on the Plumb Plan to extend federal control of railroads past the war. Ninety percent of those polled voted to strike to force Congressional enactment of the nationalization plan.

During the great strike wave of 1919, the concerns of the ''new unionism'' emerged more clearly, after a decade of maturation. These demands, David Montgomery maintains, had a distinctly syndicalist emphasis on workers' control issues. Hence, it was not surprising that ''avowedly syndicalist'' groups emerged, some of them inside of the AFL. ''The Cloth Hat and Cap Makers and the Sheet Metal Workers of New York put no faith in trade agreements or union labels and bestowed absolute power on shop committees, coordinated by executive boards of avowed revolutionaries,'' Montgomery writes. ''The Jewelry Workers, sparked by an alliance of Jewish Socialists and Italian syndicalists, boasted their shop autonomy and the direct action which won them a 44-hour week as early as 1916.''

Except for William Z. Foster's efforts to apply syndicalist strategy in the great steel strike, these groups remained localized, and so did the anarchists who were active in Italian and Russian workers' communities. The IWW had for a time attracted syndicalists and anarchists. But the Wobblies were scarred by the war, and AFL unions became the locus of most militant strike action. After the initial raids in 1917, the IWW remained active, even though it was attacked by various vigilante and employer groups. Some state legislatures enacted "criminal syndicalism" laws making IWW positions illegal. The federal government continued its harassment. It even formed a patriotic rival union, the Loyal Legion of Loggers and Lumbermen, to battle the Wobblies in the Northwestern woods. Another series of raids led to the arrest of top union leaders and to trials and convictions in Chicago and Wichita in 1918.

Like the IWW, the Socialist Party was preoccupied with defending itself against the wartime repression that led to the imprisonment of Debs and other top leaders. Therefore, it provided no national coordination for the upsurge of new unionism. During the war, the party lost its Midwestern and Western base among farmers and older immigrant workers like the miners and machinists. Still, its membership swelled to 109,000 in 1919, when East European immigrants, attracted to the Russian Revolution, flooded into the foreign-language federations. Moderate party leaders like Hillquit and Berger joined Debs in supporting the Bolshevik revolution in 1917, but they quickly parted company with Lenin and Trotsky, who prescribed revolutionary activity at a time when the American left was in disarray. In 1919, the Bolsheviks split from the Socialist Party, taking most of the foreign-language federation membership with them.

The Communists, who formed two parties of their own that year, sought to lead the new upsurge of worker militancy. They attracted leading militants from the foreign-language federations, experienced Wobblies, black revolutionaries of the African Blood Brotherhood who, like the poet Claude McKay, urged blacks to fight back against racist attacks. William Z. Foster, the nation's leading syndicalist, gravitated toward the Communists, who also won the support of Bill Haywood of the IWW. Louis C. Fraina, a protégé of De Leon, and a brilliant young theoretician, also passed through the IWW to Communism. In *Revolutionary Socialism,* Fraina emphasized the enormous potential of the unskilled, machine proletariat as the most important political base for a new left movement. Unlike the skilled workers of the labor aristocracy who had been bought off through profits from imperialism, this militant proletariat remained class-conscious. Like Lenin, Fraina dismissed the AFL completely, because Gompers and other leaders had served as agents of imperialism. As a result, Fraina failed to see that not all privileged workers had been incorporated into the new compromise engineered by capital and the state. In any case, the new Communist movement suffered immediately from official attacks, and Bolsheviks found themselves taking defensive rather than aggressive positions. State officials and a special federal anti-red squad headed by J. Edgar Hoover of the Justice Department attacked Communists without regard to free-speech rights. Wilson's Attorney General, A. Mitchell Palmer, ordered raids in late 1919 and early 1920 that, according to Robert K. Murray's *Red Scare,* affected "virtually every local Communist organization in the nation" and led to the arrest of "practically every leader of the movement, national or local." Thus, state suppression of radicalism and divisions within the left deprived the post-war phase of the "new unionism" of coordinated political leadership.

Many obstacles stood in the way of collective working-class activity. Women workers entered industry in large numbers in response to wartime labor scarcity. But according to historian Maurine Greenwald, sex segregation increased nonetheless. In railroad work, for example, the number of women employed grew from over 60,000 to over 100,000 in 1918 alone. These new workers were confined to low-paid clerical, cleaning, and repair jobs, however. The Brotherhood of Railway Clerks organized 35,000 women clericals, but the Carmen and other shop craft unions opposed the presence of women in better-paying jobs and refused to allow them union membership. Thousands of females also went to work for urban transportation systems during the war. In Cleveland, the transit workers' union struck against the employment of women as conductors. In Kansas City, though, the union demanded equal pay for 125 women transit employees and struck to enforce the demand. Women telephone operators also won the support of male workers with whom they joined in the International Brotherhood of Electrical Workers. In general, though, female war workers received help from unionized workingmen only when they organized in low-paying "women's jobs" as clericals and telephone operators. "Ironically," Greenwald concludes, "the war brought many women their first contact with highly organized, militant male workers from whom they might have learned about the advantages of trade-union protection. Instead, the opposition of organized labor taught these women to think of trade unionism and sex discrimination synonymously."

The war also afforded some immigrant workingmen a chance to attain skilled jobs, though most remained employed as semi-skilled operatives or unskilled laborers. The new unionism unified native and foreign-born workers in many industries for the first time, but employers could still manipulate the labor market and segregate their work forces effectively. The great steel strike of 1919 failed in part because Foster's organizing strategy did not bridge the gap industry, culture, and society had created between the more skilled English-speaking workers and the less skilled "Hunkies" from Eastern

Europe. "We must certainly hand it to the foreign element," wrote one native-born steelworker toward the end of the struggle. "They certainly stick to their obligations. If the American brothers would have struck like the foreign brothers, we would have won this strike long ago." Immigrants had been affected by patriotic appeals, part of a larger Americanization drive launched by progressives during the war, but the native-born skilled workers were the ones who returned to work to prove themselves "good loyal Americans." And though the strike was remarkably free of racial conflict, the strikers' cause clearly suffered from the importation of Afro-American and Mexican strike-breakers. The rising numbers of immigrants from the rural South and Mexico fitted into the steel-industry job structure just as the Slavic immigrants had before them, and epitomized the important changes in the composition of the working class during the war.

Half a million Southern blacks escaped debt peonage to come North between 1916 and 1918. The black population in Northern cities grew by 35 percent between 1910 and 1920 and topped 100,000 in New York, Philadelphia, and Chicago. In other industrial cities, this population multiplied dramatically, by over 600 percent in Detroit and over 300 percent in Cleveland. The number of blacks working in manufacturing increased by 40 percent in the same decade, while black employment in agriculture dropped by 25 percent.

Like the new immigrants before them, blacks came into industry at low wages and were rarely offered an opportunity to join unions. But unlike white European immigrants, who entered industry under similar conditions, blacks met with the kind of racist violence they thought they had left behind in the South. In July 1917, a race riot erupted in East St. Louis, Illinois, in which thirty-nine blacks died as a result of shooting, lynching, and burning by white mobs. Eight whites, including two policemen, died in two days of rioting. The AFL unions in the city appealed for action to halt the "menace" of black laborers, who were paid lower wages and sometimes acted as strikebreakers. Gompers blamed the industrialists for importing unsuspecting blacks to undermine the standards achieved by union workers, and denied charges that local AFL leaders were partly to blame for the riot. At its 1917 convention, the Federation adopted resolutions favoring the unionization of black workers, but since it refused to pass resolutions denouncing racial discrimination, its action, said W. E. B. Du Bois of the NAACP, seemed to have been taken "grudgingly, unwillingly, and almost insultingly."

In any case, little organizing followed from these resolutions, except in Chicago meat-packing industries, where a semi-industrial union called the Stockyards Labor Council recruited 10,000 black workers. When the war ended, stockyard employment fell off and labor competition became intense, as Southern blacks continued to migrate to Chicago. The Stockyards Council could not sign up many of the newcomers, who were recruited by the packing companies and pro-employer elements in the black community. Racial tensions among stockyard workers grew during the turbulent summer of 1919 when blacks replaced white strikers. Conflicts also erupted elsewhere when blacks attempted to get housing in white areas. The terrible Chicago race riot of 1919 in which twenty-three blacks and fifteen whites died resulted directly from white gang attacks and continuing tensions over housing and city politics. As William M. Tuttle shows in *Race Riot,* the bloodshed also resulted from labor competition. Even the spirited organizing of the Stockyards Labor Council could not overcome whites' long-standing prejudice against blacks, which exaggerated the role they played as strikebreakers. More established black workers responded to industrial unionism before the race riot, but most newcomers were suspicious of white men's unions. This antagonism between black and white workers presented a crucial obstacle to unionization for the next decade.

Though European immigration ceased during the war, employers continued to tap the industrial reserve army in the rural South and Mexico, and this gave them an important advantage in the mammoth struggles of 1919. Businessmen enjoyed many other advantages in the struggle for control, notably the support of the state in suppressing radicalism and labor militancy. But none was more important than the employers' ability to manipulate the domestic and international labor markets and the forms of social segregation that prevailed within them. By 1920, the workers' challenge to manipulation and segregation had been dealt a decisive blow with the defeat of industrial unionism mobilized in the IWW and in the AFL campaigns in the stockyards and the steel mills. It would be a long, terrible fifteen years before a new kind of industrial unionism reemerged to challenge corporate domination of the workers' world.

4

The New Capitalism and the Old Unionism in the 1920's

In 1927, J. B. S. Hardman, one of the shrewdest observers of the labor scene, reviewed ten years of struggle and came to this conclusion:

> In 1917, opportunity knocked at labor's door. Responding to the possibilities of the occasion, the leaders of labor then asked for recognition and collective bargaining. They asked for no more. They dreamed of no more.

As Hardman observed, workers in many industries had shown exceptional aggressiveness during and after World War I. By 1920, the House of Labor had over 5 million workers, a spectacular 74 percent increase in only one decade. Many labor leaders saw this added strength as the basis for a "new unionism" and a new labor politics based on the demand for "industrial democracy." But most of them "lacked the will to power," as Hardman suggested. To them the House of Labor still seemed much too insecure. Indeed, in perspective, it was not so strong. In Britain, for example, where a shop stewards' movement extended the "frontier of control" in many industries, and the Labour Party expressed a real will to power, over 8 million workers belonged to unions, a much larger number of trade unionists in a much smaller country. In fact, the British Trade Union Congress claimed a remarkable 46.6 percent of the industrial work force in 1920, whereas the AFL and independent unions in the United States

100

claimed, at their height, only 18.6 percent. Fearful that the open-shop drive and the judicial onslaught would return after the war, AFL leaders cautioned conservatism, preached anti-Communism, and hoped that the progressives in government would protect their newly achieved recognition and preserve their collective bargaining rights. This defensive strategy, vociferously attacked by socialists, syndicalists, and Communists, failed to safeguard the newly extended House of Labor. By 1924, it had collapsed like a house of cards, in the face of an awesome attack by employers, the courts, and the state.

The defeat of the militant railroad shopmen's strike in 1922 wiped out the last vestiges of the ''new unionism.'' For the next dozen years or so, the old business unionism was revived and even aggressive industrial unions like the UMW, the Amalgamated Clothing Workers, and the Garment Workers were forced to seek accommodation with employers, and to suppress opposition from militants in their own ranks. The Communists' attempts to revive the ''new unionism'' under William Z. Foster's leadership failed, and so did their later efforts to create dual unions modeled after the IWW. State suppression, vigilante attacks, and divisions in the labor movement extinguished the fires of worker militancy. Employers took advantage of these forces, plus a terrible depression in 1921, and renewed their open-shop drive. More important, industrialists followed the lead of Henry Ford, who devised new ways of using technology and supervision to gain enormous control at the point of production. Welfare schemes were revived, along with scientific management techniques, stock options, and a warped form of ''industrial democracy''—the company union. Essentially, the new capitalism was based on the productivity and profitability gained from Fordism and the advances it made in technical control of the workplace.

By the end of the decade, the old unionism of the AFL had been eclipsed by the employer counteroffensive. Ford even claimed to have created a new kind of machine tender who could be bent to the will of management. Ford used the carrot as well as the stick, promising workers relatively high wages for intensified labor. During the twenties, the rewards of middle-class consumer society were extended to more workers than ever before. Working-class culture in some communities began to change partly as a result of leisure-time consumption patterns. These changes were most pronounced in the lives of skilled workers of old stock who shared some of the decade's prosperity.

The world of the urban ghetto and the company town did not change so dramatically. Immigrant workers and their children had to adjust to America, especially during the patriotic hysteria of the war years, but they still lived in their own sphere and depended on traditional familial and communal resources. They still relied on the old cultural resources that had served them well in the non-union era. But they had also learned the mysterious ways of the American workplace, and passed on their knowledge to sons and daughters who developed subtle and informal ways of resisting the drive for productivity that characterized the "roaring twenties." Never before had corporate capitalism dominated the workers' world so thoroughly, but that domination was far from total. Management had not penetrated the rich group life of community and workplace that sustained the American workers through the 1920's and the Depression and became a basis for the powerful new union movement of the 1930's.

During the 1920's, United States corporate capitalism entered a new phase. The progressives' trust-busting activity had little effect on big business. Indeed, as economic historian Gabriel Kolko argues, a kind of "political capitalism" evolved in the progressive era in which corporations benefited greatly from government action. Federal regulations helped eliminate destructive competition and created a generally favorable business climate. At the start of the decade, two hundred corporations owned half the country's corporate wealth and one fifth of the total wealth. Court decisions crippled the labor movement and struck down protective legislation for women and children. Military and diplomatic policy favored the expansion of United States business abroad, especially in Latin America. Republican President Calvin Coolidge, who first gained national attention by breaking the Boston police strike, confidently proclaimed in 1925: "The business of America is business."

Using vast new financial and political resources, the big corporations renewed their struggle for control of the workplace and, by extension, for domination of social and political institutions. With radicalism and the new unionism in retreat, employers exerted power over a wide range of affairs; they created segregated residential areas to correspond to segregated job structures; they influenced municipal politics in countless ways; and used vocational educational reforms to train skilled and clerical labor for their shops and offices. Returning to the strategy employed by U.S. Steel early in the century, corporations invested in new technology, hired an expanded army of managers, supervisors, and engineers, revived scientific management schemes and various welfare reforms. By 1928, 5.8 million employees were covered by company life-insurance plans, 3.7 million by old-age pensions, while in 315 firms 800,000 employees became stockholders. Four hundred firms maintained "company unions" or "works councils" to give their employees "representation." In 1929, vice-president of International Harvester Cyrus McCormick III claimed that works councils in his firm and others had prevented strikes and demonstrated that the interests of the "workman" and employer were "one and the same." The works councils, he declared, "gave workmen an opportunity of deliberating upon and practically deciding their own destiny." Workers lost interest in the councils, however, when their representatives voted for wage increases only to have them denied. Industrial democracy was a sham when the corporation maintained veto power.

The radical economist Lewis Corey surveyed the "new capitalism" in 1927 and concluded that corporate reform had not altered the distribution of income through stock options or democratized industrial relations through employee representation. The "new capitalism," Corey argued, revealed itself when examined closely to be a series of reforms aimed at strengthening the "dictatorship of monopoly," "buttressing" the ideology of corporatism, and "erecting defenses against labor revolts by means of employee stock ownership and other measures . . . masked as industrial democracy." Workers did seem to be affected by the pro-business climate of the 1920's, but not as a result of business reforms like "profit sharing," which involved only a small number of wage earners. Indeed, after surveying stock-option plans, the economist Sumner Slichter concluded in 1927 that "the fundamental economic views" of worker-investors had not been affected significantly by the ownership of "a few shares in a huge corporation."

One of the corporations' greatest problems was labor turnover; it reached unbelievable proportions in Ford plants before the war, and spread throughout industry during the period of labor scarcity. During the 1920's, leaving a job was an important way for a worker to respond to oppressive working conditions, given the lack of collective alternatives. To combat turnover, corporations attempted to strengthen job security, especially for skilled workers. Labor stability would increase productivity, because it was discovered that workers who feared layoffs deliberately restricted output in order to "spread out the work" and save jobs. These efforts to add stability and security to the labor force conflicted with the dictates of the business cycle and the need to cut costs by reducing the work force. The Ford Motor Company, a pioneer in battling labor turnover, caused great suffering and anxiety by laying off thousands of workers when it changed models in 1927.

Attempts were also made to extend scientific management to increase productivity. The foreman's empire remained an object of reform. Many corporations set up employment and personnel departments to remove decisions over hiring, promotion, and firing from the shop floor. These decisions, along with production and pay decisions, were put in the hands of planners and managers. The foreman did not disappear, especially in smaller competitive firms. He remained the classic overseer who used his authority to hire and fire and his power to set piece rates in order to drive his gang toward greater production.

In some industries, managers actually enlisted union support for scientific management reforms to increase efficiency. Union officials in "sick," highly competitive industries like clothing manufacture supported Taylorism and hoped that the resulting increase in productivity would prevent wage cuts and layoffs. After two decades of militant resistance to bonus and incentive systems, top labor officials like Samuel Gompers extended the olive branch to the Taylorites. William Green of the UMW, who succeeded Gompers as AFL president in 1924, argued that unions should "increasingly concern themselves to see that management policies are efficient." With the exception of a few well-publicized cases, industry refused to accept the olive branch.

In any case, union cooperation could not necessarily ensure the increased efficiency and productivity promised by scientific management. Most workers remained outside of unions. And, as Stanley B. Mathewson showed in his valuable study *Restriction of Output among Unorganized Workers,* both union and non-union employees found many ways to fool the time-and-motion-study man with his ever-present stopwatch. One lathe operator in a non-union shop put it: "I would often slip a belt to a lower pulley in a lathe when being timed, and use other tricks to make the job last longer. There were a lot of rates set too low, and I felt justified in causing some to be set too high in order to get an even break in earnings." Mathewson concluded that even among unorganized workers, without union "work rules," restriction of output remained "deeply entrenched in the working habits of American laboring people." Scientific management simply "failed to develop that spirit of confidence between parties to labor contracts" essential to Taylor's scheme. The efforts of scientific managers to obtain more efficiency and productivity had been "offset by the ingenuity of workers in developing restrictive practices."

As a result, most employees, lacking confidence in Taylor's complicated bonus-pay systems, relied upon more common piece-rate pay incentives. "Most of the work done in one of the largest tire building plants in the country is on a piece-rate basis," Mathewson wrote. "In one department piece workers pushed their earnings up to $12 a day." Said an employee in this department: "The rate was immediately cut. Now we know that the maximum paid for this work is $7 a day. It would be possible for us to do much more but we are careful not to.'' The old desire to cut labor costs to increase profits prevented employers from creating rational production "incentives." In fact, given the insecurity of labor in the roaring twenties, it became more rational to restrict output than to increase production and earn more pay.

The same dynamic developed in the expanding clerical and service sector in the 1920's. Clerical work became the fastest-growing occupation in the economy because modern corporations required more secretaries and more managers and accountants.

The "feminization of the clerical labor force" occurred rapidly after the turn of the century, according to Margery Davies. And by 1930 the percentage of female stenographers and typists had surged to 96 percent. The mechanization of low-paying office jobs made them undesirable for men, who generally had better employment opportunities. And since women tended to have more schooling than men, they were better suited to jobs that required some education. They could also be paid less than men for the work. With immigration cut off by the war and then dramatically restricted by the 1924 Immigration Act, the demand for white-collar labor was met by women, who found office work more acceptable than domestic service or factory employment. The high-school curriculum was increasingly oriented to training women for office jobs; special schools were set up to teach typing and shorthand.

By 1930, nearly 2¼ million women worked in offices. This development reflected a great shift: employers clearly recognized women as the nation's largest untapped reserve army of labor. Women could be used to fill many expanding job sectors in the economy. In 1900, women worked primarily in manufacturing, agriculture, and domestic service. During the 1920's, the expansion of women's work came largely in the clerical and service sectors, as agricultural employment for women declined, and the proportion of women serving as domestics dropped from one third of all wage earners in 1910 to one fourth in 1930. The expansion of the clerical labor force clearly emerged as part of the new corporate control strategy in which the office played a central role. Lee Galloway says in *Office Management:*

Execution implies *control*—control of the factory organization—control of the financial organization—control of the marketing organization. It is the work of the office organization, under the supervision of the office manager, to devise records, methods, and systems for carrying out the function of control and for coordinating the activities of one department with those of another.

As office work changed from "something merely incidental to management into a labor process in its own right," it had to be systematized, according to Braverman. In 1917, a disciple of Taylor explained that the time-and-motion studies of "useless effort" in factories could be applied to offices. Indeed, some large offices began to apply scientific management principles in the 1920's. Eliminating much of the independent decision-making power secretaries had enjoyed, large firms organized typing pools and subdivided clerical work. They attached meters to typewriters to measure productivity. Office managers also introduced piecework payment systems borrowed from factories in order to increase output.

As "white collar" work became more proletarianized, workers adopted more and more of the tactics used in factories. In department stores, where in the twenties corporations demanded increased sales, management applied incentive-pay schemes borrowed from industry. As Susan Porter Benson points out, however, "saleswomen had a rich and varied array of tactics for keeping sales tallies down to an acceptable level, ranging from ignoring customers when their 'book' was running high to being more aggressive with customers in slow seasons than in busy seasons." "Selling work," Benson indicates, "had much in common with both sweated and machine-tending modes of manufacturing," including poor sanitary facilities, long hours, and "mandatory unpaid overtime." Management attempted to control sales workers through a variety of means, but found the "selling skill" difficult to manage. Saleswomen themselves used what freedom they had to develop a "strong work culture and durable informal work groups" that frustrated management's efforts to increase sales. The struggle for control in offices and large department stores differed from the struggle in steel mills. Women entered an already degraded and proletarianized occupation. Even without craft skills, women developed controls over their labor that enabled them to resist some of their employers' demands.

In 1927, the famous Hawthorne experiments conducted at Western Electric's giant telephone-assembly plant near Chicago focused on the work group as the key to productivity. Experimental studies of work groups revealed that lighting and other changes had no effect, but improving social relations within the primary work group did seem to increase output. This led some human-relations experts to advocate group incentives rather than the old individual piece-rate incentives. The Hawthorne experiments also showed that workers produced more when they had increased control over the labor process. The human-relations school developed to exploit this knowledge and to create the illusion of increased workers' control. It instructed managers to become less authoritarian and more manipulative of workers' informal work-group identities. Sociologist C. Wright Mills observed that by understanding group relations among employees, managers could be more effective in countering the "informal solidarities" workers had developed against management.

Small work groups had always been the essential units of production, even in the artisans' shop. During the twenties, the increased scale of production multiplied these groups. Scientific managers sought to manipulate them more effectively through the use of various studies and academic disciplines, like industrial psychology, but the growing scale of production made it difficult to maintain and control these work groupings. In Philadelphia, for example, the average number of employees per manufacturing establishment had increased to 52.6 by 1930, with department stores averaging over a thousand employees and eleven large industries employing over a hundred persons per plant. Having broken down the social or natural division of labor through mechanization and bureaucratization, industrial managers attempted to create artificial groups of about twenty workers, so they could be supervised more easily.

The worker experienced a kind of "dual control" by the supervisor on the one hand and the work group itself on the other. Management attempted to create work units it could control, but even the formal work groups, like the employer-sponsored "works councils," sometimes took on a life of their own. Furthermore, informal work groups developed along social lines (based on age, sex, nationality, family identity, etc.) that cut across the artificial lines management created. Both formal and informal work groups could be the basis of worker-controlled initiatives, such as the restriction of output.

The emergence of the modern industrial work group reflected important changes in labor relations and ultimately in class relations. As Sam Bass Warner, Jr., observes of Philadelphia's economy in the 1920's, the corporation had created a "working world of officers and enlisted men." An "us" versus "them" attitude surfaced as hierarchical organization and mechanization robbed workers of responsibility and creativity. At the bottom of the hierarchy, the degraded wage earners viewed their work as nothing but a job, while at the top a new stratum of production officers (managers, accountants, personnel experts, sales and advertising men, engineers, and corporate lawyers) saw work as a career or "calling." During the same period, other professionals in medicine, law, social science, social work, and secondary education joined the corporate drive for order, efficiency, and productivity. Many professionals shared a "calling" with corporate managers—not unlike that of the traditional bourgeoisie—which required self-discipline, self-control, and a sense of mission, a mission that centered on social control as well as personal advancement. While these professionals and managers embraced a twentieth-century faith in education and achievement, the old work ethic showed signs of deterioration. By the twenties, Daniel T. Rodgers writes in *The Work Ethic in Industrial America,* (1978), the "transformation of labor" through the modern factory "undercut virtually all the mid-nineteenth century assumptions about the moral preeminence of work." Ironically, the control corporations gained over workers in the 1920's through hierarchical organization, detailed division of labor, and mechanization meant that wage earners lacked the individual incentives and loyalties employers sought so desperately to re-create.

If the modern factory system and corporate revolution altered attitudes toward work, these radical changes also affected class relations. In a large industrial city like Pittsburgh, where "vast enterprises" controlled "centralized, rationalized, carefully-planned engineering," the increasingly polarized class structure reflected the dominance of the corporation. "The personnel of the giant mills was rigidly divided into classes, with college graduates at the top of the pyramid, followed by the skilled workers and finally by the mass of unskilled workers," Warner indicates in *The Urban Wilderness.* "Corporations rewarded each class appropriately in their own view, with steady salaries and hierarchical promotions for the educated elite, high wages and fringe benefits for the skilled, bitter poverty and unremitting toil for the unskilled."

During the "roaring twenties," employers used many methods to force more production from workers. The quickening pace and intensity of work, which impressed foreign visitors as peculiarly American, was reflected in a 64 percent jump in industrial productivity after a meager increase of only 12 percent during the previous decade of violent labor struggles. Between 1919 and 1929, the number of wage earners in manufacturing decreased slightly, but the level of production more than *doubled.* The falloff in the blue-collar factory work force contrasted dramatically with the expansion of the white-collar supervisory work force. The number of engineers increased from 77,000 to 217,000 between 1910 and 1930; the number of managers in manufacturing leaped from 126,000 to 313,000 in the same period. The growing army of professionals and managers served as commissioned officers in the corporate campaign for control. However, the modernized versions of scientific management, personnel relations, and welfare capitalism mobilized by these control officers were not primarily responsible for the great productivity of the twenties.

During the 1920's, corporations, following Henry Ford's lead, turned more to "technical control" through which disciplinary power normally exercised by the foreman became "embedded in the technological structure of the firm," as Richard Edwards discusses in *Contested Terrain*. The assembly line not only represented a technological advance in the use of machinery; it could be used as a very effective "control mechanism" in disciplining a volatile, alienated work force.

"Machinery is the new Messiah!" Henry Ford declared in the twenties. The amount of "horsepower" used per wage earner expanded noticeably between 1919 and 1929, increasing by 50 percent in factories and 60 percent in the mines, where the undercutting machine gained widespread use. Mechanization decimated whole trades, such as glassblowing. By the end of the decade, 70 percent of American industry had been electrified, making the steam engine obsolete. Ford's production empire—the symbol of the new machine age—ran on electric power produced from the immense turbines at River Rouge. Generators powered the assembly lines at Highland Park, which by 1924 contained 42,000 workers who labored at an ever-quickening pace. In 1925, Ford plants turned out 31,200 cars with the same machinery used to produce 25,000 in 1920.

The dramatic increase in productivity obtained by Ford through the use of the "endless conveyor belt" depended not so much on science and technology (the continuous-production process had been used in earlier plants) but on the control management gained over the labor process. Ford and other manufacturers also exploited specialized machine tools which allowed managers to do work formerly done by skilled craftsmen. Having gained a greater degree of technical control at the expense of the skilled auto assemblers and machinists, Ford followed his forerunners at U.S. Steel and leveled out the pay structure.

Ford drove for more productivity and control by using the continuous assembly line and new machinery, but the auto maker also instituted welfare schemes in an attempt to dominate all aspects of the workers' world. Ford's Sociology Department actually sent investigators into workers' homes to select those "right-living" employees entitled to share in the company's profits through stock ownership. These investigators sought to extend corporate control further into workers' lives by studying how workers actually lived and by undermining the family economy through prohibitions on boarding and women working outside the home. They sought to encourage a middle-class Protestant sense of domestic order by enforcing anti-liquor laws and by increasing domestic standards of cleanliness and efficiency. The Sociology Department also reached into ethnic neighborhoods, promoting the conservative role of the churches and attacking the social life flourishing in "speakeasy" drinking and gambling places. Troubled by the "petty empires" that grew up in immigrant neighborhoods, Ford's agents promoted Americanization in order to discourage ethnic loyalties, independent group life, and the use of foreign languages.

To Antonio Gramsci, the brilliant Marxist writing from a jail in Mussolini's Italy, the new capitalism seemed akin to Fascism. "Fordism," Gramsci noted, was "the biggest effort" capitalists had made "to create . . . a new type of worker and man." Unlike the old worker with irregular habits and undisciplined attitudes, the new "mass worker" would display a personality fully adapted to capitalist rationality. Like the parts of a machine, these machine tenders could easily be replaced because they, too, were interchangeable. According to Charles Reitell's 1924 description, Ford's new machine proletarian had to "maintain a constant machine pace, to be able to eliminate all waste and false motions; to follow without wavering printed instructions emanating from an unseen source lodged in some far off planning department . . ." In order to meet these standards, the new worker, said a Ford superintendent, had to live a "well-regulated home life" in which drunkenness and other signs of "careless living had been eliminated." Since Prohibition coincided with this effort to regulate the worker, Gramsci believed that "the state itself had been enlisted in the crusade for Fordism." The conjunction of control efforts through mechanization, rationalization, Prohibition, and Americanization seemed to make Fordism nothing less than the Americanism of the 1920's.

After World War I, inflation eroded the effects of the five-dollar day, and Ford's own competitive advantage began to decrease as other auto companies found the secret to productivity. By 1921, Ford had abandoned extensive welfare work and returned to the high-wage strategy, bolstered by the well-publicized shortening of the work week in 1926. Announced with great fanfare, the five-day week helped Ford attract workers, but his employees soon found that the company intended to produce the same number of cars in a given week. The effects of the speedup registered on the faces of Ford workers. A Detroit businessman, observing Ford employees at a company grocery store in 1927, said: "When a shift comes out of the factory the commissary immediately fills up with grim-looking, determined men who never smile or joke, but rush over to buy supplies in the most determined sort of way. No shopping, just speed; no unnecessary talk, no time wasted by either customer or clerk, just cold-blooded Ford efficiency.'' Using many of Ford's techniques, auto manufacturers gained a whopping 255 percent increase in productivity during the 1920's, compared to the 64 percent increase recorded by all manufacturers.

New levels of technical control provided auto makers and other manufacturers with more output while granting workers higher wages and, in some cases, shorter work weeks. In return for laboring harder and faster, factory workers in the twenties enjoyed an increase in real wages. A 26 percent gain in real income did not encroach on corporate profits, however, as dividends jumped 100 percent. Indeed, the "new capitalism" required more purchasing power for wage earners, who were expected to sustain the new prosperity by becoming consumers. Ford's Model T, a product purchased by many workers during the decade, exemplified the rewards of productivity. "To the new capitalism, the wage earner . . . is a purchaser, a partner, and a key to production," *Fortune* magazine declared. High wages would produce a new era of harmony between capital and labor. "The new capitalism" said these corporate prophets, was a radical "social conception." This new "social conception" rested on repression and exploitation more than it did on "partnership."

The new capitalism not only achieved more productivity, it began to change the workers' world in important ways. The relationship between changes in production and changes in community and family life is still obscure, but several sociological studies offer insights into the new connection between production and consumption in the 1920's. We saw earlier how craft control in Muncie, Indiana, allowed a powerful class-conscious labor movement to control many aspects of city life at the turn of the century. The Lynds' study *Middletown* three decades later revealed the devastating effects of mechanization and the new importance of consumption to the worker. By the 1920's, machine technology had virtually wiped out the skilled glassmakers who exercised so much influence in Muncie at an earlier time. In other industries, like machine tools, machinery had been sped up and "the human factor" had been eliminated from work. "It's high-speed steel and specialization and Ford cars that's hit the machinist's union," one skilled worker told the Lynds. He blamed the decline of a strong craft union not only on changes in technology, machinery, and the division of labor but also on Ford cars, which helped workers escape from the "long arm of the job."

According to the Lynds, "the psychological satisfactions formerly derived from the sense of craftsmanship" had decreased and so had "the group solidarity" of trade unionism, but Middletown people still worked very hard. Why? Piece rates and speedups provided only part of the answer. People seemed to work harder so they could spend more money, an activity greatly facilitated by the expansion of credit through "time payments." Looking for satisfaction outside the working world, workers turned to the outlawed saloons and to other "compensatory" activities like "hooking up the radio or driving the 'old bus.' " This instrumental aspect of work, rather than the "intrinsic satisfactions involved," seemed to the Lynds to be what kept "Middletown working so hard."

If developments in Muncie are indicative, many workers must have been attracted to mass-produced products like the Model T, radio, and new clothing, fashions and appliances bought through time-payment schemes. Retail outlets expanded greatly during the 1920's, from Ford dealerships to chain stores (whose units increased fivefold). Total advertising expenditures spurted from about $56 million in 1919 to $196 million in 1929. Stuart Ewen suggests in *Captains of Consciousness* that advertising opened the new world of consumption to workers alienated from the world of production. Subjected to degrading forms of discipline and control on the factory floor, the worker had a very low self-image in the 1920's, when the "dignity of labor" suffered irreparable harm. Advertising offered the worker a more positive self-image—that of an attractive, fashionable person in control of life. Denied dignity as a worker, the wage earner could gain a measure of self-respect, as well as personal satisfaction, as a consumer.

Advertising even attempted to redefine confused family roles. The traditional patriarchal family had declined drastically as a unit of production. A student of family relations in the twenties commented on how the "sense of family enterprise" had been lost. The home, no longer a center of joint production, became a center of distribution for the incomes earned by "discrete wage earners." As Rosalyn Baxandall, Linda Gordon, and Susan Reverby point out in *America's Working Women,* "by the end of the 1920's, two thirds of the national income was spent in retail stores. Shopping became part of a housewife's work, replacing home preparation." Furthermore: "Women needed different skills and a different character structure to be good shoppers and spenders than they needed as producers of their own goods. They became the objects, and victims, of sophisticated ad campaigns, which used women's fears and insecurities, already intensified by the disintegration of traditional roles, to make them seek fulfillment through purchases."

Labor-saving devices for the home were purchased largely by

middle- and upper-class women, but working-class women did buy consumer goods to reduce arduous tasks like baking bread, making clothing, and canning vegetables. As a result, women had more time to work outside the home, and the lure of consumer goods provided more incentive. Family, work, and consumer roles formed a "circle" which closed in on women in the 1920's, says Mary P. Ryan in *Womanhood in America*. "The spurious fulfillment of consumerism served to accommodate women to the monotony and depersonalization of the female work force. The purchase of clothes and cosmetics, for example, could give overworked and underpaid service workers of the 1920's a semblance of social status." In short, Ryan concludes, consumerism provided an "escape valve for the pressures built up in the female labor force; it promised release, by way of purchase, from the monotony of a deadened job."

Of course, women's increased participation in the labor force was not just the result of role changes created by advertising and consumption. By the twenties, capitalism had radically affected the workers' social and personal world. Working-class women found that they could produce and earn less at home, outside the sphere of the capitalist marketplace. With the restriction of immigration, working-class housewives lost a steady supply of single boarders who had contributed to the family income. With the availability of processed foods, fewer back-yard gardens were cultivated. "In sum," Ryan writes, "the home production so central to the nineteenth century working class was transferred to the paid public labor force."

Most working-class women still remained at home. Even those who wanted to work for wages were discouraged by low wages and poor working conditions. Advertising attempted to define a new role for the mother in the home, an alternative to the old producer role and the new proletarian role. The modern housewife spent as much time, but less energy, on housework because she could purchase appliances, detergents, disinfectants, ready-made clothing, and prepackaged food. Children were said to need more attention from the mother, even though a higher proportion attended school. Advertisers buttressed the father's primary role as provider while they boosted the mother's role as consumer. These new roles did not help to stabilize the nuclear family, however, and the divorce rate continued to rise throughout the decade, more so among industrial families than among farm families, in which more traditional roles remained intact.

Working-class women who stayed at home gained little leisure time from their new products, and found themselves cut off from each other by the increasingly more private life many workers adopted. Of the

118 working-class housewives interviewed by the Lynds in Muncie, forty had "no intimate friends." Many, of course, were "hoosiers" from the farms, who joined thousands of other native-born families fleeing rural poverty for the cash wages offered in the industrial city. But even more established Middletown women complained of isolation. "Our neighbors used to be good friends and we had lots of good times together, but in the last seven or eight years all that's gone," said one woman. "People don't pay much attention to each other any more." The Lynds found "almost universal working-class testimony" of the decline of the neighborhood as wage earners' lives became more transient and more private.

The Middletown study reflects the cultural and social changes that affected the workers' world, but it is hardly representative. In an analysis of a larger city with a more diverse work force, *The Private City: Philadelphia in Three Periods of Its Growth,* historian Sam Bass Warner, Jr., noted a variety of responses among working-class people to consumerism and the new capitalism of the twenties. In newer streetcar suburbs, skilled tradesmen joined the middle class in pursuing the new prosperity and a "more intense private family life" through homeownership, which encompassed more than half of the city's population by 1930.

In contrast, in northeast Philadelphia, an industrial district with the look of a mill town, workers still participated in an active group life. Though many of the skilled workers owned their homes, this did not lead to privatization. Neighborhoods like Kensington were not places of "isolated and alienated metropolitan workers," Warner maintains. Rather, the northeast "was the home of benefit associations, craft unions, fraternal orders, and ethnic clubs." Like the steelworkers of Homestead a decade earlier, the skilled workers in this district found that the "mill taught group work and discipline," which was in turn reflected in well-ordered group activities characteristic of the older Irish and German immigrants as well as the Polish newcomers. Unlike Homestead, however, northeast Philadelphia was not dominated by one giant corporation, and this meant, among other things, that a certain degree of "local control" developed in "job seeking and job adjustment."

In south Philadelphia, a ghetto area comparable to New York's East Side, ethnic neighborhoods displayed less discipline and less stability. "The highly organized group life of the northeast did not exist here because the industrial patterns of the district did not encourage complementary neighborhoods, union and club organizations," Warner remarks. On the other hand, these neighborhoods did not show many signs of individualism or consumerism; they were relatively settled residential areas where "poor people and working-class people could make a stable family life and a stable set of neighborhood relationships," he continues. "Parochialism, familism, the friendships and loyalties of the gang, the street and the saloon" all helped to bolster these people "against the successive crises of poverty." Isolation from the mainstream of city life allowed these neighborhoods to retain their distinctive identity in the 1920's, prevented much contact with the agents of consumerism, and offered a "refuge" for immigrants from the intense patriotism and Americanism of the decade. As Warner notes, the immigrant worker, returning home at night, could find some shelter in family and community in which the "newcomer could learn American urban culture while living among fellow beginners with whom he shared a common experience, language, and church."

Though immigrant workers were more at home in their new world, they still took refuge in the group life of the urban ghetto because the political and cultural life of the country was dominated by the business classes and nativist forces who expressed contempt for immigrant workers and their values. The public consciousness generated by the progressives and socialists in the pre-war years had all but disappeared. With the return to "normalcy" in politics, private-property rights reigned supreme. The state showed no inclination to protect the collective rights of workers, whether they were women, children, or immigrants.

The predominance of the business class and its professional allies at all levels of government reflected more than corporate economic power. The culture of the 1920's actually seemed imbued with business values. The promise of Fordism, after all, was to reward high levels of production with new kinds of consumption for the masses. The "conspicuous consumption" of the "leisure class," described by Thorstein Veblen, invited emulation by the lower classes. Of course, the intense Americanism of the early 1920's rested more heavily on patriotism and racism than it did on consumerism, which remained a mirage for most unskilled workers, native or foreign-born.

For the new immigrants in the urban ghettos, the post-war years represented a difficult period in which they faced intense pressure to assimilate. The effects of Americanization were ambiguous at best, because immigrants were being told to assimilate at the same time that their relatives and country folk were being excluded from the United States. The immigration-restriction acts approved by Congress in 1921 and 1924 reflected prejudice and the lower demand for labor by industry, which could rely on black and white migrants from rural America, as well as Mexican migrants. Closing the gates to European peasants represented much more, though, because it was accompanied by a racist campaign against the new immigrants. The militancy and radicalism immigrant proletarians displayed in the 1909–19 revolts convinced industrialists that these peasants would not adapt as well to discipline as they had hoped. Corporations like Ford and International Harvester launched ambitious Americanization programs during the war, designed mainly to teach English to foreign-speaking workers, who still suffered appallingly high accident rates because, according to employers, they could not read or understand safety instructions. Some immigrant workmen used these programs to their advantage, just as others used the public schools and settlement houses to gain new survival skills. As a second generation of workers came to maturity in the urban ghettos, Americanization programs became more ambitious. The industrialists, however, abandoned most educational efforts after the war. Whether or not they faced Americanization pressure on the job, immigrant workers were affected by the patriotic hysteria of the war, the "red scare" of 1919–20, the rise of the Ku Klux Klan, and the pressure of immigration restriction and "100 percent Americanism."

Afro-Americans and many immigrant groups created their own forms of nationalism in response to coercive Americanism. Ethnic assertiveness developed at the expense of integrationism, socialism, anarchism, and other pre-war ideologies which stressed internationalism and working-class unity. For example, among the Italian-Americans, the pressure toward Americanization produced something other than the desired effect. As Humbert Nelli indicates in *Italians in Chicago,* business values became more prominent in the immigrant community, and some peasant localism faded away. But, in response to Americanism, Italian nationalism thrived. The heroes of many Italian-Americans in Chicago and other "little Italys" were, first, Al Capone, who was not only envied and respected for his wealth and power but admired for his defiance of Prohibition laws and for his role as "a benefactor" in the mold of the old Italian *padrone,* and second, the Fascist dictator Benito Mussolini, who revived Italian nationalism.

The popularity of Italian nationalism and Fascism rose as radicalism declined. Business values gained new respect as the anti-capitalist elements lost ground. The IWW and Socialist Party strength among Italian-Americans faded after the suppression of those groups, and the new Communist movement did not attract followers as it did among East Europeans. And the troublesome anarchist movement among Italian workers and intellectuals was also repressed during the red scare. The Russian anarchists Emma Goldman and Alexander Berkman were actually deported, along with Luigi Galleani, a charismatic figure among Italian anarchists. Still, the Italian left united and rallied its people in a remarkable defense movement to save the lives of Nicola Sacco and Bartolomeo Vanzetti.

These two Italian anarchists were arrested in the midst of the 1920 red scare for a robbery and murder committed in South Braintree, Massachusetts. They were quickly tried before a prejudiced Yankee judge and jury at Dedham, Massachusetts, and sentenced to death in the electric chair on the basis of flimsy circumstantial evidence. The ordeal of Sacco and Vanzetti, who were executed in 1927 despite herculean efforts by their defenders, seemed to symbolize the fate of those who resisted Americanization and rejected the authority of the state. Sacco and Vanzetti, the shoemaker and the fisherman, were not only the romantic immigrants portrayed in left-wing literature; they were skilled labor organizers and dedicated revolutionaries. Bartolomeo Vanzetti "loved Puccini and knew Dante," but he also organized a strike at the huge Plymouth cordage factory in 1916, and toiled as a quarry worker in Connecticut and a railroad section hand in Massachusetts. He took to fish peddling only after being blacklisted in the Plymouth strike. Nicola Sacco was a skilled shoeworker, a trade that produced many radicals, but he also helped organize a strike at the big machine works in Hopedale, Massachusetts. Both men fled the country during the war to avoid conscription and both actively protested the violation of political and human rights during the red scare. Indeed, they were armed when arrested as robbery and murder suspects on May 5, 1920, because they feared for their lives. An anarchist comrade had just fallen (or been pushed) to his death from the Department of Justice Building in New York City.

Sacco and Vanzetti were condemned to death, not just because they were immigrants, but because they were anarchists active in the class struggles of their time. To John Dos Passos, the novelist, who joined other leftists in the defense work, the electrocution of the two revolutionaries epitomized the defeat a nation of "strangers" inflicted on a nation of workers. After the great funeral procession from Boston's Italian ghetto, Dos Passos wrote in *The Big Money:*

now their work is over   the immigrants   haters of oppression lie
quiet in black suits in the little undertaking parlor in the North
End   the city is quiet   the men of the conquering nation are not to
be seen on the streets

they have won   why are they scared to be seen on the streets?   on the streets you see only the downcast faces of the beaten   the streets belong to the beaten nation all the way to the cemetery where the bodies of the immigrants are to be burned   we line the curbs . . . looking with scared eyes at the coffins   we stand defeated America

The fate of Sacco and Vanzetti may have intimidated some in the Italian community, but it did not, of course, produce 100 percent Americanism.

The Sacco–Vanzetti defense movement, which attracted support in many immigrant working-class communities, bucked a trend toward ethnic nationalism among several groups, including the Italians. Various ethnocentric movements also emerged in the urban ghetto, suggesting that Americanization programs might be having a negative effect. In New York City's Jewish ghetto, the British declaration on Palestine in 1917 stimulated the growth of Zionism, while in black ghettos, Marcus Garvey's nationalist Universal Negro Improvement Association mobilized millions of oppressed black workers. As John Higham concludes in his study of nativism, *Strangers in the Land,* the excesses of the red scare and the crusade for 100 percent Americanism created a revolt among minorities. It was expressed not only in the radicals' defense of Sacco and Vanzetti but in an upsurge of ethnic nationalism. "The minority revolt against Americanization, a revolt accentuated by all of the other manifestations of 100 percent Americanism, hurled large blocs of immigrants into compensatory chauvinisms of their own," Higham observes. Unlike the socialist–Yiddish movement of the Bundists, the anarchism of Italians like Sacco and Vanzetti, or the black radicalism of the African Blood Brotherhood, these nationalisms expressed a defiant group consciousness rather than the kind of class consciousness that had emerged from the mass strikes and control struggles of the previous decade.

Americanization failed to discipline and reform ethnic workers; it also failed to homogenize the working class, which seemed as fragmented as it had been in the early 1900's. Corporate capitalism did not produce unified and militant working-class consciousness. Gone were the solidarity and combative spirit of the previous decade, in which labor radicalism and industrial unionism flourished. "If the collectivity of workers constituted a 'class,' " writes Irving Bernstein in *The Lean Years: A History of the American Worker, 1920–1933,* "it was an inert body with little dynamism or direction." And, of course, "the labor movement reflected this inertia."

The collapse of organized labor in the 1920's should be considered, then, in the larger context of Fordism, consumerism, and the emergence of a powerful "new capitalism." Gompers and other AFL leaders did lack the will to power and they did refuse to back rank-and-file militancy, which continued to grow in 1920 and 1921. But the fall of the House of Labor cannot be blamed solely on a failure of leadership. As organized labor reached its peak membership in 1920, employers launched an aggressive new open-shop drive. Taking advantage of the conservative political mood, chambers of commerce and manufacturers' associations mobilized their "American Plan" to abolish union shops. They also seized on the reactionary post-war spirit of Americanism and enlisted the support of the American Legion, the National Security League, and the Ku Klux Klan.

By 1920, the resurgent KKK had recruited millions of members by exploiting racial, religious, and political fears. Supporting the open-shop drive and denouncing all immigrants as "un-American" and "agents of Lenin," the Klan extended its membership from businessmen and professionals, who saw themselves as moral reformers, to workers and farmers in cities and towns where the AFL and agricultural organizations were weak. The Klan gained most of its support from white Protestant workingmen in places like Tulsa, Oklahoma, scene of a bloody race war in 1921, where labor competition exacerbated the tensions produced by returning servicemen, including black soldiers who militantly stood up for their rights. In Muncie, Indiana, where the once-powerful unions had disintegrated, the Klan began as a businessman's group, but then, according to the Lynds, it became a movement of white Protestant workingmen. The Klan's anti-Catholicism, anti-Semitism, and racism showed that the cultural chauvinism of the twenties affected the privileged position of the working class in many areas. In Muncie, the KKK "afforded an outlet for many of the constant frustrations of life," including economic tension as well as social insecurity, "by providing a wealth of scape goats against whom wrath might be vented." In general, unions opposed the Klan, which supported the business open-shop drive of the early 1920's. In Chicago, one of the few large industrial cities where the hooded order enjoyed support, foremen outnumbered industrial workers. Still, the race riot of 1919 and the white racism involved in the stockyards and steel strikes showed that racism was virulent among Catholic as well as Protestant workers in the Chicago area. During the 1920's, big employers were able to exploit the kind of organized racist sentiment that had long been endemic in many Southern cities. They did not need the Ku Klux Klan to do this.

In 1921, employers took advantage of a major depression (which created a frightful 19.5 percent rate of unemployment) to implement the American Plan and impose decisive defeats in union strongholds. In San Francisco, perhaps the strongest union city in the country, open-shop advocates defeated the powerful Building Trades Council, ruled for twenty-five years by political boss P. H. McCarthy, who faced a rank-and-file revolt when he accepted the employers' draconian terms. In Chicago, another center of building trades' power, the indictment of top leaders for graft and corruption weakened the fight against wage cuts and changes in work rules ordered by Federal Judge Kenesaw Mountain Landis. In Chicago and other cities, some construction unions responded to the open-shop drive just as the Structural Iron Workers had earlier in the century. In 1920 and 1921, over a hundred dynamite explosions hit open-shop sites in the Windy City. Union officials often hired thugs, or "gorillas," to "pull jobs" like this, according to Louis Adamic's account in *Dynamite!*, thus allowing "professional criminals," like Chicago's Al Capone, to begin to "muscle" their way into union affairs.

Some unions organized effectively to beat back the open-shop drive, notably the New York City International Typographical Union and the Amalgamated Clothing Workers (whose leaders also fought effectively to keep gangsters out). Both unions were especially democratic and honest.

In 1922, crucial struggles in key industries brought victories for the open-shop movement or seriously weakened unions. These struggles ended a dozen-year period of unusual working-class militancy. Labor organizations that had expanded rapidly in mass-production industries during the wartime boom suffered great losses as a result of unemployment and the open-shop drive. The Big Five meat-packing companies, for example, imposed wage cuts and an open shop after defeating the Amalgamated Association of Butcher Workmen in a crucial 1922 confrontation. The United Textile Workers, another union that had gained members in manufacturing during the war, also suffered crushing blows from employers who established the open shop in spite of militant strikes in New England mill towns, like Manchester, New Hampshire, where the employees of the giant Amoskeag complex went out for nine months.

The defeat of the six shop craft unions that struck the railroads in 1922 was crucial. Early in 1922, the leaders of these unions accepted changes in work rules, including the abolition of overtime pay for Sundays and holidays; they expected the hard-pressed membership to accept the deal. Instead, 400,000 railroad workers insisted on striking.

The chairman of the Railroad Labor Board, a holdover from the war years, called their walkout an "outlaw strike" and actually urged owners to form company unions. In the third month of the strike, Attorney General Daugherty charged the strikers with unlawful conspiracy under the Sherman Anti-Trust Act. He obtained the "most sweeping injunction ever issued in a labor dispute from a federal judge," though orders of this kind were supposedly prohibited by the Clayton Act of 1914. In fact, one year before, Supreme Court Chief Justice William Howard Taft, the old "injunction judge," wrote a decision upholding the use of an injunction against a picket line which seemed unnecessarily intimidating. This case threw into doubt the value of the Clayton Act, labor's great legislative victory of the Progressive Era. The injunction actually heightened the resolve of the 1922 strikers, but in a short time the railroad unions capitulated.

In most of the 1921–22 strikes, members supported leaders who attempted to preserve union recognition and work rules, even if this meant accepting wage cuts. The railroad unions and the United Mine Workers, however, were racked by bitter strikes, with members rebelling against compromises made by union leaders. According to Sylvia Kopald's *Rebellion in the Labor Unions,* this rank-and-file unrest also reflected discontent with the autocratic powers assumed by many AFL leaders and an attempt to extend the fight for industrial democracy to the unions themselves.

The United Mine Workers' new president, John L. Lewis, already in disfavor with his members for his leadership of the 1919 strike, assumed a militant posture in 1922: he threatened nationalization of the mines and raised the specter of the British Triple Alliance—a pact between miners, dockers, and railroad workers. But as the 1922 coal strike wore on, Lewis provoked militant miners by refusing to join with striking railroad workers and by accepting a compromise settlement. Already checked by the Supreme Court's Hitchman decision of 1917, which virtually prevented UMW organizing in open shops, the union withdrew further; its leaders refused to unionize militant Pennsylvania miners, who continued to strike after the 1922 settlement. Unlike most labor leaders, Lewis decided to try to preserve wage rates at the expense of jobs and working conditions, but he failed. Wages for soft-coal miners dropped 23 percent in the seven years after the 1922 strike. Meanwhile, the once powerful UMW lost thousands of members as mines were mechanized and others closed due to competition with open-shop mines in the South. Lewis attempted to save standards by making deals with operators and by using his influence with the Republicans in Washington; but these tactics failed. By 1929, the once-proud UMW claimed only 80,000 members; its contracts had extended to six times that many miners when Lewis assumed the presidency in 1919.

The UMW's abandonment of the striking non-union miners in Pennsylvania, combined with its losses in West Virginia, helped precipitate a rank-and-file revolt against Lewis's undemocratic administration. This movement died, but when the union lost a key struggle in 1927–28 to Midwestern operators in the Central Competitive Field, another rebellion erupted. A "Save the Union" Committee formed under the leadership of socialists, Communists, and syndicalist militants. John Brophy, a Pennsylvania UMW leader who advocated nationalized mines, challenged Lewis for the presidency, but the existing organization rigged the contest in favor of the incumbent. Lewis had already crushed various opponents in the districts, and after vanquishing Brophy in 1928, he eliminated his last serious rival. Lewis had become the archetypical labor autocrat who ruled an impoverished kingdom. As president, he appointed district officials and used patronage as effectively as any political boss.

Commenting in the 1940's on the strength of trade-union autocrats such as Lewis, the English socialist R. H. Tawney explained that special conditions in the United States favored a kind of boss rule which never developed in British trade unions. First, rank-and-filers tended to accept autocratic bosses because they were so dependent upon the union leadership for their jobs. The kind of job control the miners maintained against employers could be used to enhance the power of union officials, who became, in effect, hiring agents. They could function much like a city boss, who kept voters loyal by dispensing jobs. There was a more important source of trade-union autocracy: the violent character of the struggle for control in industries like coal mining. "Trade unionism in the United States had to fight for its existence," Tawney noted. It emerged under far more violent circumstances than British trade unionism. "Systematically persecuted by employers, and half outlawed by the courts, it had recourse, with the consent of its members, to a high degree of centralization of power as a condition of survival. Thus the dictatorship of management was countered by tolerating dictatorial methods in the leaders appointed to mobilize resistance to intolerable conditions." Revolts against the machine occurred periodically, but in a union like the UMW they failed to affect the centralized power of the Lewis organization, which prevailed from the 1920's through the 1960's. Lewis frankly stated throughout his rule that democracy was a luxury the hard-pressed miners could not afford.

The open-shop drive, the Depression, and the growing anti-labor posture of the courts cost the AFL over a million members. Furthermore, the decline of powerful industrial unions like the UMW, Garment Workers', and Brewers', all victimized by "sick" industries in the 1920's, allowed the craft unions to regain controlling interests in the AFL. William Green, Gompers's mild-mannered successor, came from the UMW and continued to wave the banner of industrialism, but in most cases he kowtowed to craft unionists. Commenting on the 1926 AFL convention, journalist Benjamin Stolberg remarked ironically that Green's weakness was actually his strength. "He can continue to lead the American Federation of Labor as long as the hard men on its Executive Council . . . think he is safe. At Detroit they all tested his strength. They found him weak. They are for him."

Most of these men on the Executive Council were conservative business unionists; they were typified by William Hutcheson of the Carpenters, whose ranks actually expanded during the building boom of the mid-twenties. Unlike P. J. McGuire, Hutcheson had little use for rank-and-file democracy: the union was a business. Unlike John L. Lewis, who demanded complete loyalty from his district leaders, Hutcheson and other international presidents allowed great autonomy for local barons like Theodore Brandle, who served as business agent of an Iron Workers Union and as president of the Hudson County, New Jersey, Building Trades Council. As a businessman, a banker, and director of an employer's association, Brandle served both sides. He milked business unionism for all it was worth. The AFL's international officers refused to intervene against local bosses like Brandle.

During the 1920's, business unionism led, on the one hand, to corruption and gangsterism, and, on the other hand, to more legitimate forms like "labor banking." Tsar Brandle himself established the Labor National Bank in Jersey City and made himself president. In the heady business climate of the 1920's, business unionism became something more pretentious, "trade union capitalism."

This kind of trade unionism could adapt itself easily to imperialism. The AFL had opposed U.S. colonialism since the days of the Spanish-American War, and in the 1920's its leaders still objected to the existence of colonies like Puerto Rico and the Philippines, which sent cheap labor back to the mother country. During World War I, Gompers became an agent of Wilson's foreign policy, a leading opponent of the Bolshevik revolution, and a defender of Western imperialist attacks on the new Russian regime. The AFL helped to organize the Pan-American Labor Federation during the war to stop the growth of a "revolutionary labor movement" in Latin America. In this sense,

Gompers and his conservative associates functioned like the "labor aristocrats" Lenin and the Bolsheviks condemned as traitors to the working class. According to Lenin's theory of the "labor aristocracy" and imperialism, the business union aristocrats accepted the "bribe" of higher pay offered by monopoly corporations which had secured cheap raw material and lucrative markets abroad. To Lenin, it seemed as though "something like an alliance" had developed between labor aristocrats and monopoly capitalists in the imperialist nations, an alliance opposed to all revolutionary movements at home and abroad. While some AFL unions undoubtedly benefited from U.S. overseas expansion in the 1920's, they were not significant actors in defense of imperialism. In fact, the finance and corporate capitalists involved in importing and exporting scarcely needed to bribe labor unions when they could defeat them.

Furthermore, capitalists and labor unionists clashed over the use of the international labor market, which supplied employers with cheap labor. The AFL had succeeded in obtaining legislation which virtually excluded Asians, and it actively supported new restriction laws in 1920 and 1924, drastically limiting emigration from Southern and Eastern Europe. Some employers, of course, opposed this restriction on the labor supply. Union leaders also hoped to check the emigration from Latin America. Roughly 70,000 Mexicans, mostly single men, crossed the border each year during the 1920's. Employers successfully argued that Mexicans should be excluded from immigration quotas. They said these immigrants were needed to perform jobs whites refused. These jobs were primarily in the Southwestern extractive industries, but Mexicans also worked in Midwestern steel mills. As usual, the AFL unions refused to organize the immigrant workers, even though the Mexicans had proven to be militant labor unionists.

With immigration reduced so drastically, employers relied more during the 1920's on the domestic reserve army in rural areas. Blacks came to Northern industrial cities in large numbers during World War I, and during the 1920's industrialists continued to recruit them from the cotton farms. In the aftermath of the 1919 race riots and the collapse of industrial unionism, employers were able to take full advantage of the animosity between black and white workers. Sterling D. Spero and Abram L. Harris surveyed the depressing decade of the 1920's in *The Black Worker* and concluded that the industrial reserve army in the South had been effectively tapped. The use of blacks as strikebreakers in conflicts like the Chicago stockyards strike of 1922 confirmed the white workers' view that blacks were being used to undermine them, but, in fact, Spero and Harris concluded, black strikebreaking was greatly exaggerated. Black workers rarely displaced white workers. "The most distinctive characteristic of the Negro's position in the world of labor is his relegation to occupations in which he does not compete with white workers—in short, the perpetuation of the tradition of black men's and white men's jobs."

The segregated nature of the job structure emerged clearly in the steel industry. U.S. Steel hired blacks and Mexicans almost entirely for the dirty, dangerous jobs the Slavs had once dominated. In the corporation's Gary and South Works, nearly 80 percent of these dark-skinned men worked as unskilled laborers by 1928, while whites held 85 and 95 percent of the semi-skilled and skilled jobs, respectively. U.S. Steel placed a quota on the hiring of blacks and blocked any prospects for advancement. At the same time, it allowed whites to move up slightly on the pay scale and the job ladder. Skillful manipulation of the labor market and segregation of the work force promoted racism and group conflict and helped prevent the reemergence of industrial unionism. In addition, the corporation executives who controlled company towns like Gary encouraged segregation in housing, recreation, and education.

The AFL unions, whose leaders and members generally supported segregation before the war, capitulated almost entirely to racism in the "tribal twenties." The all-black Brotherhood of Sleeping Car Porters, headed by socialist A. Philip Randolph, was admitted to the Federation, but it was admitted on a segregated basis. The AFL denied Randolph's remarkable new union the status of a full-fledged "international" organization. Further, it continued to allow its affiliates to openly discriminate against minorities. A letter from the NAACP to the AFL in 1924 expressed the depth of the estrangement blacks felt.

> For many years the American Negro has been demanding admittance to the ranks of organized labor.
> For many years your organizations have made public profession of your hatred of the black "scab."
> Notwithstanding this apparent surface agreement, Negro labor in the main is outside the ranks of organized labor, and the reason is first that white union labor does not want black labor and secondly, black labor has ceased to beg admittance to union ranks because of its increasing value and efficiency outside the unions.

Women industrial workers maintained a hard-won foothold in the labor movement through the Ladies' Garment Workers and the Amalgamated Clothing Workers. The decade began auspiciously when each union claimed over 100,000 members. At the same time, women labor unionists joined their sisters in celebrating the successful ratification of the Nineteenth Amendment, which guaranteed female suffrage. The result of nearly a century of struggle, the suffrage victory bene-fited from the support of working women, and union men, mobilized by Rose Schneiderman and other Women's Trade Union League leaders. The final ratification demonstrated the skill and tenacity of women as organizers, and it represented an important social and politi-cal advance for all women. Public life could no longer be regarded as man's domain. Schneiderman, the WTUL vice-president, hoped that the vote would allow women to win more political reforms and to ad-vance the cause of unionization. Instead, protective legislation was struck down by reactionary judges during the 1920's. Furthermore, the number of women in unions declined. By the end of the decade, only 250,000 of the 4 million women wage earners belonged to unions, half of them to the Garment and Clothing workers' organizations. On the eve of the great Depression, one of every nine male workers enjoyed union protection, as compared to one of every sixteen female work-ers. Moreover, the House of Labor again closed its doors to women. The AFL's executive denied a WTUL request to organize separate fed-eral locals for women. Denied access to most AFL international unions (five internationals explicitly excluded women in their bylaws), women were now prohibited from organizing separately. "Women coming into the trade union movement have an optimism and fresh-ness that men officials are likely to resent. They upset the traditional routine," noted Ann Washington Craton in 1927. "The struggles of promising rank-and-file girls for recognition have met not only lack of cooperation but often direct sabotage from their trade union brothers."

Under the circumstances, the Women's Trade Union League con-tinued to move away from unionization toward protective legislation. This tactic proved discouraging, however, when the Supreme Court in the 1923 Atkins case ruled that minimum-wage legislation for women was unconstitutional. Women gained some recognition when the De-partment of Labor established a Women's Bureau in 1920, but the agency, headed by Mary Anderson of the WTUL, could do little more than document sex discrimination in the labor market. At the same time, feminists, led by the Women's Party, rejected protective legisla-tion entirely in favor of an Equal Rights Amendment to the Constitu-tion. When this amendment was actually proposed to Congress in 1923, it met with strong opposition from Mary Anderson and women trade unionists. The women's rights movement, so united around the Suffrage Amendment, split over the issue of Equal Rights versus pro-tective laws. In any case, neither strategy proved very effective during the 1920's. Despite the franchise, women, along with blacks, immigrants, and wage earners generally, seemed powerless in the face of conservative political domination.

The eclipse of the AFL during the 1920's reduced workers' political and economic power drastically. Labor leaders assumed a defensive posture and openly collaborated with employers to save jobs and wage rates. Lewis of the UMW accepted the loss of thousands of jobs to mine mechanization in order to maintain wartime wage levels; Gompers made peace with the followers of Frederick Taylor; and his successor, William Green, took peacemaking talks a step further by arguing that wages should be tied to productivity and that unions had a responsibility to insure industrial efficiency. "Under Green's gentle leadership in the twenties the Federation assumed a new posture, one that it had never taken since its inception in the eighties," Bernstein indicates. "It shifted from militancy to respectability. With business supreme, the AFL sought to sell itself as an auxiliary of business."

As the organizational power of the unions grew weak, labor politics floundered after a promising period of activity in the early 1920's. In late 1921, William Johnston, the former socialist who headed the Machinists' union, called for a Conference of Progressive Political Action (CPPA). Socialists and Farmer–Labor Party supporters active in several states responded quickly to the call. They were impressed by the restiveness of the railroad brotherhoods. The members of these unions, the most powerful labor bloc in the country, had favored nationalization of their industry. When Congress voted to end wartime controls over the railroads and return them to full private ownership, the unions affected responded angrily. The depression of 1921 and the growing agrarian movements in the Midwest also fueled insurgent politics. The Progressive Conference did not call for a third party, however. And when the CPPA convened again in 1922, it still refused to declare its independence. With this, the Chicago Farmer-Laborites, headed by AFL radical John Fitzpatrick, bolted and moved to form a new third party in 1923. The socialists preferred to remain in the CPPA, but their Communist rivals decided to join the Chicago insurgents in an attempt to create a British-style labor party. The Communists hoped that their most influential leader, William Z. Foster, could strengthen their young movement by working with Fitzpatrick, an old ally from the stockyard and steel-mill organizing efforts.

In 1920, Foster had formed the Trade Union Educational League in Chicago, in an attempt to channel in a radical direction the rank-and-file militancy that had exploded all over the country. Using his influence as the country's best industrial organizer, Foster gained support from many AFL unions to consolidate "scattered craft unions" and to form a labor party. In 1921, Foster joined a reorganized Communist party (known as the Workers' Party) formed when the Bolsheviks abandoned underground activity. He maintained his tested strategy of "boring from within" the AFL unions. The TUEL did not capture many followers, however, aside from Russians, Finns, and other groups of ethnic workers who already gave some support to the Communists. The "new unionism" Foster had helped to stimulate during the war years had been defeated, and the "old unionism" of the AFL proved impervious to left-wing influence.

Despite the TUEL's failure, Foster had emerged as the nation's leading labor radical. Other revolutionary leaders had died or faded from the scene. Mother Jones was in her waning years. Eugene Debs polled over a million protest votes in 1920 when he campaigned for President from a federal penitentiary cell, but it was his last race. A strong protest movement won Debs's release in 1921, but he died five years later, weakened by his incarceration. Big Bill Haywood died in 1928, a lonely refugee in the Soviet Union. Elizabeth Gurley Flynn, who saw him there, said Haywood "longed for the land of baseball and burlesque, big steaks and cigars, cowboys and rodeos, strikes and picket lines, to see the Mississippi River and the Rocky Mountains, the America which was his home." Flynn herself collapsed after a furious period of defense work on behalf of persecuted radicals; it was, she recalled, a "brutal period of reaction" that lasted from the red scare to the execution of Sacco and Vanzetti. Flynn spent the next ten years recovering, mentally and physically, from the effects of what she called a "hideous nightmare." Swimming upstream against the reactionary flow of the twenties, William Z. Foster and his comrades struggled to build a new revolutionary movement.

Born in Taunton, Massachusetts, in 1888, he grew up in "a poor workers' family." He lived in Philadelphia's West End, and ran with an Irish gang who hated Jews, blacks, and strikebreakers with equal venom. After a brief apprenticeship to a sculptor, young Foster worked his way around the world as a sailor, a laborer in a fertilizer plant, a logger in a Florida lumber camp, a piece-rate car repairman in Chicago, a motorman in New York, a homesteader in Oregon, and a shepherd in Wyoming. He was a "hard-line mule skinner" on the Columbia River in Washington, before he fell in with the Wobblies. He went to jail during the Spokane free-speech fight and went underground at Coeur d'Alene, Idaho, to organize for the IWW, where the Western Federation had already been "smashed."

Foster agreed with the IWW class point of view but after a trip to Europe, where he met revolutionary syndicalists working in established unions, he rejected the IWW's dual-union approach. After founding the Syndicalist League during the Harriman strike in 1912, Foster became the most successful industrial union organizer in the AFL. He became a subject of nationwide ''red-baiting'' during the steel strike of 1919 and was later denounced by AFL leaders as the ''arch prince of Communism.'' But Foster gave as good as he got, inheriting the role of Debs and Haywood as critic of AFL business unionism and craft unionism.

One of his favorite targets was William Green. Green was raised in a strict Baptist home in Ohio, and while Foster was booming and hoboing around the world, Green advanced through the UMW hierarchy. When he took over from Gompers in 1924, he had become the perfect business unionist. A heavyset man with a round cherubic face, Green wore metal-rimmed glasses, a conservative business suit, and a gold watch chain. The blue spots under his skin—evidence of years in the mines—were the only signs of his proletarian past. ''He exuded respectability,'' says Bernstein, and ''enjoyed addressing business and banking leaders as well as students at prominent universities.'' Though he was nominally an industrial unionist, he ''accepted the legacy . . . handed down by Gompers without question.'' Bill Green was not an impressive man. His timid leadership and vacuous mind seemed to personify trade unionism in the 1920's. John L. Lewis, who worked with Green in the UMW, said cruelly: ''Explore the mind of Bill Green? Why, Bill and I had offices next door to each other for ten years . . . I have done a lot of exploring in Bill's mind and I give you my word there is nothing there.''

Bill Green was the perfect foil for William Z. Foster's attacks on the AFL ''aristocrats'' and their brand of ''trade-union capitalism.'' But scoring rhetorical points did not build the Communist movement or the TUEL. The Communists' efforts to capture the national movement for a farmer-labor party ended badly when Fitzpatrick and the Chicago insurgents split with the revolutionaries. Fitzpatrick accused the Communists and his old ally, Foster, of trying to take control of the third-party initiative by ''ruthless force.'' These charges, coming from a respected radical, reinforced the view among many independent militants that the Communists could not be trusted. The party's cadre worked much more effectively in the Minnesota Federated Farmer-Labor Party, however, and by 1924 this organization had become the basis of a revived movement for a national third-party campaign.

When Senator Robert La Follette, the veteran Wisconsin progressive, agreed to head a third-party ticket, radicals throughout the country expressed optimism, but La Follette denounced the Minnesota reds. The Communists, following a new policy determined in Moscow, responded by attacking La Follette and launching their own campaign for Foster, thus isolating themselves completely from the labor party. La Follette polled an impressive 5 million votes from farmers, workers, intellectuals, and others who were disgusted with the two-party system. But the Progressive Party campaign proved to be an end rather than a beginning of independent labor politics. Before his death in 1924, Gompers joined other AFL chiefs in repenting their brief departure from politics as usual. This prompted Eugene Debs, whose Socialist Party was a ghost of its former self, to remark that "the hope for an American labor party lies not in the official labor leaders, but in the rank and file." Of course, this was a wistful hope, because rank-and-file militancy and the "new unionism" it generated had been defeated decisively by 1922.

After the Labor Party debacles of 1922–24, the Communists turned almost exclusively to trade-union work, and this suited Foster, who maintained his syndicalist convictions. The TUEL captured leadership of some locals in the Ladies' Garment Workers' Union by opposing a socialist reorganization plan that restricted rank-and-file democracy, but it quickly lost this foothold by pushing for a 1926 strike that ended in disaster. The Communists also led a mass strike of Passaic, New Jersey, textile workers in the same year, but this, too, ended in defeat. Their only victory came in the New York City fur industry, where the Communists, led by Ben Gold, won a stunning strike victory in 1926 and held power after another bitter strike one year later. By this time, many Communists felt totally exiled from the House of Labor, so when Stalin called for a more revolutionary political line in 1928, the party in the United States quickly responded by leaving the AFL and forming the Trade Union Unity League as a dual union. Foster, who had always opposed this course in favor of "boring from within" the AFL, was displaced as the party's labor leader. In *Ambiguous Legacy,* James Weinstein argues that the new policy hurt the party. It removed leftists from the unions just at a time when rank-and-file opposition had begun to revive, notably in John Brophy's left-wing "Save the Union" movement in the UMW, which Foster had effectively initiated. By adopting an ultra-revolutionary line, in which other leftists were branded as "social Fascists," the Communists furthered their reputation as impossible sectarians. Ironically, says Weinstein, the radical change of policy did not alter the party's basically syndicalist approach, which focused more and more on workplace organizing to the near-exclusion of political organization and education; this effect seemed clear from the drop in party membership. Finally, though, the Communists' dual unions failed to develop, largely because of the frightening repression they sustained. Like the IWW a decade earlier, the TUUL intervened in spontaneous protests against wage cuts and speedups, notably in a series of surprisingly militant revolts of poor white Southern textile workers, culminating in the great strike at Gastonia, North Carolina, in 1929.

The party did its most effective work in the Detroit auto plants, participating in most of the hundred "quickie strikes" that broke out in the late 1920's. Roughly three hundred Workers' Party members formed "shop nuclei" in about a dozen shops, where they also distributed colorfully written newspapers, denouncing Fordism as Fascism, attacking racism and "trade union capitalism"; these papers, according to socialist auto worker Frank Marquart, won a wide audience because they also "bristled with on-the-spot shop reports exposing flagrant health hazards" and other forms of oppression. "These papers had the smell of machine oil about them," Marquart recalled. The Communists were well aware of the difficulty in sustaining the shop cells in the face of layoffs and company spies; so they also organized within the ethnic clubs and benefit societies of Detroit's immigrant neighborhoods, the very ones Ford's Sociology Department had failed to penetrate. This community organizing took place outside the arena of corporate control and proved invaluable to Communist organizers when industrial unionism revived as a social movement.

During the late 1920's, the Communists established themselves as fearless organizers and vocal critics of AFL business unionism and craft exclusionism. More important, the syndicalist approach they adopted throughout the 1920's gave the party's cadre valuable experience. It helped them tap sources of worker resistance in informal work groups on the shop floor and in ethnic societies which remained impervious to corporate domination. Despite the eclipse of unionism in the 1920's, the struggle for control had not ended and the Communists knew it. By patiently organizing at the shop-floor and community levels, they were able to expand beyond the old Jewish-Finnish immigrant networks and reach new groups, notably native-born blacks and whites. Unlike the IWW, however, the TUUL did not mount a serious threat to the AFL; it attempted to organize through the strike, at a time when workers lacked the strength to win by walking out. Indeed, by 1929, most workers abandoned the strike as a weapon. More than 4 million people struck in 1919. A decade later, fewer than 300,000 walked out, and they only won in 28 percent of their confrontations with employers.

Still, the revolt that swept the textile plants and company towns of the Southern Piedmont in 1928–29 showed that workers were willing to risk nearly certain defeat to protest speedup and wage cuts. These strikes also showed that the Communists could play important leadership roles, even among poor whites, who held very conservative views on many social issues.

The new capitalism had overwhelmed the new unionism and labor radicalism, and it nearly eliminated the old AFL unionism as a force in industrial relations. Using the techniques of Fordism, industrialists achieved the kind of productivity that had been denied them in past decades. But there were cracks in this efficient new capitalist machine. In the 1930's those cracks would become fissures and workers' resistance would widen and broaden into a new industrial union movement of unprecedented size and strength.

5

The Depression, the New Deal, and the New Industrial Unions

With the stock-market crash of 1929, a great Depression hit the nation and traumatized the world of the worker. While some skilled workers and a few others in strong trade unions enjoyed some protection, most faced the crisis without significant organizational power. In 1930, unions represented only 12 percent of the industrial work force. And even those who remained within the shelter of the House of Labor wondered if their protection would survive the storm. Most rank-and-file workers seemed to have given up hope in the labor movement. And yet, within a decade, the labor movement revived itself and the House of Labor more than doubled in size; by 1941, 27 percent of all industrial workers belonged to unions. What accounted for "labor's new millions"?

The origins of working-class militancy in the great Depression and the ways in which it stimulated the growth of the new industrial unionism in the mid and late 1930's are important. So, too, is the relationship between rank-and-file militancy and the leadership of figures like John L. Lewis, who seemed to be transformed by the mass strikes of the early 1930's. Lastly, the relationship between the resurgent labor movement and the New Deal reforms introduced by President Franklin D. Roosevelt and liberal Democrats is vital. This relationship was a complex one. On the one hand, worker militancy and the threat of radicalism pushed the New Deal to the left. On the other, the new unions benefited significantly from the protection and support offered by New Deal politicians. Government actions and policies helped the new unions gain a foothold in basic industry, but intervention by the state, and especially by the courts, also restricted the new unionism and harnessed its more radical tendencies.

The organization of mass-production unionism in the 1930's took place under circumstances determined by corporate capitalists and New Deal reformers. Nonetheless, workers made their own history and reshaped their world. The expansion of the labor movement and the extension of workers' rights was especially important for those immigrants who entered the mines, mills, and factories during the early 1900's. They had spent most of their working lives in industrial America, and those who survived saw their sons and daughters enter the same dreadful world. In the 1930's, these workers, no longer intimidated by red scares and cross burnings, claimed their constitutional rights; they refused to be relegated to second-class citizenship any longer. To an important degree, the common experiences of the workers' world provided the basis for unity among a diverse group of immigrant workers, from the Slavs in the Homestead mills to the Jews in the Lower East Side's garment shops. Social and economic conditions had not created a homogenized working class, but in the militancy and creativity of the 1930's, industrial workers forged a new identity for themselves as part of a class and a nation.

Mechanization made industry productive in the 1920's, but it also created more goods than society could consume. Ford's high-wage policy was not widely followed, and though real income increased, the country was still glutted with consumer goods. Moreover, the job security many corporations promised could not be guaranteed. Even Ford laid off thousands of workers in 1927, while seasonal and cyclical unemployment prevailed in many industries. As Thorstein Veblen, the iconoclastic economist, pointed out in 1921, the new prosperity was based on an "inordinately productive" form of "mechanical industry." Unwilling to sacrifice the possibility of short-run profits for long-run stability, industrialists turned up the dials and ran the system flat out, creating periodical layoffs and contributing to the depression that hit after the stock-market crash in 1929. Faced with such capitalist irrationality, workers had no choice but to "withhold efficiency" as best they could to spread out the work and prepare for layoffs. Despite the productivity of the 1920's, workers held back, using the discipline of the informal work group to resist management demands for still greater efficiency. Reluctant to strike and risk almost certain defeat, most workers withdrew from organized activity and depended on family and community networks for survival. One year after the stock-market crash, 6 million people suffered the effects of unemployment. By 1933, 8 million were out of work, and the system of private relief had collapsed. The industrial cities suffered profoundly as breadlines stretched for blocks—one million on the dole in New York City alone. Joblessness reached ghastly rates in the industrial heartland—50 percent in Cleveland, 60 percent in Akron, 80 percent in Toledo.

The worldwide capitalist collapse had struck the United States hardest. In three years after the crash, manufacturing output plunged by 54 percent. The auto industry, engine of the new capitalism, operated at 20 percent capacity in 1932. Along the Allegheny and Mahoning rivers, the valleys were clear for the first time in human memory. U.S. Steel's smokestacks no longer belched. The foundry fires were banked, the giant rolling mills were silent.

Republican President Herbert Hoover resisted business demands for deflationary policies. Instead, he increased federal construction, urged state and local spending, and encouraged investments, but these policies had little effect. To counter a Congressional bill that provided direct relief to the unemployed and large-scale public works, the President supported increased lending to states and cities by the new Reconstruction Finance Corporation. But RFC loans did not make for adequate relief programs. Private charities had exhausted their funds, and by 1932 states faced bankruptcy and cities, unable to tax corporations, lacked the resources to feed the hungry. In fact, courts issued countless evictions to the very homeowning families who were supposed to pay taxes. Tenants, unable to pay rent, also ended up on the streets.

Thrown out of work, evicted from farms, houses, and tenements, thousands of dispossessed families joined the single men and women roaming aimlessly across the country. Many huddled in rusted-out car bodies and orange-crate shacks on the outskirts of cities—in makeshift slums the people derisively called "Hoovervilles." Children picked through garbage dumps in search of food, women fought railroad police to get coal, while millions lined up at Salvation Army soup kitchens. In the Pennsylvania coal towns, miners and their families lived on grass and roots, and in rural Alabama poor white babies died with nothing but dirt in their stomachs. "The majority of people were hit and hit hard," recalled Mary Owsley of her days in the Oklahoma City Hooverville. "They were mentally disturbed you're bound to know, 'cause they didn't know when the end of all this was comin'."

Of course, the Depression had a serious effect on working-class family life. In *Hard Times,* Studs Terkel's oral history of the great

Depression, many people spoke about the strain on family relations. Larry Van Dusen said that his father, a skilled worker, refused to take jobs that were "beneath his dignity." Van Dusen thought of his father as a failure. "The shock, the confusion, the hurt that many kids felt about their fathers not being able to provide for them" was reflected in many quarrels.

The structure of the nuclear family remained intact during the Depression. Indeed, the family was the last refuge for most of its victims. But roles changed within the family. John Steinbeck's controversial novel, *The Grapes of Wrath* (1939), depicted the Joad family which migrated from Oklahoma to California along Route 66. In the traumatic process of changing from tenant farmers to fruit pickers, "Ma Joad" held the family together. E. Wight Bakke, who studied families of the unemployed in New Haven, found a similar development. His *Citizens without Work* included this case study:

> The impact of unemployment did not destroy the Raparka family, but the adjustments made necessary did lead to a complete reorganization of the structure of family relationships. When Mr. Raparka lost his job in the fall of 1933 he dominated the family. Two years later it was Mrs. Raparka who was the center of authority. . . .

When she took the initiative and secured relief for the family, a shift in organization took place. Mrs. Raparka supervised her husband's search for work and went to look for a job herself. "The change wrought in him," Bakke reported, was "evidenced by the fact that for the first time in his life he submitted to his wife's insistence that he help with scrubbing the floors and doing the washing (though he refused to hang out the clothes, in which activity 'he would be seen')."

The economic crisis had important effects on race relations. During the early years of the Depression, racism became especially threatening as blacks were made scapegoats and lynchings spread. The uprooting of the black population during the early 1930's created the fear among many whites that blacks no longer knew their place. The Ku Klux Klan did not revive, but other organized hate groups flourished in some localities, openly embracing Fascism and anti-Semitism. In retrospect, it seems remarkable that racist attacks were not more severe during the Depression. Nothing comparable to the 1919 race riots took place. And though lynchings increased during the first few years of the Depression, the number of blacks murdered declined to 119 during the 1930's, from 568 in the 1900's, and 281 in the 1920's.

The general uprooting of the white and black population undercut the forces of institutionalized racism to some degree. Woody Guthrie, the Oklahoma folksinger, who grew up in a profoundly racist oil boom town, wrote about a rough sense of racial equality that prevailed among some of the unemployed who rode the rails. Louis Banks, a black wanderer, recalled that railside "jungle camps" were "friendly." "Black and white, it didn't make any difference who you were 'cause everybody was poor." The egalitarianism of the dispossessed can easily be romanticized. Under certain conditions, white unemployed workers could turn violently against blacks. Hard times as such did not necessarily change attitudes. Most of the changed patterns in race relations during the early 1930's resulted from determined organizing, especially in the interracial movement of the unemployed, which involved an extraordinary degree of black participation.

The Unemployed Councils organized by the Communist Party won widespread black support, especially in major cities. In Chicago alone, party members and other radicals mobilized over 2,000 demonstrations demanding relief and blocking evictions, especially in the South Side "black belt." In Harlem, where unemployment reached 60 percent by 1933, the Councils used direct action, including sit-ins at relief offices, to win their demands. This approach contrasted clearly with the timid posture of established black-community leaders. In addition to building a significant interracial movement of unemployed workers, the Communists gained respect among blacks by leading a defense movement for the "Scottsboro boys," who were unjustly tried and convicted of rape in an all-white Alabama court. At first, the mass marches in support of the Scottsboro defendants were composed mainly of white party supporters, but gradually blacks joined in, and the Communists were able to advance black-white unity in many Northern cities. The Scottsboro case was part of a remarkably vital black civil-rights movement in the 1930's which included sit-ins, boycotts, and picketing, as well as lobbying in Washington for anti-lynching legislation and other anti-racist measures.

The Communists' involvement in the civil-rights struggle and their leadership in protesting various racist attacks gained them strong black support. Hosea Hudson, a black steelworker in Birmingham, Alabama, said that he joined the party after being impressed by its role in defending the Scottsboro boys. To Hudson, the plight of these young black men symbolized "the frame up of the Negro people in the South"—a frame-up that included Jim Crow laws and lynchings as well as unemployment and speedup.

The unions organized by the party as part of the Trade Union Unity League (TUUL) failed to win many victories, however. The same repression that hit them in the textile strikes during the late 1920's continued in the 1930's, when, as Woody Guthrie wrote, the shadow of the "vigilante man" was seen all over the land. The National Miners Union, for instance, met with violent opposition when it attempted to organize East Kentucky miners in "Bloody Harlan" County. The iron heel of repression descended hardest when blacks attempted to organize themselves, as they did in rural Alabama, where a Communist-led Sharecroppers' Union suffered from attacks by armed posses. The urban-unemployed movement made much more tangible gains, but it also met with brutal opposition from authorities. In Chicago, three black activists were killed attempting to resist an eviction. Four died and over fifty were wounded when the Detroit Unemployed Council led a "hunger march" to Ford's River Rouge complex in 1932.

The unemployed movement was not led entirely by Communists. The Socialist Party built up several strong Unemployed Workers Committees, and the American Workers' Party, led by a revolutionary socialist ex-minister, A. J. Muste, built a surprisingly large Unemployed League in several states, notably Ohio, where the League claimed a membership of 100,000 in 187 locals. By 1935, the combined unemployed movement had organized an estimated 450,000 workers. These interracial organizations agitated and demonstrated to prevent many relief cutbacks and evictions and won many additional demands for the unemployed. The movement drew on self-help groups and neighborhood networks that operated informally in working-class areas.

The repression visited on the unemployed was not restricted to Communist-led organizations. The World War I veterans who conducted a Bonus March on Washington in 1932 to claim immediate payment on their insurance certificates were not led by revolutionaries. But after a two-month sit-in they were routed by tanks and army troops commanded by a saber-wielding general, Douglas MacArthur.

Direct action by the unemployed did win significant gains. Before 1932, these actions helped provide and protect relief to the unemployed. And when Franklin D. Roosevelt took office in 1933, after defeating Herbert Hoover, his decision to provide massive direct relief was influenced by the insurgency of the organized unemployed. By the winter of 1934, 20 million people were on the dole, roughly one sixth of the total population and 30 percent of the black population. For the first time in United States history, the national government had taken major responsibility for the human suffering brought about by business collapse. In the fall of 1934, another downturn wiped out the gains of the early New Deal measures, and political forces of the right and left began to appeal to the discontented masses. Father Charles Coughlin, the anti-banker radio priest, had a massive following, as did Louisiana's Populist Senator Huey Long. Roosevelt viewed them both as threats. "To contain these dissident movements and to consolidate them behind the New Deal, Roosevelt promulgated a series of reforms which, though they hardly met the demands of insurgent leaders, were nevertheless sufficient to steal their thunder and capture their followers," write Frances Fox Piven and Richard A. Cloward in *Regulating the Poor*.

Initially, Roosevelt favored direct relief through the Federal Emergency Relief Agency (FERA). Harry Hopkins, who headed the agency, argued that the unemployed were not tramps but America's "finest working people." Direct relief was only an emergency measure, however. By 1934, FERA officials reported to Hopkins that they were less worried about the "red menace." Indeed, the militant unemployed movement had already been tamed by repression. Rather, they worried about the atrophy of the work ethic. The New Dealers believed work relief was required, to restore respect for work and for the workingman, before family and community life disintegrated any further. Roosevelt's program for 1935 included protection of labor unions, tax reform, social security, regulation of utilities and monopolies, and a massive dose of work relief which would take the form of the Works Progress Administration (WPA) and other agencies designed to get Americans back to work. In the short run, the federal government's relief policies affected employers' unrestricted ability to tap the reserve army of the unemployed. And this was an advantage during the period of resurgent union organization in the mid-1930's. In the long run, the government's attempts to "regulate the poor" through relief could be readily incorporated within employers' efforts to manipulate the labor market. In any case, the New Deal established federal responsibility for the unemployed, and influenced the world of the worker in a profound way.

Attitudes among the unemployed varied. In Muncie, Indiana, the Lynds found that "fear, resentment, insecurity, and disillusionment" were experienced largely as "individual" problems, and not "generalized into a class experience." In New Haven, Bakke found a stronger sense of class among jobless workers, but that sensibility remained latent because the city lacked a militant movement of the unemployed like those found in larger industrial cities. In New Haven, the unemployed never mobilized, partly, Bakke suggested, because they feared repression. In Chicago, New York, and elsewhere, left-led insurgency risked confrontations and won real gains. These efforts also helped overcome racial divisions which immobilized the poor in many localities. In Baltimore, where the socialists organized a large interracial movement, an important educational goal was attained, according to one organizer, because white men and women were persuaded to work with and under black men and women. Though the dynamics of insurgency in the early 1930's require further study, it is likely that the unemployed movements broke down patterns of accommodation and other obstacles to mass organization.

Attitudes among the unemployed were also affected by earlier traditions of radical and union organizing, extending back to the pre-World War I era. The writer Sherwood Anderson picked up many hitchhikers as he traveled the stricken land of plenty. The "defeated factory hands of the city"—who had never been organized—tended to blame themselves for their "hard luck" and apologize for being out of work, Anderson observed. The coal miners, however, expressed anger and resentment. They did not act like "defeated men."

The resurgence of union activity began with the early New Deal and was mobilized by the industrial unions with a strong, fighting tradition, the miners and the garment workers. The National Industrial Recovery Act (NIRA) passed by Congress in June of 1933 included a section 7(a) giving workers the right to "organize unions of their own choosing" and to engage in collective bargaining. The NIRA exempted businesses from anti-trust laws and allowed them to stabilize their industries through price fixing if they agreed to conform to codes establishing minimum wages, maximum hours, child-labor prohibitions, and collective-bargaining rights.

John L. Lewis of the UMW, who had lobbied for the NIRA, was surprised by its galvanizing effect on rank-and-file miners, who actually organized themselves into UMW locals. In just a few weeks in June and July of 1933, the coal miners took decisive action and once again proved themselves to be the "shock troops of American labor." They revived the spirit of industrial unionism that helped to make the UMW the nation's most powerful labor organization. In the minefields, this almost religious revival took place rapidly once the miners realized that the state might no longer be their implacable enemy, and that the government might even protect the miner's right to organize. Once the resurgence began, Lewis and his organizers could hardly control it. Wildcat strikes erupted in many minefields and UMW officials won major concessions from operators still shaken by the effects of the Depression and the New Deal. Rank-and-file militancy kept constant pressure on the negotiations, allowing Lewis to use the National Recovery Act effectively. Fearing a national coal strike, President Roosevelt approved a major concession to the UMW through the bituminous coal "code," which extended to all soft-coal operations and included the following: a minimum daily wage of $4.20, which drastically narrowed the traditional pay differential between Northern and Southern mines; an eight-hour day and a five-day week; the right to select check weighmen; the abolition of scrip payment and the operators' monopoly on retail trade and housing in the company towns; a dues checkoff, which enabled the UMW to build up a sizable war chest; and, finally, the end to child labor which had condemned several generations of "breaker boys" to sorting coal in dark, sooty tipples.

Though the NRA codes excluded many women workers, such as domestics, they did help the predominantly female clothing workers' unions to reorganize themselves. Both the International Ladies' Garment Workers and the Amalgamated Clothing Workers had suffered from the same problems that afflicted the UMW during the 1920's: chaos in the industry that resulted in shop closings and layoffs and internal faction fights within the union. Both organizations were headed by aggressive Jewish immigrant socialists who maintained some of their original commitment to progressive industrial unionism. Both Sidney Hillman of the Amalgamated and David Dubinsky of the ILGWU came to the United States after fleeing Tsarist oppression and suffering persecutions as Jews and as socialists. Both were tough, resourceful leaders schooled in the militant tradition of the Bund and the practical politics of industrial relations. They were quick to support Roosevelt's New Deal and to seize the opportunity presented by the NRA to rebuild industrial unionism in the clothing industry.

In other industries, however, resurgent unionism actually suffered under the NRA because employers used section 7(a) to form company unions. In still others, independent unions developed, but the AFL failed to support them and the employers prevailed. The NRA's section 7(a) gave workers the right to organize; but it offered them no other tangible protection and did not prevent employers from engaging in anti-union tactics. Events in the steel and auto industry illustrate the difficulties of organizing under the NRA.

In 1933, the New Deal and the NRA had an "electric effect" up and down the valleys where the steel towns were located, according to Harvey O'Connor, a labor journalist and former Wobbly.

> The mills began reopening somewhat and the steel workers read in the newspapers about this NRA section 7(a) that guaranteed you the right to organize. That was true, and that's about as far as it went; you had the right to organize, but what happened after that was another matter. All over the country steel union locals sprang up spontaneously. . . . These

locals sprang up at Duquesne, Homestead, and Braddock. You name the
mill town and there was a local there, carrying a name like the "Blue
Eagle" [symbol of the NRA] or even "New Deal" Local . . .

Steelworkers flooded into the old Amalgamated Association, but this
moribund craft union and its conservative leaders actually inhibited
unionization. The steel masters refused to negotiate and adopted their
old union-busting tactics.

In Detroit, a series of militant auto strikes galvanized the production
workers, but the only real victory resulted from the activity of the
skilled tool-and-die makers. In 1933, a strike against speedup, wage
cuts, and unsafe working conditions affected the Briggs "butcher
shops" in Detroit. The Communists, who had been active in the
shops, took a leading role, but "red-baiting" hurt the effort. *Business
Week* called this the first "depression strike" because workers attempted to set limits on how much they would pay for the crisis. The
Briggs strike was followed by an important walkout at the Murray auto
body shop, where the Industrial Workers of the World had established
one of their few remaining locals. This strike was also defeated, but the
IWW's brand of direct action, industrial unionism, was becoming popular again. Unlike the Communists and the Wobblies, the AFL attempted to organize federal unions for auto workers from the top
down. Thousands of production workers joined these locals, hoping to
take advantage of section 7(a). The Communists even abandoned the
TUUL to join some of these upstarts. When the federal unions called
strikes, they received no assistance from the AFL. The automobile
manufacturers, with their networks of labor spies, their arsenals of
guns and tear gas, and their armies of guards, were unimpressed by
the AFL organizing effort.

The skilled trades made the first breakthrough in the auto-industry
battle line. AFL craft unionism had failed miserably in the 1920's. In
1933, the tool-and-die makers formed an independent organization,
the Mechanics Educational Society of America (MESA), after revolt-
ing against the high dues charged by the AFL Machinists' union.
Using the NRA to organize locals, MESA struck Detroit machine
shops and demanded a uniform contract. When federal mediation
bogged down, a motorized brigade of 3,000 strikers hit the shops with
spectacular acts of sabotage. Clearly, something new was in the wind.
Led by Matthew Smith, a militant socialist trained in the British shop-
stewards movement, MESA won recognition and a master contract
from the employers and cracked the open-shop fortress in Detroit.
Skilled tradesmen would again take on key roles in organizing their

own unions and in forging the new industrial unions of mass-production workers.

In 1933, MESA used the power and strategic importance of its skilled members to win major concessions, but unskilled auto workers fared poorly under the NRA codes. When strike sentiment grew among assembly-line workers in the AFL federal locals, FDR intervened. Concerned that a big auto strike would hurt recovery, he helped to postpone the strike by setting up an Auto Labor Board. This Board wrote an auto code that did little for the AFL locals and actually gave administrative sanction to company unions. In short, the auto companies gained more than the workers from the application of section 7(a) to their industry.

Though few workers took advantage of the New Deal to win permanent gains in 1933 and 1934, labor militancy continued to erupt in the industrial heartland and in strange places, such as Hollywood, where Boris Karloff and Groucho Marx organized the Screen Actors Guild to win better working conditions from the big studios. Newspaper reporters, led by Heywood Broun, formed the American Newspaper Guild. Agricultural workers, who labored under shockingly oppressive conditions, struck, against all odds. From the fruit groves of California to the hop fields of Washington's Yakima Valley, from the citrus groves of Florida to the tobacco fields of Connecticut and the cranberry bogs of Cape Cod, migrant workers struck to win better wages and better working conditions.

In California, the Communists organized foreign-speaking agricultural workers (Mexicans, Filipinos, Japanese, to name a few) into their Cannery and Agricultural Workers Union and waged militant strikes against growers, who responded violently. The Communists, who had no faith in section 7(a) or the rest of the "Fascist" NRA, adopted the Wobblies' old direct-action tactics and took on the growers. They lost almost all their strikes. Critics like John Steinbeck questioned the Communists' motives in leading migrant workers in these "dubious battles," but the workers seemed as militant as their leaders. Cesar Chavez remembers that "labor strikes were everywhere" in those days, and his family was one of the "strikingest"—"always honoring someone else's grievance."

Despite these bloody defeats, the resurgence continued as workers followed the example of the miners and clothing workers. In 1932, only 324,210 workers engaged in work stoppages (roughly the same number as each year after 1925), but in 1933 strikes and lockouts involved over 1,168,272. Many workers began to feel that the tide of history had finally turned. In 1934, a violent outburst of working-class militancy signaled the beginning of a new era, as nearly 1½ million workers engaged in industrial actions. In three major cities, general strikes produced class warfare. More important, the long-suffering textile workers, who had struck desperately against wage cuts and speedups in the late 1920's, went out from Alabama to Maine in one of the most important industrial conflicts in United States history.

On February 23, 1934, electrical workers at Auto-Lite's Toledo, Ohio, plant struck after forming an AFL federal union. They returned to work at the Federation's request and submitted their case to an NRA labor board. Frustrated with stalling, the Auto-Lite workers struck again and refused to deal with the NRA. When the courts issued an injunction against the strike, the county's Unemployed League, led by the radical American Workers' Party, defied the court order and literally imprisoned 1,500 strikebreakers inside the plant. After a seven-hour battle between pickets and deputies, 900 National Guardsmen intervened, but they, too, failed to break a massive picket that involved 10,000 workers from the entire area.

At the same time, Teamsters Local 574 in Minneapolis, Minnesota, whose leaders were revolutionary Trotskyists, closed down the trucking industry and tied up the whole city, using motorized "flying squadrons" of pickets. When 35,000 construction workers and the city's taxi drivers struck in sympathy, the scene was set for a spectacular two-day battle on May 21 and 22 in which strikers routed police and deputies from the central market. After this "Battle of Deputies Run," Minnesota's Governor Floyd B. Olson of the Farmer–Labor Party worked with federal mediators to arrange a settlement; they failed. International Teamster president Dan Tobin denounced the revolutionaries leading Local 574, and the police beefed up their forces for another confrontation. On "Bloody Friday," July 20, it came, as police fired at pickets in the central market, wounding sixty and killing two. Governor Olson ordered in the National Guard and had the Trotskyist leaders arrested, but the warfare continued as "marauding bands of pickets roamed the city," striking at moving trucks. The strike had been organized in a democratic way, reported Charles R. Walker in *American City,* so that when the radical leaders went to jail, "a thousand lesser leaders 'came out of' the ranks," infusing the strike movement, "at least temporarily, with demonic fury." Unable to intimidate the strikers, the governor backed down, released the strike leaders, and ordered a raid on the anti-union Citizen Alliance. After a month of violence and nearly unbearable tension, the employers surrendered, opening the way for a Teamster organizing drive that would extend throughout the Midwest. This "civil war," Walker concluded, had not only produced a key union victory, it had "challenged and broken" the "historic dictatorship" of the Citizen Alliance and open-shop employers.

On May 9, 1934, West Coast longshoremen struck from San Diego to Seattle, after organizing into AFL locals under section 7(a). The workers soon became disgusted with the corrupt leadership of the International Longshoremen's Association, because it refused to challenge the notorious "shape-up" through which hiring bosses tyrannized the work force. Led by Harry Bridges, a gaunt Australian with Communist sympathies, discontented workers mobilized a rank-and-file movement within the ILA. When Teamsters, sailors, and other seamen honored the ILA picket lines, a general strike closed down the port of San Francisco. After federal mediators failed to end the dispute, the police mobilized to open the port. On July 3 and again on July 5, the Embarcadero rang with gunfire, as police and National Guard moved in to secure the docks with barbed wire and machine guns. The battle on the second day was, said one reporter, "as close to actual war" as anything he had seen. After this confrontation, freight began moving, but again the Teamsters struck in sympathy, and NRA chief Hugh Johnson arrived to call the strike a "menace to the government." On July 18, AFL president Green condemned the action and the city's Central Labor Council used its influence to end the walkout. The longshoremen won the right to have union dispatchers in hiring halls, though employers retained the final choice of workers. However, the hiring hall was "to all intents and purposes controlled by the union through the dispatcher," Mike Quin wrote in *The Big Strike*. "The longshoremen were perfectly capable of managing the hall and they, better than anyone else, could judge the efficiency and qualifications of the men."

The 1934 general strike in San Francisco helped to smash the shape-up, which employers had used to divide and conquer longshoremen and warehousemen. The strikers had restricted a key management power and advanced their own struggle for control in the process. The San Francisco strike included all the issues that made the 1934 conflicts into epic struggles. They were led by radicals determined to use any means necessary to extend workers' rights and to increase their control on the job. Despite widespread red-baiting, the strikers won support from other AFL unions and even from the public at large. They raised class warfare to a new level of violence, but out of the brutal conflict the strikers emerged victorious rather than vanquished. Finally, the activists seized the new opportunity presented by the NRA but did not depend upon either the federal government or the AFL internationals. They knew that in the final analysis the struggle was theirs to win or lose.

Coincidentally, the AFL's 1934 convention met in San Francisco that fall. The Executive Council recognized a "virtual uprising of workers for union membership," but maintained its traditional defense of craft unionism. Many of the pure craft unions had been amalgamated or transformed into semi-industrial unions in order to draw unskilled workers into an alliance with beleaguered skilled workers but pure industrial unionism still seemed a threat. In a revealing vote, the convention removed jurisdiction over beer drivers from the Brewery Workers Union, an old industrial organization, resurgent after the end of prohibition in 1933, and granted it to the International Brotherhood of Teamsters, whose president, Dan Tobin, used this victory over the Brewers to reaffirm the sanctity of exclusionary craft unionism. Tobin, a Boston motorman who gained the IBT presidency in 1907 and held it until 1952, warned that the uprising should not lead to a "scramble" for unionization that would grant charters to the "riffraff or good-for-nothings." The Teamsters, he said, used "force" to keep out the "rubbish that have lately come into other organizations." Concerned with the rise of revolutionary leadership in his Minneapolis local, Tobin drew conservative conclusions from the 1934 eruption.

John L. Lewis, still consolidating the gains his own members had made through mass strikes, drew different conclusions. He must have been especially impressed with the amazing national strike of cotton-mill workers, who closed virtually the whole industry, only to be sold out by their conservative AFL leaders. "Lewis watched the unrest and flareups of violence through the summer of 1934," Saul Alinsky notes in his "unauthorized biography" of the UMW chief.

> Before that year was out, seven hundred thousand workers had struck. Lewis could read the revolutionary handwriting on the walls of American industry. He knew that workers were seething and aching to be organized so they could strike back. Everyone wanted to hit out, employers against worker and worker against employer . . . America was becoming more class-conscious than at any time in its history . . .

Within a year, Lewis would decide to lead a revolt against craft unionism from within the House of Labor. By that time, it would be clear that the mass-production workers, dying to be organized, could expect little from either the AFL or the NRA. In fact, wrote William Z. Foster of the Communist Trade Union Unity League, "the big strikes of 1934" actually amounted to "struggles against the N.R.A.," with its low minimum-wage scales, its acceptance of company unions, its delayed hearings, and its discriminatory rulings. The Communist Party, still focusing on the recruitment of black cadre, branded the NRA a "Negro Removal Act" because employers, forced to pay minimum wages, managed to fire blacks and replace them with unemployed whites; the bosses thought new minimums gave "too much money to Negroes." The party's dual unions attracted some support in 1934 from rebellious workers frustrated by the AFL and NRA labor boards.

Black and white steelworkers, for example, had in some cases joined the party's TUUL union, the Steel and Metal Workers Industrial Union (SMWIU), as they became disgusted with the old Amalgamated. In 1934, rank-and-file militants in the AFL locals established under section 7(a) attempted to link up with the Communists' industrial union. This potentially important alliance failed to materialize, according to historian Staughton Lynd, because the TUUL union leaders wanted to maintain their independent organization and their own locals. In fact, local Communists were already complaining about this dual-union strategy. For example, in Warren, Ohio, where the SMWIU lost a bitter strike that led to the departure of a whole community of radical Finnish workers, the local CP was convinced that it was impossible to organize independent unions in opposition to the AFL affiliates. Later in 1934, when many steelworkers were actually ready to abandon the old Amalgamated, the CP abandoned its dual unions and returned to its old boring-from-within strategy. Though the party missed a chance to lead rebellious steelworkers out of the AFL, it gained new leverage in the labor movement by reentering the House of Labor. The party's TUUL unions had fought on bravely for four years against the most brutal kind of anti-union violence, and they had kept the banner of militant industrial unionism waving. In 1935, the CPUSA followed Moscow's directions and allied with liberals and other radicals to form a united front against the rising tide of Fascism. After sharply attacking the New Deal and its "Fascist" NRA, which favored the growth of corporate cartels, the Communists became less critical of Roosevelt and the New Deal.

Roosevelt responded to the discontent of 1934 rather dramatically. Work-relief and tax-reform proposals were designed to meet discontent among the unemployed and the followers of Populist critics such as Huey Long, whose numerous "Share the Wealth" clubs expressed popular unrest over the issue of economic inequality, a problem only compounded by the NRA. Roosevelt also kept an eye on the socialist writer Upton Sinclair, who launched a program to "End Poverty in California"; it almost made him governor of that state. Dr. Francis

Townsend gained great support for his plan to provide monthly pensions of $200 for the elderly. Townsend's movement surely influenced Roosevelt's plans for social-security legislation. The Democrats swept the 1934 Congressional elections, but the New Deal was still in trouble, even with union leaders who had hailed the passage of section 7(a). AFL president William Green, normally a very cautious man, threatened to mobilize the unions against F.D.R. Labor leaders, *The New York Times* reported, were "almost in despair of making headway toward union recognition in the face of powerful industrial interests and an unsympathetic administration." Senator Robert Wagner of New York was working on labor legislation to put teeth into section 7(a) and to provide federal protection for union organizing. But Roosevelt still hoped to win business support for the NRA and opposed the labor reforms.

The militancy of the 1934 mass strikes precipitated a menacing reaction on the right. The New Deal officeholders did not respond adequately to the threats made against civil liberties in this violent time. As strikers became bolder and more organized, right-wing groups moved to the forefront. Father Coughlin abandoned his pro-worker stance after 1934 and turned hysterically against the New Deal. His appeal remained strong, especially among Irish Catholics. Former New York governor and Democratic Presidential candidate Al Smith attacked the New Deal and allied himself with a bitter old foe, the reactionary publisher William Randolph Hearst, who had praised Hitler and Mussolini. The Black Legion was intimidating union members in Michigan, and the Fascist paramilitary groups were active in several areas. During the year beginning in June of 1934, the American Civil Liberties Union "recorded a greater variety of serious violations of civil liberties than in any years since the war." Many of these violations resulted not from Fascist activity but from anti-union measures taken by employers. It was clear that the struggle to build a new union movement would also have to be a civil-rights movement.

The remarkable struggle of the Southern Tenant Farmers Union illustrated the poor working people's determination to organize and highlighted the New Deal's failure to protect the collective-bargaining rights and civil liberties of the new unions. Two Southern-born socialists, Clay East and H. L. Mitchell, organized the Southern Tenant Farmers Union in 1934 to prevent planters from stealing subsidy payments intended for sharecroppers under the Agricultural Adjustment Act. The socialists insisted on interracial organizations and directly challenged the Southern system of control based on paternalism and racism. The cotton planters had used violence against sharecroppers' unions before, notably in the 1919 Elaine massacre, when, according to some estimates, seventy-three blacks were murdered in Phillips County, Arkansas. They did not hesitate to bring violence down upon the STFU. But in the 1930's socialists and liberals immediately protested to Washington and drew national attention to the violation of civil liberties in the Delta. F.D.R. was reluctant to take any action to defend the union. He did not want to offend the influential Senate Majority Leader from Arkansas, Joe Robinson, and refused to order federal intervention. In 1935, this crisis led to the purge of liberals in the Department of Agriculture, who wanted to extend federal relief and protection to the sharecroppers. After conducting a remarkable interracial "marching strike" in that year, the STFU was driven underground by the planters' gunmen, but not before its members had drawn attention to the "raw deal" the rural poor received from Washington. Emerging in the Southwest, where the pre-war Debsian socialists had sunk their deepest roots, the Southern Tenant Farmers Union quickly abandoned the hopes its leaders had for reviving the party and turned instead to direct action through interracial industrial unionism. The STFU, whose members became very distrustful of the new welfare state, had joined with labor's "new millions" to revive the syndicalist spirit of the IWW and the "new unionism."

The STFU provided tenant farmers with some protection against the planters and their allies, but in most Southern states sharecroppers bore the full brunt of the Depression and dislocation caused by New Deal policies. The Agricultural Adjustment Act of 1933 took 53 percent of the South's cotton acreage out of production. Planters released their tenants from bondage in order to receive subsidies for uncultivated land. Black migration from the South jumped, as 425,000 left the Southeastern states alone during the 1930's. Evicted from the land, black sharecroppers joined the vast army of unemployed workers already seeking federal relief. Those who remained in the South became proletarianized, as planters turned away from the archaic tenancy system to wage labor, which could be manipulated easily, depending on supply and demand. During the early years of the Depression, black unemployment rates were recorded at about two thirds greater than the white rates. As the Depression continued, it became clear that blacks would become an important new element in the reserve army of the unemployed. The relative position of the black labor force actually declined. In the Northern cities, only half the black men had regular full-time employment. It was not only rural migrants who crowded the relief rolls. Urban blacks who had industrial jobs during the twenties were laid off at a much higher rate than whites. "The rationing out of unemployment operated in such a way as to reinforce the demarcation of 'Negro jobs,' '' Harold M. Baron writes. And the ''limited openings available to black job seekers were in precisely those fields that were defined as 'Negro jobs.' '' Still, blacks were able to obtain government relief and did not have to rely on employers as completely as before. Indeed, blacks played a militant part in the unemployed movement to demand more direct relief. In spite of the extension of racial segregation in the labor market, blacks showed a new willingness to ally with whites in a number of common struggles, from the relief lines in Chicago to the cotton fields of the Arkansas Delta.

The Southern Tenant Farmers Union's criticism of the Agricultural Adjustment Act and lack of government protection for civil liberties corresponded to much wider discontent with the pro-business character of the early New Deal. Roosevelt was well aware of this discontent and in 1935 began to propose more progressive policies aimed at winning the support of workers and farmers. After calling for tax reform, social security, and work relief, FDR shifted gears and supported Senator Wagner's labor-reform bill. Congress had already approved the Norris–La Guardia Act to limit the use of court injunctions, and liberal Congressmen were pushing hard for legislation offered by Senator Robert Wagner of New York that would outlaw the ''unfair labor practices'' that flourished under the NRA. The President at first opposed Wagner's bill to create a National Labor Relations Board to conduct elections for collective-bargaining units and to regulate labor practices, but when the bill cleared the Senate, F.D.R. gave his support. The Wagner Act passed in the House in June 1935 and was signed into law by the President on July 5, 1935; it was, correctly, regarded by business interests as the most radical labor legislation ever enacted. The National Labor Relations Act, which resulted mainly from the resurgence of labor militancy in 1933 and 1934, finally gave federal recognition to the rights workers had been asserting for more than a century: the right to engage in collective bargaining, the right to free speech in advocating unionism, the right to freely elect a representative union, the right to protest unfair labor practices and to seek redress of grievances. The Wagner Act represented a great advance for the workers' rights movement, though it would later be restricted by the courts, frustrated by employers, and perverted by the Taft-Hartley Act of 1947. It encouraged worker militancy by demonstrating that the New Deal Congress would protect and defend the workers' right to organize and bargain collectively. But the Act did not have a tangible effect, because it was tied up in court challenges for two years. Industrial workers did not wait for the legal question to be decided. They resumed the militant struggle against open-shop employers begun in 1933 and 1934 and continued to rely on direct action rather than legal protection.

In Akron, Ohio, a smoky industrial city that produced most of the nation's rubber, workers who had joined AFL federal unions struck against speedup and piece rates, only to be criticized by AFL leaders. Rubber workers continued to unionize in 1935 and were prepared to strike again. The Federation dissuaded them and pushed instead for federal mediation. The resulting settlement enraged workers, who stood on street corners, tearing up their union cards, refusing even to vote on the contract. "You can't do nothin' about that," said one tire builder. "They run the union, and they run it for the bosses, not for us." AFL unions actually seemed to be blocking the workers' efforts to organize and win recognition. This sentiment, which existed in many industrial cities, burst forth at the AFL convention in 1935.

John L. Lewis, having read the handwriting on the wall, rose to the occasion, attacking the Executive Council's unwillingness to support industrial union organization. A powerful orator, Lewis spoke in terms that turned the struggle for unionization into a much broader crusade against monopoly and tyranny. "Great combinations of wealth," he declared, had assembled "tremendous power and influence" to block the old tactics advocated by the AFL. Equating Fascist aggression abroad with capitalist oppression at home, Lewis called on the AFL to live up to its founding principle: the strong should aid the weak. "Heed this cry from Macedonia," Lewis appealed. "Organize the unorganized . . ."

Unmoved by Lewis's eloquence, the delegates voted down industrial union strategy and removed jurisdiction over a group of skilled workers from the Mine, Mill and Smelter Workers, whose industrial-union roots went back to the old Western Federation of Miners. At one point in the convention, William Hutcheson, burly boss of the Carpenters, insulted a speaker from the rubber workers by interrupting him. Lewis jumped to his feet and accused Hutcheson of lording it over the minor delegates. A hot argument ensued and Lewis floored Hutcheson with a right cross. With this historic punch, Lewis signified the formal beginning of the industrial-union rebellion within the House of Labor and made himself the leading rebel. Following the convention, Lewis met with industrial union leaders, including Hillman and Dubinsky, and on November 9, 1935, they formed the Committee for Industrial Organization. For the next five years, the CIO was Lewis's movement. He seemed to personify the power and confidence of the industrial workers.

In his early career, however, Lewis had behaved like a conservative business unionist. Like Bill Green, he was a skilled bureaucrat who left the mines early in life and became a self-educated career man in the UMW. In 1907, the young Lewis, son of a Welsh coal miner, left Iowa for Illinois, where he organized a political machine to win office in his local. He then became a lobbyist in the state capital, where his skillful work attracted Sam Gompers's eye. The ambitious young man used his post as AFL legislative representative and UMW statistician to learn the economics of coal mining and to develop a national network of contacts. In 1918, Lewis became UMW vice-president and really ran the union, because the chief executive, Frank Hayes, was an alcoholic. In 1919, Lewis was elected president in his own right, despite the rank-and-file opposition to his role in the mass strikes of that year. Throughout the 1920's, the UMW chief displayed an uncanny ability to undercut his opponents in the union and to consolidate his power. He also attempted to use his Republican contacts in Washington to aid the miners, but, as we have seen, Lewis ruled over an impoverished kingdom in the 1920's. At the onset of the Depression, Lewis seemed, says David Brody, "merely a labor boss of the most conventional kind, and a largely discredited one at that." What, Brody asks, was "hidden behind this sad spectacle that drove Lewis . . . to play so extraordinary a role over the next few years"?

Clearly, the man's imposing personal qualities made a difference. John L. could be intimidating. Just under six feet, with 200 pounds distributed over a broad frame, he oozed power. His famous bushy eyebrows and piercing blue eyes drew attention to a frightening scowl. He used a booming voice and a withering wit to great effect, whether he was quoting Shakespeare to puzzled politicians or casting aspersions on a union rival. Like his forerunner, John Mitchell, Lewis considered himself a business executive, if not an entrepreneur, and lived the style of a moderately well-to-do corporation man. He felt no sense of inferiority before the mine operators, bankers, and politicians with whom he negotiated, and he conveyed this confidence to his men. These qualities, though impressive, had not saved Lewis from being discredited by the collapse of the UMW during the 1920's; it was only with the reorganization of the UMW in 1933 and with the mass strikes of 1934 that Lewis transformed himself into a militant industrial union leader. He accurately sensed the discontent among the masses and expressed their anger and frustration with economic tyranny and the bureaucracy of the NRA and the AFL. By doing so, John L. Lewis became one of the century's greatest working-class leaders.

Lewis organized the CIO after landing the symbolic blow against craft unionism on Bill Hutcheson's jaw. The rank-and-file revolt in mass production in 1936 and 1937 made the new organization a real movement, the greatest of its kind in labor history. Like all great organizational surges, the industrial unionism of the mid-thirties required a new tactic to replace the AFL's hopeless strategy. The workers themselves revived the sit-down or stay-in strike, pioneered by the Wobblies when they occupied the General Electric plant at Schenectady, New York, thirty years before. Late in 1935, Goodyear led the tire industry in imposing an extended work day and a layoff of 1,500 workers. Though the employees of the Big Three rubber companies had given up on the AFL, they prepared to fight the speedup anyway. When management started adjusting piece rates to fit the longer working day, spontaneous work stoppages slowed down production. On January 29, 1936, Firestone tire builders secretly planned and carried out a sit-down strike on the night shift. The plant occupation began at 2 a.m. According to Ruth McKenney's account in *Industrial Valley,* a "tire builder at the end of the line walked three steps to the master safety switch and, drawing a deep breath, he pulled up the heavy wooden handle. With this signal, in perfect synchronization, with the rhythm they had learned in a great mass-production industry, the tire-builders stepped back from their machines." An eerie silence kept the workers themselves quiet for a few seconds, until someone shouted: "We done it! We stopped the belt! By God, we done it!" Hysterical cheering erupted as the rubber workers shouted and howled "in the fresh silence."

Within ten days, sit-downs had spread to Goodrich and Goodyear as the workers' bold tactics took management completely by surprise. The largest confrontation occurred at Goodyear, where pickets had to defend an eleven-mile plant perimeter. During this conventional strike 10,000 Akron trade unionists prevented the sheriff from enforcing an injunction. The rubber workers stayed out despite the intervention of Roosevelt's labor mediator; they also reorganized their AFL union as the United Rubber Workers and affiliated with the new CIO. At first, the URW leaders opposed the sit-down as a tactic, but they soon had to support it. To the workers, the sit-down offered a new way to control their own strikes, ensure speedy negotiations, and prevent the sellouts they had experienced in the past.

Following the dramatic Akron victory, CIO organizers pushed into other mass-production industries. In the summer of 1936, Lewis created the Steel Workers Organizing Committee (SWOC), headed by his loyal lieutenant, Phil Murray, and staffed with battle-scarred steelworkers, UMW organizers, and sixty experienced Communists.

SWOC strategy involved, first, union organizers, notably the Communists, who used ethnic associations and black organizations as beachheads from which to attack the company towns. Ethnic steelworkers, including the sons of Slavic immigrants, showed some support for the CIO, as did a few skilled black workers. Second, SWOC supporters tried to capture the company unions from within, an effective strategy that also brought results for union organizers at General Electric, RCA, and other corporations. Third, the CIO took advantage of New Deal support. Since Roosevelt favored the Wagner Act, the organizers argued, he wanted steelworkers to join the union. CIO activists were encouraged by the shift in New Deal policies and by F.D.R.'s rhetorical attacks on "economic royalists." SWOC also urged Senator Robert La Follette, Jr., to use his civil-liberties investigating committee to examine the arsenal of anti-union weapons employed by the steel corporations.

Roosevelt was campaigning for reelection to a second term in 1936. He wanted more support from organized labor than he had had in his first campaign, but many unions were alienated by the NRA. Some labor leaders supported the formation of an independent labor party. The Socialist Party, revived by an influx of young activists, backed the idea, and so did the Communists, who favored a labor party built from below and not dependent on the AFL bureaucracy. However, Roosevelt's new progressive policies won widespread support from the unions. CIO and AFL political activists formed Labor's Non-Partisan League in 1936 in order to back F.D.R.'s bid for reelection. The League also supported independent labor parties on a state and local level, and hoped that these organizations would channel even more support to the President. In New York, for example, needle-trades unionists, led by David Dubinsky of the ILGWU, could not stomach an alliance with the conservative Democrats in Tammany Hall, but they wanted to win votes for Roosevelt. Therefore, they abandoned their historic ties with the Socialist Party and created the American Labor Party to help reelect the President and to boost their own candidates in state, Congressional, and local elections. The Communist Party had softened its criticisms of F.D.R., but it did place its own ticket in the field, headed by Earl Browder. The Communists worked with the ALP in New York and urged Labor's Non-Partisan League to build other state and local labor parties; they were worried that the support mobilized for Roosevelt in 1936 would remain permanently tied to the Democratic Party. Their fears proved to be well grounded. Though some labor unionists continued to push for political independence, Roosevelt's sweeping reelection in 1936 committed most AFL and CIO members firmly to the New Deal Democratic coalition. Organized labor played no direct part in Roosevelt's second administration, but many labor leaders believed that the Democrats could still be transformed into a kind of labor party. The votes mustered for F.D.R. by Labor's Non-Partisan League convinced many unionists that they now had allies in the federal and state governments.

Shortly after Roosevelt's 1936 election, a number of sit-down strikes took place: first at a Bendix plant in South Bend, Indiana, then at Midland Steel in Detroit, where Communist leaders claimed a big victory, and then at a General Motors plant in Atlanta, where auto workers protested a cut in piece rates. After the key breakthrough at Midland steel, sit-down strike fever swept Detroit, and many smaller manufacturers surrendered to the new United Auto Workers union of the CIO. These early plant occupations were largely spontaneous actions against typical Depression grievances, but the timing was hardly accidental. The strikers seemed to have waited until sympathetic New Deal politicians were returned to office. In fact, the plant occupations were generally not broken up by local police or state militia. The strikers had picked a good time to test the pro-union Democrats.

On December 28, 1936, employees at the Fisher Body plant in Cleveland took their new UAW officers by surprise when they occupied the factory. Their action triggered the most important single strike confrontation of the century, the great sit-down strike against General Motors in Flint, Michigan. The Flint strike was the most spectacular of the sit-downs. It began as a spontaneous protest against speedups, wage cuts, unsafe and unsanitary working conditions, and the kind of corporate tyranny that prevailed in many plants. Wyndham Mortimer, the top Communist in the new UAW leadership, had been slowly organizing in this totalitarian company town. When the news came in from Cleveland, he rushed back to his home town and told the Fisher sit-downers to hold out for a national contract settlement that would involve the plants at Flint and other cities. On December 30, 1936, an UAW cadre took the Fisher plant in Flint, and the great struggle was on. Communists like Mortimer, Bob Travis, and Bud Simons played important roles at Flint in designing a military strategy to seize a key Chevrolet engine plant, which helped to paralyze the G.M. empire. Once the auto workers began the sit-downs, the leftists were thrust forward as leaders and organizers. The Communists abandoned sectarianism and worked closely with socialists such as the Reuther brothers in Detroit and John Brophy of the CIO. The Communists had already learned to work under John L. Lewis in SWOC and they did so again when the CIO leader assumed negotiations with

G.M. Once strikers seized the plants, radicals and other militants articulated demands for better wages and working conditions and the recognition of their new industrial unions.

The sit-downs usually involved widespread community support. In
fact, the sit-down strike required firm support from the outside in order
to succeed. In Flint, women mobilized much of that support. Genora
Johnson, a socialist, led in organizing a Women's Emergency Brigade
consisting of women auto workers, who had been asked to leave the
plants, and wives of male strikers. The Brigade gave critical support to
the sit-downers. Its members joined with a small army of auto workers
from other cities to defeat sheriffs' deputies in the "Battle of Running
Bulls." And together with the Ladies' Auxiliary, the Women's
Brigade made the Flint strike a community mobilization. "I found a
common understanding and unselfishness I'd never known in my
life," wrote the wife of one sit-down striker. "I'm living for the first
time with a definite goal. Just being a woman isn't enough any more. I
want to be a human being with the right to think for myself." "A new
type of woman was born in the strike," noted one observer. "Women
who only yesterday were horrified at unionism, who felt inferior to the
task of speaking, leading, have, as if overnight, become the spearhead
in the battle for unionism."

The determination of the sit-downers and their supporters made it
possible for Lewis to exert maximum pressure on General Motors and
on political officials. Michigan's new Democratic Governor Frank
Murphy was persuaded not to order a military attack on the strikers.
When the sit-downers defied a court injunction and wired Murphy that
they would rather die than evacuate, General Motors gave in and
began negotiations with Lewis through the offices of Murphy and Secretary of Labor Frances Perkins. On March 12, 1937, the largest corporation in the world, General Motors, a firm controlled by J. P.
Morgan and the Du Ponts, capitulated to the auto workers and signed a
contract with the UAW. The strikers had used the sit-down tactic to
maximum effect and taken the utmost advantage of the reluctant support offered by the New Deal Democrats.

The rubber and auto workers' plant occupations had already stimulated a wave of sit-downs, and the recognition of the UAW turned the
wave into a flood. After the General Motors victory, the UAW immediately opened negotiations with Chrysler. When they bogged down,
6,000 workers staged a sit-down at plants in and around Detroit,
where mass pickets again engaged in street warfare with police to protect the sit-downers. Eventually, John L. Lewis—who opposed the sit-
down tactic—persuaded Chrysler workers to leave the plants and ac-

cept the G.M. settlement, which included union recognition. In a candid article, an unnamed UAW organizer admitted that the sit-down strike was really a use of force and "a violation of property rights." Violating the law did not trouble him, though. "We recognize the law only as long as it doesn't interfere with our plans; after that we ignore it." The sit-downs "made it plain to management that our forces are very strong," and that, he said, is the "objective we are striving for— recognition."

In March 1937 alone, 167,210 people engaged in 170 occupations of their employers' property. Within a year, 400,000 workers engaged in sit-downs. In Illinois, Chicago's workers contracted a kind of proletarian spring fever, organizing sixty occupations in the first two weeks of March. Downstate, inmates staged sit-downs in the Joliet prison yard and housewives in Bloomington even staged a sit-down protest. Factory workers passed along the tactic to a wide variety of others: sales clerks and stockboys, garbage collectors and laundry workers, gravediggers and WPA employees followed suit. "The sit-down idea," writes Jeremy Brecher in *Strike!*, "spread so rapidly because it dramatized a simple powerful fact: that no social institution can run without the cooperation of those whose activity makes it up." Once people saw what the sit-down could accomplish, they applied it to their own plants. Workers in large mass-production industries, who were mainly concerned with speedup, tried to use the occupation to gain some control over the process of production. The G.M. contract, like the others that followed, conceded control over the pace and organization of production to management. But union recognition allowed organized workers to reduce speedup through concerted actions and to begin to humanize their workplaces. For example, at G.M., slowdowns plagued production after the contract was signed. As one Fisher Body worker declared in the euphoric days of March 1937: "The inhuman speed is *no more*. We now have a voice, and we have slowed up the speed of the line. And [we] are now treated as human beings, and not as part of the machinery."

In *The Dynamics of Industrial Democracy,* Clinton Golden and Harold Ruttenberg, two CIO staffers, explained that the informal work groups which restricted output in the pre-union days continued to function after union recognition. In one auto plant they studied, these groups became the basis of the new UAW local. Officially, management maintained full control over the speed of production, but the work groups "continued to participate in setting assembly speeds and rates of pay through the indirect methods they had perfected over a long period of years." The field of forces had changed, however.

When restrictive practices became more obvious, management charged sabotage and fired the ringleaders in the groups. The rank-and-file members promptly struck in support of the leaders and stopped production completely. Unable to fire the men, the company began negotiating with the UAW. The strike ended when management agreed to consult with the union over changes in assembly-line speed. Workers had never had this power before.

In 1937, the National Association of Manufacturers printed millions of pamphlets charging that the CIO was "trying its utmost to control industry at the point of production." John L. Lewis had been converted to William Z. Foster's ideas and was trying to create Russian "soviets" in American factories. Lewis and other CIO leaders denied any intention of taking away management's power to control production. But the NAM and other employers were understandably concerned. The sit-downs had directly challenged private-property rights, and the new CIO unions, through their shop stewards and other elected leaders, were already exerting new kinds of power on the shop floor.

Propelled by the sit-down strike movement, 4.7 million workers struck in 1937, as compared to 2.1 million in 1936. Revived by the challenge of the CIO and the effects of the second New Deal, the old AFL added 886,000 new members. The gains came mainly in construction, transportation, and services, where its affiliates faced no competition from the new unions. But the most impressive growth took place in the new CIO unions such as the UAW, whose membership jumped from 88,000 in early 1937 to 400,000 in the fall. The new unions had by this time enrolled a startlingly large membership of 4 million in thirty-two international unions and six hundred independent locals. The members ranged from lumberjacks, sailors, and smeltermen in the West, who remembered the IWW, to rubber, packinghouse, and auto workers in the Midwest who had given up on the AFL. In only two years, the CIO had eclipsed its parent body and played an important role in a national election. This great achievement, unique in the annals of unionism, came about in part through the favorable climate created by the New Deal. But, as labor historian David Brody explains, the "emergence of mass production unionism" was not the result of governmental reform. The CIO's biggest gains came when the Wagner Act was being challenged in the courts and "virtually ignored" by employers. The workers themselves really made the breakthrough. Their "accommodation to the industrial system had broken down under the long strain of the Depression."

This accommodation had been enforced by the new kinds of technical control Ford developed, by the fear of unemployment, by court injunctions, labor spies, and thugs, but it also rested upon certain ideas—the sanctity of the law and especially of private-property rights. The effects of the Depression undermined some of these ideas, and the workers' demands for rights challenged others. A survey of CIO rubber workers in Akron during the late 1930's revealed that the vast majority of these industrial unionists supported workers who violated the law by bootlegging coal, occupying factories, and blocking evictions; they also supported actions that would force a company to "sign away its . . . traditional right to move its property" wherever its owners pleased. By contrast, other groups in Akron, including skilled workers, opposed these illegal violations of property rights.

As millions of industrial workers abandoned accommodation and accepted the risks of confrontation, they learned, as the Wobblies had, that the organization of United States industry could be accomplished through direct action and industrial union tactics. The biggest fortress of all fell without a violent struggle, however. U.S. Steel, the nation's largest open shop, agreed to accept SWOC as a bargaining agent for its workers, rather than risk sit-down strikes at a time when the international demand for steel was rising. Myron Taylor, the corporation's chief officer, preferred to negotiate with Lewis and Phil Murray, whom he referred to as "experienced, responsible union officials," rather than face the unpredictable results of bargaining with a union like the UAW whose leaders exercised little control over the rank-and-file. "The tumultuous democracy of the early Auto Workers horrified the CIO big shots," wrote Len DeCaux, the left-wing editor of the *CIO News*. Murray and Lewis, who appointed all SWOC organizers and controlled the committee from the top, warned against the dangers of "rank-and-filism." The undemocratic structure of SWOC and some of the other organizing committees would later come back to haunt the CIO unions.

In fact, in the 1930's, the top leaders depended upon mass participation at the local level in order to build the unions. And with this kind of participation came considerable democracy and local autonomy. The Packinghouse Workers Organizing Committee, for example, issued these instructions to a group of supporters in a Fort Worth, Texas, meat-packing plant:

It takes Organizers inside the plant to organize the plant. The Committee that organized the Oklahoma City plant was a voluntary committee organized inside the plant.

You cannot wait for the National Organizer to do all the work . . .
You people here can have a Union, but you will have to work to build it.

The local organizers of the new unions hoped to avoid "bureaucratic rule," by placing leadership, not in the hands of a few, but in the "whole body, in one, acting as one." Democracy prevailed in many CIO unions well into the forties, when, for reasons explained in the next chapter, the international officers began to exert more control. In 1936 and 1937, a heady sense of democracy prevailed wherever the CIO arrived. For example, in Homestead, where corporate despotism had existed since the great strike of 1892, SWOC supporters used Independence Day 1936 to celebrate their freedom from economic tyranny and political domination. "Through their control over the hours we work, the wages we receive and the conditions of our labor, and through their denial of our right to organize freely and bargain collectively, the Lords of Steel try to rule us as did the royalists against whom our forefathers rebelled," a CIO activist declared. The end of "industrial despotism" would come through a "great industrial union" which enabled all steelworkers to band together.

The great potential of industrial unionism seemed finally to be realized. The CIO unions organized all workers "en masse" and, as one UAW organizer wrote, "let them decide their problems as a class rather than a craft." Writing in the summer of 1937, this anonymous organizer added: "We are doing much to create, if nothing else, a class-consciousness of the laboring people, who are now beginning to feel just as important and necessary in the general scheme as the business and middle-class . . . ."

For the first time since World War I, organizers found that class appeal could overcome differences of race, nationality, and gender. The UMW and the Packinghouse Workers recruited thousands of blacks, including many who came into the mining and packing towns as strikebreakers. SWOC organizers, led by the Communists, used industrial union tactics to overcome some of the ethnic and racial divisions that had benefited the steel masters for decades. "Organizers in Chicago and Pittsburgh reported that in some cases Negroes joined S.W.O.C. in even greater numbers than did white workers," according to Horace R. Cayton and George S. Mitchell, who concluded, in *Black Workers and the New Unions,* that the CIO helped to break down racist divisions. Like the Mexican-Americans first brought into the mills as strikebreakers in 1919, the Afro-Americans who helped build industrial unions in steel were experienced workers who had suffered even more from corporate despotism than their white fellow workers. SWOC locals included blacks in leadership positions from the start, along with representatives of the various East European ethnic groups who had also been deprived of their rights on the job. The

Steelton, Pennsylvania, local leadership, for example, included two Croats, two Serbs, two Italians, an Irishman, and three blacks. Though they had lived different social lives, they shared a common experience in the mills. The CIO unions did not dissolve ethnic and racial group consciousness or end cultural antagonism, but they did give a highly divided work force a basis for cooperation on issues of common concern.

The pathbreaking interracial movements of the early 1930's, the unemployed organizations, and the sharecroppers' unions in the South were extended greatly by the CIO unions. The new unions helped to create a different attitude toward race relations in many industrial communities. For the first time, many white workers supported black workers. Many whites even rooted for black sports heroes. Two decades earlier, a racist reaction followed when black heavyweight Jack Johnson beat a popular white fighter. In the thirties, Jesse Owens and Joe Louis became national celebrities by beating white opponents from Nazi Germany. For black workers, accustomed to viewing white workers as their main enemy, the CIO brought even more dramatic changes. In supporting the new unions, black industrial workers rejected black middle-class leaders, who had always opposed unions, and, according to Cayton and Mitchell, class consciousness increased within many black communities.

Many blacks were attracted to the CIO unions because they had been an economic arm of a civil-rights movement active throughout the decade. Since the NAACP and other organizations led by middle-class blacks opposed the CIO, a new leftist group called the National Negro Congress was formed in 1936 to represent class-conscious blacks. Led by John P. Davis, the NNC aimed to create a "united front against Fascism and the repression of the rights of Negro people." The organization included many Communists as well as a number of black trade unionists and intellectuals such as Ralph Bunche and Alain Locke of Howard University. Davis saw the steel organizing campaign as a chance to write a "Magna Carta for black labor," but he refused to issue a blanket endorsement of the CIO. At the first NNC convention, congress president A. Philip Randolph of the Sleeping Car Porters underlined the connection between the civil-rights and industrial union movements. He linked together a variety of struggles ranging from opposition to Mussolini's Fascist attack on Ethiopia to support for "strikes and lockouts of black and white workers." The NNC would carry on the fight to free the Scottsboro boys and Angelo Herndon, a black Communist convicted of sedition in Atlanta, and would fight against any violation of Negro rights or workers' rights protected by the new Wagner Act. Though civil-rights groups had failed to win anti-discrimination clauses in the Act, they still hoped it could protect blacks who wanted to organize together with whites.

White workers also linked the struggle for collective-bargaining rights to a broader struggle for democratic rights and human liberties. While the La Follette committee in the Senate documented corporate violations of civil rights, F.D.R. and John L. Lewis denounced the economic "tyrants" and "royalists" who ruled the country. Lewis clearly identified the struggle for industrial democracy at home with the fight against Fascism abroad. Metaphors from the American Revolution seemed appropriate. Stanley Zelinka, a steel-union committeeman, picked up the reference and urged his fellow workers to retain the CIO spirit of equality and liberty "in spite of the Tory enemies of labor." In the 1937 elections, workers threw out of office the steel-town political bosses who had ruled since the turn of the century. As Mary Heaton Vorse wrote ecstatically in *Labor's New Millions:* "Union men or their sympathizers were elected up and down what had been called the dark valleys." In Homestead, one of the many towns where workers faced political intimidation, the Republican bosses were defeated for the first time since the great strike of 1892. Emphasizing the significance of the CIO as a workers' civil-rights movement, Vorse declared: "There has been a social awakening throughout the country, the coming of democracy in towns and industrial valleys where the Bill of Rights, such things as free speech, free assembly, and even the right to vote as one pleased, had been unknown."

The Communist Party expanded its political influence dramatically during the mid-thirties by taking a leadership role in building the CIO and defending workers' rights. The party ended a long period of political and cultural isolation in 1935 when it entered a Popular Front against Fascism and joined with other liberal and radical movements in defending democracy. Party members, who were largely first-generation immigrants from Eastern Europe, could now be part of a quasi-patriotic crusade to defend the principles of the Republic against tyranny and autocracy. They could fight side by side with native-born Americans.

During the Popular Front period, the party mobilized significant working-class support for the new unions, for the Republican government in Spain, and for the civil rights of blacks in the North as well as the South. Party leader Earl Browder exaggerated the new mood when he hailed "Communism as Twentieth Century Americanism." There was, however, greater tolerance of the left, especially in the labor movement, because the Communist cadre had built many of the new unions. Party members played strategic roles in the Flint and Detroit sit-downs, among others, and in the organization of key CIO unions such as SWOC and the United Electrical Workers (UE). The party also maintained its emphasis on interracial struggle and recruited impressive numbers of black workers. In Harlem, where the party organized unions and mass anti-Fascist rallies, CP membership jumped from 300 to 700 in 1935, though turnover remained high. Overall party membership increased from about 20,000 in 1934 to 50,000 in 1938. At that point, about 10 percent of the membership was black, a remarkable proportion.

The Communist domination of CIO unions was raised as a specter by employers and right-wingers. In fact, party members never accounted for more than a tiny minority in giant unions like the UAW. In the early days, however, leftists exerted influence far beyond their numbers. Ronald Shatz's study of United Electrical Workers' pioneers shows that union organizers were often skilled workers with a radical or industrial union background. In Schenectady and East Pittsburgh, the union founders tended to be skilled middle-aged men influenced by the pre-war traditions of Debsian socialism, which exerted a strong hold in both cities, and by the small groups of Communists active in the 1920's. "Male union pioneers in the electrical industry were," Shatz observes, "loosely supervised workers who possessed considerable freedom to move about and determine the means by which they would execute their tasks." Many of the skilled workmen were political radicals, and in "organizing workers less skilled than themselves," they carried on a long tradition. The early CIO unions were organized by a militant minority of workers in informal work groups and political organizations in which the Communists and other radicals often played leadership roles.

On a national level, the Communists actually controlled only a few unions, and in others they expanded their influence by allying with various progressives and militants. In the UAW for example, they formed a bloc with the progressive faction that controlled the international office until 1946. In other unions, the CP worked intimately with party supporters such as Harry Bridges of the West Coast Longshoremen's and Warehousemen's Union and Mike Quill of the New York Transport Workers. And in still other unions, the party worked with more opportunistic leaders such as Joe Curran of the National Maritime Union and James Carey of the UE. Even in unions such as the Woodworkers and the Mine, Mill and Smelter Workers in which Communists were elected as top officers, opposition blocs limited their ability to make and carry out union policy. On a national level, Lewis and his allies exerted firm domination of the CIO, and the left never gained the kind of strength the old socialists mobilized against Gompers in the AFL.

The Communist Party deemphasized its socialist program after 1936 in order to increase the appeal of the Popular Front against Fascism. In fact, the party's earlier program for a Soviet America had little appeal. Unlike the Debsian socialists, the Communists offered no vision of socialism that appealed to the political and cultural traditions of the American worker. In the late 1930's, the party Americanized its program and won support for a populist kind of radicalism that did have broad appeal. At the time, many party members were convinced that by organizing for the CIO, advocating racial equality, defending democratic rights, and generating opposition to Fascism, they were actually creating a working-class socialist movement, at least implicitly. Democracy within the CIO unions was undercut by the policy changes demanded by Moscow to meet international objectives. Again, the Communist Party, U.S.A., had to sacrifice a consistent approach to building socialism in this country in order to support policies determined in Russia.

Alarmed by the breakthroughs in auto, steel, rubber, meat-packing, and electrical manufacturing, open-shop owners struck back. In 1936, Remington Rand, the typewriter manufacturer, developed the "Mohawk Valley formula" to defeat organizational strikes with coordinated propaganda campaigns. Employees and local citizens received intimidating messages, including threats to move plants if they went union. When SWOC tried to extend its victory over U.S. Steel to the other major corporations, the so-called "Little Steel" companies employed the Mohawk Valley formula as a major weapon. According to the La Follette investigating committee, the four largest steel companies in the United States purchased more tear-gas equipment during the mid-thirties than any law-enforcement agency in the country. These weapons were employed to the utmost in the brutal "Little Steel" strike of 1937, in which the CIO sustained its first serious defeat. Republic Steel, which owned ten times more riot-gas equipment than the Chicago police department, found its own resources taxed, nonetheless. On Memorial Day, the Chicago police fired into the backs of SWOC pickets at the Republic Steel plant and killed ten. The Memorial Day massacre served notice on the CIO that it could expect no more quick, nonviolent victories. The steel strike also showed the limits of New Deal political support. F.D.R., who refrained from criticizing the Democratic mayor of Chicago after the massacre, actually wished a plague on the houses of labor and capital. This statement prompted Lewis to say: "It ill behooves one who has supped at labor's house to curse with equal fervor and fine impartiality both labor and its adversaries when they are locked in deadly embrace." When the UAW attempted to organize at the Ford Motor Company, it was beaten back by the vast security army headed by Harry Bennett. Another open-shop fortress remained unconquered. In 1938, the La Follette committee concluded its inquiry into violations of civil liberties and amassed evidence to prove what most American workers already knew. As historian Jerold S. Auerbach notes in *Labor and Liberty,* the committee's findings showed that labor relations had been "poisoned by the cruel acts of predatory employers." These findings seemed "to confirm the most pessimistic Marxist forebodings about the nature of capitalistic society." The La Follette committee documented the existence of class warfare in America and the industrialists' willingness to win that war by any means.

The CIO's defeat in the "Little Steel" strike was followed by a big jump in unemployment. During the "Roosevelt recession" of 1937, the number of jobless surged back to 11 million. Union organizers again faced the debilitating effects of a full-scale depression. The UAW lost 90,000 members, largely as a result of layoffs. Other CIO unions struggled to consolidate their positions in plants where they had already signed contracts. Virtual guerrilla warfare raged in some factories as the new unions struggled to unionize the whole work force. CIO prestige suffered when the resurgent AFL attained a larger membership. While industrial unionists were suffering major defeats, old AFL affiliates were making big gains. The Teamsters, for example, benefited greatly from the organization of over-the-road truckers. Led by the Trotskyist Farrell Dobbs and other radicals in the Minneapolis local, the Teamsters organized the long-haul drivers in the Northwest. By 1938, Dobbs and his comrades had formed a District Council with forty-six locals in eleven states and had negotiated a master contract covering 2,000 companies and 250,000 employees. Dobbs's strategy was soon adopted by Jimmy Hoffa of Detroit, who organized a council in the Midwest, and Dave Beck of Seattle, who headed up the Teamsters in the West. By 1940, when the Ladies' Garment Workers returned to the old House of Labor, the AFL claimed 4.2 million members, compared to the CIO's 3.6 million.

In March 1937, the Supreme Court upheld the constitutionality of the Wagner Act in the Jones and Laughlin case, and the machinery of the National Labor Relations Board began to work, but not in time to save the CIO from some serious defeats. Having accepted the NLRB as a legal body with authority over employers engaged in interstate commerce, the court then set about restricting workers' rights under the Wagner Act. In 1939, it outlawed the sit-down strike in the Fansteel case, and decided that the Wagner Act could not force employers to make concessions to workers. In other decisions, the courts reinforced employers' rights and limited workers' rights by holding: (1) that the Act did not interfere with the employer's right to select employees or discharge them; (2) that, if the employers bargained to "an impasse," they could unilaterally impose terms, but the workers could not strike while under contract; (3) that the employees' right to strike did not include the license to "seize the employers' plants" as in sit-down strikes; (4) that unions were institutions apart from their members and that union leaders, therefore, had to police their unions and ensure "responsible behavior." In sum, the courts allowed unions to engage in collective bargaining over a limited range of issues, but prohibited them from using the kind of militant, direct action that had built the CIO.

At the same time, union officials were also clamping down on rank-and-file militancy. The Steel Workers Organizing Committee, for example, had been established with what labor historian Irving Bernstein calls an "authoritarian government." SWOC became even more dictatorial "in the wake of the defeat in the Little Steel strike and a severe decline in employment in the latter part of 1937." "Murray felt that organizational survival depended upon tight control and internal discipline," notes Bernstein in *The Turbulent Years*. "Moreover, the oligopolized steel industry required that a union, to be effective, must also be centralized. Democracy could wait." By 1942, when SWOC officially became a union with elected leaders, steelworkers in the locals discovered that they had waited too long.

The CIO had overcome some of the old antagonism between native "buckwheats" and foreign "hunkies" and even between blacks and whites, but other important distinctions remained. Employers maintained wage differentials and other distinctions in job structures, and they continued to use a segregated labor market to their advantage. Union seniority clauses prohibited some discriminatory practices in firing, but racism and sexism could still be applied in hiring, job assignment, and upgrading. As a result, some of the black enthusiasm for the CIO began to wane. "In New York City," indicates Mark Naison, "CIO organizing drives ultimately disappointed those black leaders who had hoped that union activity would rapidly improve the position of blacks in the economy or eliminate job discrimination." The CIO unions took strong positions against racial discrimination in New York and other cities, but "they concentrated their efforts on winning union recognition for workers already employed not on ensuring unemployed workers equal access to jobs."

Women in industry made significant gains during the union upsurge. The number of female union members increased by 300 percent in the 1930's, reaching a total of 800,000 in 1940. Wages were increased and hours were reduced; more important perhaps was the new dignity and freedom women won through their unions. Before the ILGWU came to her shop, said Anna Weinstein in 1940:

> No girl would say anything or even complain . . . because she was afraid she would lose her job. The boss would do everything in his power to rob the girl of her self-confidence, and in a short period of time she became nothing more than a robot. With the coming of the union all these things changed. Now the girls have a power stronger than the bosses to back them. We are no longer robots. We are independent. We are strong. No longer can a boss cheat us out of pay. We now have the courage to tell him he is doing wrong and he must stop.

By taking advantage of renewed militancy among women clothing workers and the opportunities offered by the NRA and the Wagner Act, Anna Weinstein's union grew to 200,000 members during the decade, a 500 percent increase. Three quarters of these members were women, but in 1940 the ILGWU only had one woman in its twenty-four-person executive board. Much had changed but much remained the same. Women organizers played crucial roles in the organizational battles of the 1930's, but they were denied leadership roles. Oral histories indicate that the female pioneers of unionism were generally single and from union families or from nontraditional families, where women had not stayed within their sphere. Working wives and mothers were discouraged from participating in union affairs except during community-wide conflicts like the Flint sit-down strike. Stella Nowicki, a coal miner's daughter who was active in the Packinghouse Workers and the CP when she was single, recalled: "The union didn't encourage women to come to meetings," and the male leadership "didn't take up the problems women had." And their union brothers still believed women's place was in the home, not in the factory or the union hall. As a result, the CIO generally failed to halt patterns of discrimination against women in industry. Some even agreed to sign contracts with unequal-pay provisions for men and women and separate seniority lists that preserved male privilege in the job and pay structure. In general, the new unions mobilized women in the industries they organized, but they did not fight to change the status of women in those industries. And they did not effectively organize women in other sectors.

Women continued to enter the labor force during the 1930's despite the opposition of men. Single women and widows still needed to support themselves, especially at a time when family support networks were taxed. And despite laws in twenty-six states restricting or prohibiting employment of married women, wives continued to enter the labor market. The short-term reason was that men's employment was so irregular that women had to contribute to the family income. The long-term reasons were that female jobs continued to increase in the clerical and service sectors, while the possibilities of producing income at home continued to decline. New Deal labor legislation outlawed child labor and homework, and forced more women into the wage labor market. The uprooting of poor white and black women from the Southern cotton farms had a similar effect. The Depression forced families to rely more upon home-grown and homemade commodities, but it did not reverse the trend toward consumer capitalism. By the end of the decade, working-class women and men were more dependent on the consumer market and the wage labor market than ever before. Despite the sacrifices necessary in hard times, working people kept their sights on consumer items. Indeed, as the Lynds found in *Middletown in Transition,* the promise of consumption helped keep the work ethic alive. "If the automobile is by now a habit with the business class, a comfortable, convenient, pleasant addition to the paraphernalia of living, it represents far more to the working class," they noted. "For to the latter it gives the status which his job increasingly denies, and, more than any other possession or facility to which he has access, it symbolizes living, having a good time, the thing that keeps you working."

The Depression challenged traditional family roles in many ways, but the traditional family structure remained intact. Sex segregation still prevailed in the wage-labor force. Few were willing to question the separation of women's sphere from the man's world at home or at work. During the 1940's, this situation became far more acute; women's work roles finally became a subject that required public debate and political activity.

The struggles of the decade involved unprecedented working-class militancy and solidarity and a revival of political radicalism. The new unions overcame some of the ethnic, racial, and sexual conflicts that had long separated workers who toiled side by side. A remarkable workers' rights movement won respect and dignity for millions of wage earners, as proletarians and as citizens. But these struggles did not lead many workers to question the basic social and cultural relations that prevailed in their world. Familial and communal relationships that had sustained workers for generations were altered by the hard times, but not radically transformed. Workers had a new sense of ethnicity and race and gender. Many white workers now accepted women and minority workers as allies. But a strong sense of differences still existed on the shop floor. And these differences were still exacerbated by the employers' discriminatory use of the labor market and of the power they had to classify and segregate their employees.

While workers struck angrily at many forms of exploitation and oppression on their jobs in their communities, they also relied more upon the traditional familial and communal institutions that had always sustained them. Popular culture reflected a new sensibility about class and race and a kind of populist sympathy for the downtrodden, but it also contained strong doses of sentimentality, and reverence for established values. In an essay on the culture of the thirties, Warren Susman notes that the "new age of sound" represented by the radio—now a fixture in nearly all working-class homes—brought with it a "newly developed media" with "special kinds of appeal" that helped sustain a "rapidly disintegrating" social order. Even the soap opera, one of radio's most successful innovations, "played a role in reinforcing fundamental values and in providing the intimate experience of other people's lives so that millions of housewives knew that they were neither alone nor unique in their problems," he maintains. Timeless portrayal of "crisis and recovery" in the "soaps" helped to provide "a sense of continuity, assuring triumph of generally shared values and beliefs," no matter what the "reality." The media "helped create an environment in which the sharing of common experience . . . made the demand for action and reform striking and urgent." Franklin D. Roosevelt, whose fireside chats demonstrated his mastery of the radio, used the media to help create a new unity. "Whatever else that might be said about the New Deal, its success and failures, it is obviously true that it was a sociological and psychological triumph," Susman observes. "Roosevelt on the radio was to reach out to each American in his living room and make him feel that the Administration was thinking specifically of him, that he had a place in society."

This appeal of the New Deal retained the loyalty of millions of working-class Americans even when Roosevelt's programs failed in the late 1930's and drew radical criticism from a variety of labor leaders. A coalition of conservative Republicans and Democrats gained control of Congress and kept the Administration on the defensive. When New Dealers seemed to be surrendering to the reactionary tide, union leaders spoke out. In 1939, CIO officials criticized F.D.R. for cutting the relief rolls of the WPA, whose employees had been unionized. Black leaders were distressed by the lack of Administration support for anti-lynching legislation. A. Philip Randolph of the National Negro Congress complained about the layoffs of blacks from the WPA and the lack of support for civil-rights concerns. The New Deal, he said, provided no real "remedy" for black people's problems, because it did not "change the profit system" or "place human rights above property rights." More generally, there was concern for the enforcement of the Wagner Act, especially after the failure of legislation proposed by Senator La Follette to outlaw the use of labor spies, strikebreakers, and tear gas or firearms in labor disputes. The NLRB represented a great achievement for protecting collective bargaining, but it often failed to check unfair labor practices. Reviewing the NLRB's activity in the decade after 1937, Harry Millis (who served as Board Chairman part of that time) concluded that workers' "democratic rights" were "never fully protected" under the Wagner Act because the Board "failed to push vigorously for enforcement and compliance with the Act."

Indeed, by 1939 the limits of New Deal reform itself were becoming clear. As William Leuchtenberg indicates in *Franklin D. Roosevelt and the New Deal:*

> Even the most precedent-breaking New Deal projects reflected capitalist thinking and deferred to business sensibilities. Social security was molded, often irrelevantly, on private insurance systems; relief directors were forbidden to approve projects which interfered with private profit-taking. The HOLC (Home Owners' Loan Corporation) gave no relief to homeowners who were unemployed; had a commercial agency investigate each applicant to determine whether he was a sound "moral risk"; and foreclosed more mortgages than the villain in a thousand melodramas.
>
> Roosevelt's program rested on the assumption that a just society could be secured by imposing the welfare state on a capitalist foundation.

But with the exception of the Communists and socialists, few in the labor movement wanted to break with Roosevelt and the Democrats. John L. Lewis was the only leader who could possibly precipitate such a revolt. He had been demanding more action from the Democrats ever since organized labor helped win the 1936 elections. Indeed, he embarrassed F.D.R. by calling for improvement of faltering New Deal programs, by advocating the unionization of federal employees (whose collective-bargaining rights the President denied), and by resisting the efforts of Secretary of Labor Frances Perkins to reunite the AFL and the CIO. Zeroing in on the pro-business aspects of the Administration, Lewis threatened to revive the old movement for an independent farmer-labor party, for which there was growing sympathy in areas of militant CIO strength.

Though Lewis had an ego to match Roosevelt's and may have harbored Presidential ambitions, the conflict between the two leaders was much more than a clash of "great men." As Melvyn Dubofsky and Warren Van Tyne point out in their biography, *John L. Lewis,* Lewis "functioned as the leader of a militant working-class movement," while Roosevelt represented the corporate liberals in the ruling class and other sections of society who wanted workers to function as a responsible interest group, subservient to big business. "Where Roosevelt sought to contain working-class militancy through reform," Dubofsky and Van Tyne argue, "militant workers pressured Lewis to demand more than the President and the ruling-class were willing to concede." Len DeCaux, the *CIO News* editor, recalled: "No matter how much Roosevelt did for the workers, Lewis demanded more, he showed no gratitude, nor did he bid his fellows to be grateful."

Roosevelt and Lewis also clashed over foreign policy. As the President adopted more interventionist policies toward the war in Europe, the CIO head clung to the old position of a progressive isolationist who believed that workers never gained anything from wars. The war issue finally caused Lewis to break completely with Roosevelt in 1940. He threatened to resign the CIO presidency if F.D.R. won the election. Instead of forming a labor party to challenge the Democrats, Lewis revived his ties with the Republicans and endorsed their candidate, Wendell Willkie. Roosevelt, of course, swept to victory in 1940. In a brilliant piece of political maneuvering, the President's main operative, Sidney Hillman, forced Lewis to keep his promise. He was replaced as CIO chief by his protégé Phil Murray of SWOC. Lewis retreated to the United Mine Workers headquarters, where he carried on as an old-fashioned but still militant labor boss.

Sidney Hillman's star rose accordingly. He had helped to organize the American Labor Party in New York to win socialist votes for F.D.R. in 1936. But he abandoned the Socialist Party in 1940 because its Presidential candidate, Norman Thomas, who ran a weak campaign, opposed United States intervention in the European war. Though many workers, especially in immigrant communities, had opposed World War I, there was strong popular support for intervention to stop Hitler's Nazi war machine. It was a long road from the revolutionary days of the Bund in the early 1900's to the brink of World War

II, from Debsian socialism to New Deal liberalism, but many union leaders traveled that road with Sidney Hillman. Unlike Lewis, the Amalgamated Clothing Workers' leader had no voluntarist reservations about state intervention in industrial relations. And unlike the UMW chief, he had none of the old progressives' reservations about intervening in a second world war. Hillman would become Roosevelt's right-hand man in mobilizing labor support for a massive war effort. Lewis would be his greatest opponent. Despite serious defeats and embarrassing rebuffs, most labor leaders followed Hillman's lead. Lewis realized too late that the massive labor vote the CIO helped to mobilize for F.D.R. in 1936 had become firmly wedded to the New Deal and the Democratic Party, in spite of its increasingly obvious business orientation.

These two industrial unionists, along with Dubinksy and a few others, were the first to see that the New Deal represented a critical new opportunity for organized labor. They took full advantage of the opportunity to rebuild their devastated unions under the NRA, and they took the lead in using New Deal political support and later the Wagner Act to build the newer CIO unions in other mass-production industries. The labor history of the 1930's is often written with these great leaders at center stage. In fact, as one CIO labor organizer put it, industrial workers made "their own labor history" during the Depression. Like their AFL rivals, the CIO chiefs were suspicious of rank-and-file militancy and the role radicals played in organizing it. Men like Hillman and Lewis took full advantage of that militancy in rebuilding their unions and negotiating contracts, but once those goals were achieved, they were anxious to keep the rank-and-file under control, and to keep Communists out of the rank-and-file. The institutionalization of the new unions began soon after their explosive creation in the mass strikes of the mid-thirties. The top leaders hastened this process, especially after the employers' vicious counterattack in 1937. Moreover, the whole structure of collective bargaining, as determined by the courts and the NLRB, favored a more routinized, businesslike relationship between top leaders of labor and management, with the government as referee. As a result, many of the issues, such as speedup, that precipitated the original labor revolts were shunted aside. Control issues became the grist of guerrilla warfare on the shop floor and of wildcat strikes, but not of collective bargaining at the national level.

Still, the gains workers made in the 1930's were enormous. During the decade, when powerful workers' organizations fell before the Fascist threat in Germany and Spain and floundered in democratic countries like Britain, workers in the United States made historic advances despite the effects of the Depression and the cumulative effects of corporate oppression. In organizational terms alone, the growth of the CIO and the revival of the AFL were impressive. The number of unionized employees tripled from 2,805,000 in 1933 to 8,410,000 in 1941. During the strife-ridden decade, the proportion of workers enjoying union rights and protection jumped from 9 to 34 percent in manufacturing, 21 to 72 percent in mining, 23 to 48 percent in transportation, and 54 to 65 percent in construction. A new kind of workers' power had been mobilized in countless factories and communities. For the first time, millions of industrial workers asserted rights that had to be respected, and created organizations that finally gave them some control over their world.

6

The House of Labor Divided

In 1941, CIO militants again took the offensive and breached several important open-shop citadels, notably Ford and "Little Steel." During the period of United States involvement in World War II, the House of Labor established itself as a powerful force. Labor-union membership soared from 10.5 million to 14.7 million, and many unions made significant contractual gains. Union officials took positions in the high councils of state and found that wartime labor scarcity increased their bargaining power with many employers. Unions became even more firmly attached to the Democratic Party and the federal government. These gains did not, however, yield a proportionate expansion of organized labor's political and economic power. In 1946, a wave of strikes of unprecedented scale produced disappointing results, and Roosevelt's successor, Harry S. Truman, openly attacked striking unions. In 1947, Congress passed the Taft-Hartley Act and seriously restricted the rights organized workers had won in more than a decade of struggle. The Act also gave management valuable new weapons to use in its struggle to regain some of the shop-floor control lost to the new unions in the 1930's.

Why did this radical change occur in such a short time? The effects of World War II on the working class were profound. Through the wartime no-strike pledge, the government convinced labor leaders to sacrifice the right to strike and to keep their own members in line. During the war, union officials, especially in the CIO, strengthened and consolidated their unions, but they also divided themselves from the rank-and-file, who showed a remarkable tendency to engage in wildcat strikes in certain war-related industries.

In addition to this bureaucratic division within organized labor, there were other ways in which the House of Labor was divided. The lingering separation of the AFL and CIO was less important than other tensions. Wartime labor scarcity introduced masses of new workers into basic industry, and many of them were women and blacks. This created a problem for the unions, notably at the shop-floor level. The war disrupted the informal work groups that had been the basis of CIO organizing in the 1930's. Some of the new war workers were integrated into existing work groups, but blacks and women were still not at home in the House of Labor. Despite the great opportunities opened up by the war, divisions based on race and sex segregation remained strong. There was also a growing political division within the House of Labor between the Communists and the anti-Communists. This political division weakened the whole labor movement. During the Cold War, CIO leaders isolated the left and removed leading militants from the movement. Conservatives gained unchallenged power in many unions and hastened the "main drift" in the movement toward business unionism and accommodation with employers.

As early as 1939, when war preparations began, unions demanded representation in the Office of Production Management. After a good deal of lobbying, union representatives were appointed to serve on advisory committees. But businessmen were already moving into dominant positions in the mobilization effort, and they kept the union representatives from gaining real power. The National Defense Advisory Commission, created in 1940, included a noted labor representative, Sidney Hillman. He pushed for a policy that would require defense contractors to conform to the Wagner Act and other federal labor laws. In 1941, President Roosevelt appointed his key labor advisor as co-director of the Office of Production Management. In that office, Hillman hammered out a defense labor policy that included a forty-hour work week, overtime pay, and observance of federal, state, and local labor laws. He could not, however, enforce the policy because the OPM, like other war-mobilization agencies, was controlled by businessmen, who wanted to maintain management prerogatives. The Roosevelt Administration's willingness to make major concessions to business, already apparent in 1939 and 1940, now became obvious. Hillman's most embarrassing setback came when the federal government decided to award defense contracts to firms that had violated the Wagner Act. For a time, Hillman was billed as a "labor tsar." Unions were told to "clear it with Sidney" if they wanted something. But Hillman's humiliation by the Administration indicated that organized labor's influence in Washington was limited.

During the late 1930's, as we have seen, the CIO suffered serious setbacks. Membership dropped and the political power the new unions mobilized for the 1936 elections seemed to have evaporated as the conservative Congress cut back on New Deal programs. In 1940, with unemployment still hovering at over 8 million (14.5 percent of the eligible work force), worker militancy receded and the number of workers involved in strike action decreased to the pre-New Deal level. In 1941, however, defense production started booming, unemployment fell to 5.6 million (or 9.9 percent), and the CIO unions took the offensive again. Over four thousand work stoppages took place in that year, involving more workers (2.4 million) than any previous year except 1919. The 1941 strikes were long and brutal and involved the biggest open-shop employers in the nation, notably "Little Steel" and the Ford Motor Company. Many of these strikes also pitted workers and their unions against the federal government for the first time in many years. The clashes between striking unions and the Roosevelt Administration were sharpest in defense industries involving UAW locals in which Communist leaders were prominent. The Communist Party in 1939 abandoned the relatively moderate line of 1936–38 and attacked Roosevelt's interventionist policies in Europe and criticized the pro-business character of New Deal domestic policies. The party leaders warmly supported John L. Lewis, who led his miners in a series of militant 1941 walkouts against government orders and continued to espouse an isolationist position on intervention in the European war. Unlike Hillman, who used his position in government to discourage strikes in defense industries, Lewis refused to hold back worker militancy in order to support mobilization. Like the Communists, he was very aggressive and political in his attitudes toward some of the 1941 strikes.

In late 1940, FBI agents and other federal troubleshooters intervened in a UAW strike at the Vultee Aircraft plant in Los Angeles, charging that the walkout was Communist-inspired. In fact, Wyndham Mortimer and other party activists were involved, but red-baiting and government intimidation did not daunt the strikers; they carried on with the help of sympathy strikes by local AFL unions, including building trades unions involved in defense-plant construction. When the Vultee management, anxious to resume production, acceded to UAW demands, CIO organizing revved up throughout the West Coast aircraft and auto industry. In March 1941, strike activity had become so alarming that Roosevelt created the National Defense Mediation Board (NDMB) to reduce industrial conflict.

In the spring and summer of 1941, the strike wave gained new force. Two bitter UAW strikes pitted the unions against the federal government. A seventy-five-day walkout at the Allis-Chalmers plant near Milwaukee, in which the Communists again played a key role, provoked F.D.R. to threaten to seize the plant. And when 12,000 UAW members closed down the North American Aviation plant in Englewood, California, Roosevelt ordered federal troops to the scene for the first time in his tenure as Chief Executive. Sidney Hillman, who supported the use of troops to keep up war production, was branded a traitor by John L. Lewis and the Communists, whose strange alliance continued. The Communist Party's activists gained some prestige among rank-and-file militants through their defiance of the government in the 1941 strikes. They also became a political target within the CIO for the first time. At the UAW's 1941 convention, pro-Hillman forces, including socialists such as the Reuther brothers as well as the Association of Catholic Trade Unionists, used the Nazi–Soviet pact to their advantage. They won an endorsement for a resolution denying union office to a member of "any political organization, such as Communist, Nazi, or Fascist, which owes its allegiance to any foreign government." Unwilling to make an all-out fight and risk losing their influence within the UAW, the Communists unsuccessfully sought to amend the resolution to include socialists. This ineffective attempt to embarrass the socialists, especially the Reuthers, completely ignored the principle involved: that members of political organizations should not be denied the right to hold office. The Communists also sacrificed principle to political expediency when they approved of the federal suppression of their Trotskyist rivals. A group of these revolutionaries, which included the militant Teamster leaders from Minneapolis, was tried and convicted under the Smith Act of 1940, which made it a "federal crime to teach, advocate and encourage revolution." Exactly one decade later, Communist Party leaders would be tried and convicted under the same repressive Act.

The political strikes led by Communists and the factional fighting that resulted in the UAW were important. But these events were overshadowed by the CIO unions' smashing victories over Bethlehem Steel, the Ford Motor Company, and the "captive coal mines" owned by U.S. Steel. The Steel Workers Organizing Committee's effective walkout against Bethlehem Steel struck at the heart of the "Little Steel" empire. With the bloody defeats of 1937 still fresh in their minds, steelworkers held their lines, notably in pitched battles at Lackawanna, New York, and the main plant in Bethlehem, Pennsylvania. The racial unity created by SWOC organizers helped the union gain a crucial victory. Race also proved a critical issue in the 1941 strike against Ford, which had mastered the tactic of dividing white and black workers. Blacks in Detroit remained skeptical of the UAW because of its ineffectiveness in battling discrimination at General Motors. But the success of SWOC and the influence of the National Negro Congress helped win the support of key black leaders such as Walter White of the NAACP, who then mobilized black support for the UAW in the 1941 Ford strike. The UAW boldly challenged the authoritarian control of Harry Bennett's Service Department. Using motorized pickets, the union closed down the huge River Rouge complex and surrounded it with marchers carrying signs that read: "Fordism is Fascism." Black workers, who were a pivotal force in the Bethlehem strike, again turned the tide, breaking their paternalistic ties with Ford and coming over to the UAW by the thousands, despite the anti-CIO sermons of black preachers in Detroit who had served as Ford recruiting agents. Blacks had never played such a crucial role in the organization of American labor unions. Conscious of their increased importance, these workers began to make new demands on the government as well as the unions.

A. Philip Randolph had resigned as head of the National Negro Congress because he thought it was being used by the Communists to support Russian foreign policy, but he remained the most influential black labor leader in the United States. And in 1941 he planned a mass march on Washington to demand defense jobs and anti-discrimination laws for blacks. Randolph's prestige had risen after 1937, when his reorganized Brotherhood of Sleeping Car Porters finally won a contract from the Pullman Company. By 1940, the Brotherhood had about 10,000 members and was the largest independent black labor union ever organized. It provided Randolph and his organizers with a powerful independent base from which to challenge the racial segregation in the job market which had prevailed despite the New Deal and the rise of the CIO. Randolph maintained close ties with the Socialist Party, which had helped to finance the rebuilding of the Brotherhood, but he remained critical of the New Deal and middle-class leadership in the black community. He also opposed those blacks who joined the Communist Party and followed the party line. As Randolph and the Brotherhood organized the March on Washington in 1941, they met with opposition from the Roosevelt Administration, the NAACP, and other black groups, and from the Communists, who had once again changed their position on the war in Europe. When Hitler invaded

Russia in 1941, the party called for all-out mobilization against Nazism, and suddenly abandoned its militant labor activity. Its leaders opposed any strikes or other demonstrations, such as the March on Washington, that would disrupt preparation for war against Germany. The Communists also objected to the fact that the March was an all-black movement, but Randolph and his Brotherhood persisted. A. Philip Randolph was a strong leader. Tall and dignified, blessed with a wonderful voice and eloquent diction, Randolph personified the dignity the Pullman Car Porters had won in their long struggle to form a union. Born at Crescent City, Florida, in 1889, Randolph grew up in the poor but proud home of a Jacksonville preacher in the African Methodist Church, where he learned a bit of black nationalist philosophy from his father. He received a classical education at Cookman Institute in Jacksonville, and was inspired by W. E. B. Du Bois's *The Souls of Black Folk*. He may also have been influenced by Dr. Du Bois's occasional advocacy of socialism, for after a few years in Harlem, he joined the Socialist Party, a decision also influenced by the socialistic milieu of City College, where he matriculated. After some frustrating efforts to organize New York's hotel and restaurant workers, Randolph moved further to the left, and his newspaper, *The Messenger,* took a revolutionary line during and after the war, urging armed self-defense for blacks during the 1919 race riots. During the 1920's and on the long road to organizing the Brotherhood of Sleeping Car Porters, Randolph joined the Socialist Party's move toward moderation and shared the anti-Communism of his Jewish comrades in the garment unions. Randolph joined forces with Du Bois against Marcus Garvey, who had mobilized a massive black-nationalist movement in the Northern ghettos. Unlike the black Communists, who saw the radical power of Garveyism, Randolph held to a traditional socialist position on the need for unified class struggle. Though he was a head of an all-black organization and would later lead other movements that excluded whites, Randolph could not embrace black nationalism wholeheartedly. He continued to stress the need for white allies, even in the racist AFL unions.

In 1925, some Pullman car porters asked Randolph to help them form a union. He helped obtain funding and hired Frank Crosswaith, the West Indian socialist, as organizer. Though he had not worked the Pullman cars, Randolph became the first president of the Brotherhood of Sleeping Car Porters. The early years were discouraging, but the Brotherhood recruited several thousand porters and threatened to strike in 1928. At the last minute, Randolph called off the strike, partly because of a lack of support from AFL president William Green. The

Brotherhood quickly declined and its president was criticized in many quarters for not being more militant. It was not until 1937 that the Brotherhood finally won a contract from the Pullman Company, which, among other things, reduced the porters' inhuman work load from 400 to 240 hours monthly. As historian Manning Marable indicates, many of Randolph's critics, both black and white, argued that these and other accomplishments would have been achieved earlier if the president of the Brotherhood had a little less faith in the system and his white allies and more faith in the ability of black workers to act militantly and independently.

In 1941, though, Randolph did organize a militant, all-black march for jobs on Washington. Despite accusations of treason, the organizers persisted with their plans and refused to be daunted by the criticism of the NAACP and other middle-class black organizations. When the March was officially scheduled for July 1, 1941, the black Brotherhood's organizers promised that at least 100,000 marchers would descend on the capital. Roosevelt backed down and signed Executive Order 8802 on June 25, prohibiting racial discrimination in government and in defense industries. The success of the threatened March in winning black demands was a culmination of the civil-rights movement in the 1930's. Its emphasis on massive direct action and black independence, and its focus on the federal government previewed the civil-rights movement of the 1960's.

Of course, the executive order and the creation of a federal Fair Employment Practices Commission (FEPC) did not guarantee equal access to jobs and promotions. Rather, the civil-rights movement that culminated in 1941 created black pressure, especially in the CIO unions, for a change in racist hiring practices. During the 1940's, several CIO unions, notably the UAW and the Packinghouse Workers, became more involved in supporting black demands for equal rights. In Detroit, for example, the country's largest NAACP chapter worked with black unionists and some white UAW officials to protest discriminatory hiring and promotion practices at Ford, which suddenly stopped hiring blacks after the union's 1941 strike victory. Black UAW activists gave special attention to discrimination against black women, who were virtually excluded from better-paying defense jobs. In December 1942, the FEPC forced Ford to hire a number of black women as a result of pressure mobilized by the UAW, especially black union activists, and a militant Citizens for Jobs in War Industry. For the first time, at least in Detroit, an alliance had formed between the workers' rights and black civil-rights movements.

Before 1941 ended, thousands of other workers adopted mass action to win major concessions. In the summer of that year, the UMW achieved a remarkable settlement in which bituminous-coal miners in the South finally achieved parity with their Northern fellow workers. In September and again in October, coal diggers struck the "captive mines" owned by steel companies, despite the fact that their patriotism was questioned. John L. Lewis rose to the occasion, as usual. Still an outspoken isolationist, he made no apologies. The strike did not involve patriotism or national security; it was a fight between "a labor union and a ruthless corporation"—U.S. Steel. Speaking directly to Roosevelt, his great antagonist, the UMW boss declared: "If you would use the power of the state to restrain men, as an agent of labor, then, Sir, I submit that you should use the same power to restrain my adversary in this issue who is an agent of capital."

When the miners went out again in November, the corporation capitulated. The UMW won a closed shop in the "captive mines" and Lewis emerged victor over F.D.R., but his triumph went unnoticed. The terms of the contract were announced on December 7, 1941, just after the Japanese attacked Pearl Harbor, making United States entry into World War II inevitable. John L. Lewis and the Miners, of course, supported the declaration of war, but they had no intention of giving ground to their employers during the hostilities.

The miners' militancy had discredited the National Defense Mediation Board, so after Pearl Harbor, Roosevelt created a more powerful War Labor Board (WLB). At a conference in mid-December 1941, leaders of industry and labor agreed voluntarily to end all strikes and walkouts for the duration of the war. The WLB, which included one-third labor representation, created a system of compulsory arbitration to prevent labor disputes from erupting into strikes. By July 1942, the WLB had developed a set of guidelines called the "Little Steel formula" which allowed only those pay increases that brought wages up to the January 1941 level, readjusted to include the intervening cost-of-living rise. This wage-stabilization policy made "legitimate and equitable wage adjustments" impossible, according to the *CIO News*, and so, as a form of compensation, the WLB offered a union-security policy to assist unions in retaining and expanding their dues-paying membership. Thus, in return for the no-strike pledge, the acceptance of compulsory arbitration, and a wage freeze, the WLB gave the unions a modified union shop.

Blacks, who had been treated so viciously after serving their country in World War I, remained skeptical about World War II. But most white workers responded patriotically to the United States declaration of war that followed the Japanese air attack on Pearl Harbor on

December 7, 1941. Immigrant workers had opposed the First World War in large numbers, but they followed the leadership of labor leaders like Hillman in giving all-out support to the war against Nazism. A wide range of labor leaders, from Communist CIO organizers to conservative AFL chiefs, pledged their unqualified support for F.D.R. as Commander in Chief. Phil Murray, who replaced Lewis as CIO chief, caught the spirit when he declared: "Heed the call of your Commander in Chief and Work, Work, Work, PRODUCE, PRODUCE, PRODUCE."

The President's call for "equality of sacrifice" did not, however, produce the desired results, and workers soon protested their treatment on the home front. While corporate profits rose at an unprecedented rate, prices climbed much faster than wages, which were frozen by the "Little Steel formula." Many employers complained of lax discipline in the shops. With unemployment wiped out overnight and labor scarce, workers could sometimes defy foremen or switch to better-paying jobs in other defense plants. Nonetheless, workers complained about long hours and dangerous makeshift conditions. Those who were unwilling or unable to use the grievance procedure took matters into their own hands and conducted hundreds of wildcat strikes. In 1941, for example, the CIO labor leaders reaffirmed the no-strike pledge, but 2,968 work stoppages took place in one year, mostly in auto, rubber, and shipbuilding industries. This was the largest number of job actions ever recorded, except for 1919, and nearly all of them occurred at the plant level, without permission of national officials. Top labor leaders had agreed to sacrifice the right to strike and to increase production in order to gain government protection, but millions of rank-and-file workers felt compelled to violate the pledge their leaders had made.

Among the hardest hit on the home front in the winter of 1942 were the coal miners of Pennsylvania, who, according to a UMW survey of eighty coal towns, experienced a 125 percent increase in food costs while laboring under increasingly hazardous conditions. On January 2, 1943, Pennsylvania anthracite miners left the pits in an illegal walkout. They ignored the WLB's back-to-work order and returned to the mines only at the insistense of local leaders. Lewis, who initially opposed the walkout (because it was partly an internal protest against the cost of dues), soon assumed his belligerent posture. He denounced the "miserably stupid Little Steel formula for chaining labor to the wheels of industry without compensation for increased costs, while other agencies of government reward and fatten industry by charging increased costs to the public purse."

Thus began a tortuous struggle in which the miners waged "rolling strikes"—including four national strikes—to break through the wage freeze. Despite threats to call out troops, seize the mines, and draft strikers, the miners held firm, saying: "You can't dig coal with bayonets." In an additional effort to intimidate the strikers and to enforce industrial discipline, the Democratic Congress overrode Roosevelt's veto, to enact the first federal anti-strike legislation. The Smith-Connally War Labor Disputes Act gave the WLB subpoena power over union officials; made it a crime to advocate, let alone organize, a strike or a slowdown in a defense plant; authorized government seizure of struck plants; and required a thirty-day "cooling-off" period before any action could be taken on a grievance. Nevertheless, coal miners held their line and in a last general strike in November 1943 forced the federal government to abandon the "Little Steel formula" and grant them wage increases.

Emboldened by the miners' year-long struggle and the continuing inflation of prices, defense-plant employees defied the no-strike pledge in 3,572 work stoppages. Nearly 2 million workers struck in 1943 (twice the number who went out in the previous year), causing the number of "man days" lost in strikes to skyrocket from 4.2 to 13.5 million. The auto industry, converted to produce aircraft, tanks, and other war material, experienced the most wildcat strikes. Detroit was a storm center of discontent during the war. Five hundred thousand people, sixty thousand of them blacks, migrated to the Motor City in search of war work, putting an impossible strain on the city's housing. Thousands of jerry-built structures or corrugated-aluminum huts sprang up in makeshift communities like the one near a giant bomber plant at Willow Run. By 1943, Detroit was a time bomb ready to explode. Workers, who were putting in long hours of overtime, conducted 377 wildcat strikes in 1943 and 1944, protesting everything from unsafe working conditions to overheated plants. Shops with especially authoritarian managers, like Ford and Briggs, were especially hard hit. Newer workers from Appalachia and other rural areas simply rebelled against factory discipline, and older workers continued to use informal work groups to restrict production. In demanding the no-strike pledge from unions, government and industry relied heavily on arbitration to settle disputes. But to get to arbitration through the established grievance procedure took time, energy, and money. War workers in Detroit and other cities were unwilling to wait when a "quickie" strike in a certain department could resolve an issue in a few hours. The vast majority of wildcat strikes centered on working conditions, but in a few cases white workers struck against the hiring and upgrading of black workers. After three hate strikes hit Packard in 1943, UAW officials removed the white strike leaders. The union also worked to ease racial tension and defend minority civil rights by supporting the blacks who occupied the federally funded Sojourner Truth Housing Project, despite the protest of white mobs. A race riot started in Detroit on July 20, 1943, and lasted for three more days; it cost thirty-four lives. Again, UAW leaders supported the blacks and mobilized shop stewards to reduce the violence. The worst racially inspired strikes occurred elsewhere, notably in the shipyards, where "hate strikes" in 1943 checked efforts made by the federal Fair Employment Practices Commission (FEPC) to improve the position of black workers. And in the auto industry the vast majority of the wildcats hit at the speedup and the deterioration of working conditions, and not at black workers.

Wildcat strikes not only interrupted war production; they created serious problems for the UAW. The union's president, R. J. Thomas, noting that there were more strikes in the first eleven months of 1944 than at any time in the organization's history, declared that the UAW faced its greatest crisis. Under the WLB maintenance-of-membership agreements, local and international officers were held responsible for the behavior of their members. In other words, union officials had to enforce the no-strike pledge or lose maintenance-of-membership protection and even face possible legal action. In some cases, the international suspended local leaders for participating in wildcats and put their locals into "receivership" by removing the elected officers. Over 2 million workers had engaged in 5,000 wildcats, and since most of these actions were taken by CIO members, Phil Murray worried about the effects of this growing conflict between leaders and members. In fact, local officers complained that the international forced them "to line up with management against the workers" in order to contain strikes. "A union cannot survive under such conditions," one local officer reported. "The gap between the rank-and-file and their elected leaders will grow so wide that our whole structure will collapse." For their part, the international officers feared that rank-and-file militancy would destroy their unions. United Rubber Workers president Sherman Dalrymple faced a virtual rebellion by Akron members who demanded a revocation of the no-strike pledge. Dalrymple expelled hundreds of members who had wildcatted in violation of the pledge, arguing that "too much local autonomy" spelled "disaster." When rubber workers at Goodyear and Firestone conducted long strikes in June and July 1943, the army took over the plants, and Dalrymple was forced to resign as URW president. In most cases, however, officials in the rebellious unions remained in power and strengthened their control over the members. In his study of the CIO during World War II, labor historian Nelson Lichtenstein concludes that "the 'gap' between union leaders and the rank and file was bridged only by increasingly bureaucratic methods of control." Government labor policy assured the growth and stability of the new CIO unions, but it also created internal tension. In outlawing the strike and emphasizing arbitration and other bureaucratic procedures, the state stressed the role of the international officers as disciplinarians, and placed penalties on "local union initiative and rank and file militancy." Certain trends toward bureaucracy and hierarchy had been evident in CIO unions during the late 1930's, especially in highly centralized organizations like SWOC that were organized from the top down. Government and labor policy during the war accelerated those trends.

Before the 1944 UAW convention, President Thomas declared that strikes were "destroying the UAW." At the convention, leaders failed to win an endorsement for the no-strike pledge. Ben Garrison of the Highland Park Ford Local, where the assembly-line speedup began, spoke for many disgruntled militants when he said: "Management has taken advantage of the war to break down collective bargaining and to render our grievance procedure inactive and void. The gains labor has made have been steadily taken away from us." Responding directly to those who challenged the patriotism of wartime militants, he argued that refusing to renew the no-strike pledge would not in fact hurt "our boys in uniform." "I want to make damn certain that a just share of victory means that a union will be here when they do come home."

The no-strike pledge was later reaffirmed by the UAW membership in a mail-referendum ballot which allowed unionists to consider the issue outside the highly charged atmosphere of a union convention. Still, only a small number of UAW members voted. In fact, more members wildcatted during the war than voted to renew the pledge. Workers who engaged in unofficial strikes were not necessarily unpatriotic or unwilling to make sacrifices for the war effort; they simply refused to allow management to abuse them by taking advantage of the war situation. As wildcat strikes continued in 1944–45, a Rank and File Caucus was formed to oppose the no-strike pledge, to regain the UAW's collective-bargaining rights, and to win decent wages from industry and government. The Caucus also tied the issue of the no-strike pledge to the questions of local autonomy and democracy, but its militant leaders failed to transform their movement into a permanent caucus.

The CIO's new Political Action Committee, headed by Hillman, was designed in part to undermine rising labor-party sentiment. In New York, for example, Hillman's followers in the Amalgamated Clothing Workers allied with their Communist enemies (who actually disbanded their party in 1944 to work for Roosevelt's reelection), and together these strange political bedfellows took over the American Labor Party, making it a stronger ally of the Democrats. During the 1944 primary, PAC helped to defeat some anti-labor Democratic Congressmen, and in the 1944 Presidential election it mobilized union support for F.D.R., who was triumphantly elected to an unprecedented fourth term. If Roosevelt's image as "Dr. New Deal" had been tarnished, his new persona as "Dr. Win-the-War" redeemed him in the eyes of most American workers, including those whose loyalty to the Democratic Party faltered.

Maintenance-of-membership clauses in union contracts helped organized labor add 4 million new members to its ranks during the war, but despite these gains and despite canvassing by PAC, the unions failed to regain their pre-war influence in Congress. The AFL and CIO were battling the conservative resurgence that attacked the New Deal in 1939 and 1940. That trend continued after the war. Moreover, as C. Wright Mills noted, the locus of power was shifting in the 1940's from "representative bodies, such as Congress, to administrative bodies, such as labor boards." The unions gained token representation on these bodies during the war, but they were often controlled by business and the military. Some labor leaders such as Sidney Hillman hoped that the state, under the aegis of the New Deal, would be a neutral umpire, but the war disproved this liberal view. Old-time anti-statist union leaders like John L. Lewis saw this clearly and refused to surrender the right to strike in favor of the government's bureaucratic solutions to industrial disputes.

Nonetheless, the trend in labor politics changed radically. The intense involvement of rank-and-file members and local leaders that took place in the initial mass strikes of the 1930's faded. The war dispersed these militants in some cases, or set them against their own leaders. Despite Hillman's efforts with PAC, the intense politicization of the 1930's also faded. In Michigan, an exceptionally militant, well-organized CIO virtually took over the Democratic Party during the war. But the political power mobilized by the UAW and PAC proved difficult to institutionalize. Labor candidates lost narrowly in Detroit city elections in 1943 and in 1945 because of confusion created by ethnic and racial friction and by nonpartisan elections which worked against the labor-party concept. Electoral politics could not be transformed overnight. "As the special conditions of the 1930's steadily re-ceded with time, the outer limits on labor's political power within the present system became increasingly clear to the Detroit area labor movement itself," notes J. David Greenstone in *Labor in American Politics*. As these limits became apparent, the Detroit labor movement "came to terms with the entire political system by moderating its goals" rather than by attempting to alter the status quo in electoral politics and local government. Given their frustration with the system and their preoccupation with union affairs, it was easy enough for CIO leaders to be wooed and won by professional politicians. Politics had become more professionalized during the war, just as union affairs now seemed to require the services of highly paid labor lawyers and arbitrators. By the end of the war, C. Wright Mills observed, politics had become largely "a battle between various pressure organizations represented by lawyers and technicians," a battle in which the "masses of people" did not participate. This "main drift" in national politics was later reflected in the extraordinarily low voter turnout recorded in the 1948 Presidential election, when only 51.1 percent of those eligible voted.

The Communist Party had regained much of its influence in the CIO during the war years, but its attempts to influence national electoral politics ended in disaster after the 1948 Progressive Party campaign, and in 1949 the Communists were purged from the CIO. By support-ing the war effort a hundred percent, by reemphasizing the coalition politics of the Popular Front, and by popularizing the wartime Soviet-American alliance, the Communists gained a new position in political life. "At last," the party's immigrant members said, "we are now Americans." Of course, the party abandoned the militant posture it had taken during its anti-war phase in 1939–41. Its leaders now sup-ported F.D.R. Indeed, the organization disbanded as a party in 1944 and became a Political Association. To keep as many votes as possible in the Democratic column, Communist canvassers played an active role in campaigning for F.D.R. and other New Deal Democrats in the 1944 elections. Communist leader Earl Browder, spokesman for the Americanized organization, deluded himself and others into thinking that the Political Association, which had 63,000 members by the war's end, would make it possible for the party to play an influential role in national politics.

The Communists attracted new worker support during the war. About half the Association's membership was composed of workers, though turnover was very high in industrial areas. This was not only the result of wartime transiency. Many local militants and blacks quickly became disillusioned with the party, because it seemed to abandon their demands in order to maintain war production. In part, party officials in the unions were overwhelmed by the effects of the war. There did not seem to be time to engage in political education. The United Electrical Workers, for example, surged from a membership of 154,000 to 600,000 during the war. James Matles, Julius Emspak, and other top leaders supported the no-strike pledge and downplayed Communist politics, but they did fight for new gains for union members. The UE used its new power to challenge management prerogatives through joint management-labor production committees, the equalization of wages between regions and between men and women, and through the organization of white-collar workers. Of special significance was the UE's use of WLB machinery to force G.E. to reduce wage discrimination against women. Matles, the UE's secretary-treasurer, admitted, however, that management took advantage of the no-strike pledge, and implied that the union leadership lost support when workers had to engage in work stoppages to prevent violations of their contracts.

The Communists lost support from many militants when Browder called for a national campaign to use incentive pay to increase war production. Rank-and-file auto workers, who were already violating the no-strike pledge, rejected the scheme. The CP's reputation declined further when Communist-inclined leaders like Harry Bridges of the West Coast Longshoremen and Joe Curran of the National Maritime Union called for the extension of the no-strike pledge after the war. This attempt to build stronger unions through bureaucratic means hurt the CP, Foster later admitted, because it flew in the face of the rank-and-file's use of the strike against management contract violations and government controls.

After two decades of militant struggle on behalf of rank-and-filers generally and black workers in particular, the party's activists became less combative during the war and concentrated on forging high-level alliances with progressive CIO officials. The alliance between the left and the center helped expand Communist influence in the top leadership of unions like the UAW, the United Steelworkers (formed out of SWOC in 1942) and the Packinghouse Workers. But the center-left alliance began to falter immediately after the war. In 1946, Walter Reuther, who had shown his adeptness as an anti-Communist in 1941, won a narrow victory as UAW president by red-baiting the incumbent administration and its Communist allies. Reuther also won the support of the Rank and File Caucus, and other union members frustrated with the no-strike pledge. He used the CP's advocacy of a incentive-pay scheme to win votes from discontented militants.

When William Z. Foster again returned as party chief in 1945, having replaced the deposed Earl Browder, the party took a more aggressive stance on a number of trade-union issues, notably on the issues raised by blacks in the CIO. The Communists also joined with their ally in Congress, Representative Vito Marcantonio of Harlem, who was fighting to save and strengthen the Fair Employment Practices Commission. After Roosevelt's death, the party reconstituted itself and became more critical of the new President, Harry S. Truman, who showed little interest in preserving the Soviet-American alliance or the Popular Front politics that had allowed the CP to become part of the New Deal coalition. With the start of the Cold War, the party concentrated essentially on foreign-policy issues, the very issues their enemies would seize upon to purge them from the labor movement in 1949. But before we describe the "red purge" of the late 1940's and assess its impact on the CIO, we must turn from political to social history and examine the changing composition of the working class.

During the war, the most important single change in twentieth-century working-class life was rapidly accelerated: the entry of women, married and single, into the paid labor force. During the war, 8 million became wage earners, and their proportion in the work force jumped from 25 to 36 percent. War propaganda urged women to work in defense plants. They would receive high wages and demonstrate their patriotism without jeopardizing their femininity. Many of the taboos about women leaving the home and doing men's work suddenly vanished as female labor power became crucial. Depression-era laws against hiring married women were swept aside. Women wage earners and housewives, relegated to low-wage or unpaid occupations, needed little encouragement. They abandoned traditional female jobs in homes, restaurants, and laundries and headed for the shipyards and aircraft plants. Hundreds of laundries across the country, unable to replace their female help, closed. By the time the war ended, two thirds of women waitresses had shifted to other work. Over 400,000 domestics left their exhausting, degrading jobs to do war work. The percentage of black women performing paid housework dropped from 69 to 35 percent, as industrial jobs opened to them for the first time. A large percentage of these new workers were married women; as the traditional supply of single women workers quickly evaporated, wives and mothers entered industry in large numbers. By 1944, 75 percent of the new women war workers were married, most of them with children. Mothers went to work, even though Congress refused to pass adequate child-care legislation. The male leaders of the unions failed to press the issue, because they, like their counterparts in government, expected women to work only for the duration of the war.

Women found war work challenging and exciting, if not liberating. They clearly demonstrated their ability to operate lathes, service aircraft, fell giant redwoods, and wield rivet guns. As Augusta Clawson stated in *Diary of a Shipyard Worker:*

> I, who hate heights, climbed stair after stair till I thought I must be close to the sun. I, who hate confined spaces, went through narrow corridors, stumbling my way over rubber coated leads . . . I welded in the poop deck lying on the floor while another welder spattered sparks from the ceiling . . . I did overhead welding, horizontal, flat and vertical. I made some good welds and some frightful ones. But now a door in the poop deck of an oil tanker is hanging, four feet by six of solid steel, by *my* welds. Pretty exciting!

Women took pride in their work, and the public seemed to take pride in them. "Rosie the Riveter" was a cartoon character that appeared regularly on magazine covers, reflecting what seemed to be a new sensibility about women and work. Rose Schneiderman of the Women's Trade Union League went so far as to say that, after a century of struggle for rights, the female worker had at last become a first-class citizen instead of a "social inferior living on the fringe of American life." Women found new earning power in war work, which paid 40 percent higher wages on the average than traditional female jobs. The important issue of equal pay for equal work was raised, notably in unions like the leftist United Electrical Workers, which took advantage of the War Labor Board's egalitarian policies to win equal-pay clauses in various contracts.

However, the promises of the war era were not fully realized. The War Labor Board's equal-pay-for-equal-work rulings were not usually enforced, and few unions followed the UE's example of forcefully attacking wage discrimination based on sex. In 1945, as in 1940, women employed in manufacturing earned only 65 percent of what their male counterparts earned. Women workers were not well served by male-led unions in World War II. Women in the UAW complained that their grievances were buried in the union's multi-step procedure. Others won little support from union brothers when they criticized the separate seniority lists that existed in many plants, thus preserving the segregation of the labor force. Union leaders favored seniority for women only for the duration of the war. In short, the CIO unions that represented most of the defense workers did not respond to the demands of women as permanent wage earners or as union members.

Near the end of the war, the Women's Bureau of the Labor Department found that 75 percent of the women working in industry expected to remain in the labor force after the conflict ended, including 57 percent of the married women. And 86 percent of these workers expected to stay in their wartime occupations. They would soon be disappointed. With demobilization and reconversion, women were forced out of higher-paying defense jobs. Women's participation in the labor force dropped from 37 percent in 1945 to 31 percent in 1946. Married women were actively discouraged from working by a campaign to return "Rosie the Riveter" to the kitchen. Since fertility rates climbed with the post-war baby boom, and day-care facilities, such as they were, disappeared, many women did return to the home. The "feminine mystique," wrote Betty Friedan, strongly encouraged this trend by celebrating domesticity, romanticizing motherhood, and revitalizing the traditional notion that women belonged in the home.

The post-war decline in women's work outside the home should not be exaggerated. Working-class families now depended on the women's income. Post-war inflation and increased consumption of housing, clothing, recreation, and education, only added to this dependency. And so, while the relative percentage of women working for wages declined after the war, the actual number rose, reaching 18.4 million in 1950, a total more than 5 million higher than the number of females working for wages in 1940. By 1952, two million more women worked than at the wartime peak. More important, the number of married women working outside the home grew from roughly 5 million to 9.3 million during the 1940's. "Rosie the Riveter" did not disappear entirely. She did not return to domestic life, but rather moved from relatively well-paid defense-plant work back to clerical and service jobs. The number of female office workers expanded by a hundred percent during the 1940's, for example. Women did not generally return to domestic service, though. This occupation, still one of the largest in 1940, dropped from 2.3 to 1.5 million workers. More women, including ethnic women, now had a choice of doing clerical work. Moreover, the increased availability of home appliances and other conveniences convinced middle- and upper-class women that they could do their own housework, while the "feminine mystique" reinforced the desirability of clean, efficient housekeeping. Even working-class women could now spend money on time- and labor-saving appliances, and could shop in supermarkets and use processed foods, coin-operated laundry facilities, ready-to-wear clothing, and "miracle" cleansing agents. The hope was to reduce the drudgery of housework and increase the time available for wage work and child rearing. Overall, consumption of household furniture, equipment, and supplies (affected by declining expenditures in the 1930's) multiplied strikingly from $4.9 million in 1940 to $16.6 million in 1950. It is reasonable to believe that working-class families, which had been denied consumer items throughout the Depression, contributed to this leap in household expenditures.

Later studies show, however, that housewives in the 1940's spent as much time working in the home as their mothers had spent. Advertisers and other exponents of the "feminine mystique" had subtly raised the standards of home cleanliness, the complexity of home cooking, and the time required for child rearing. Dr. Benjamin Spock in his popular baby-care book joined the chorus of voices discouraging mothers from working. After the child reached school age, mothers were advised that they could get a job, as long as they were home when their children returned from school. "Thus the directives of the child-rearing theorists seemed to mesh neatly with the demands of the female labor market," Mary P. Ryan observes in *Womanhood in America*. "They encouraged women to seek employment outside the home after the interruption of child rearing, when they were preoccupied with family affairs and consequently well suited for and satisfied with low-paying, low status, part-time jobs."

In sum, most of the progressive changes in the status of working women promised during the war went unfulfilled. Management hiring practices, government and union policy, and the traditional ideology of domesticity that pervaded popular culture helped to restore the status quo ante bellum. The war experience had, however, raised crucial issues for working women that would reappear in the late 1960's when a women's liberation movement emerged: equal pay for equal work, government-subsidized day care for working mothers, an end to sex discrimination in employers' job classifications and in unions' seniority systems, and the Equal Rights Amendment, which the Women's Party revived during the 1940's. More important, the steady rise in women's participation in the labor force throughout the decade indicated that these issues were here to stay, just as the women workers who raised them during the war had said.

Randolph's threatened March on Washington in 1941 was a spectacular victory in the struggle for black job rights. But the war did not reduce the effects of racial discrimination and segregation, any more than it did sex discrimination and segregation. More black men and women now worked in industry, just as more married white women did, but the inequalities in pay and conditions prevailed. Blacks had increased their share of defense jobs from 3 to 8 percent between 1942 and 1944 as a result of pressure from labor and civil-rights groups on the FEPC and on employers. With immigration from Europe reduced to a low level for nearly two decades, rural blacks and whites were the main supply of surplus labor during the war. And blacks took advantage of the demand for their labor to secure a foothold in manufacturing industries like auto, steel, and meat-packing. Despite the impact of demobilization on black war workers, many Afro-Americans could hope to find factory jobs. Black women were not entirely restricted to domestic service, and black men were no longer restricted to menial jobs in the Northern cities. Indeed, Randolph and other black leaders had consciously used this added demand for black labor as leverage in their civil-rights struggles.

Some CIO unions had made progress in improving race relations. In Detroit, where the union alliance with the black civil-rights groups was strongest, relations on the shop floor improved in spite of the bloody 1943 riot. One black militant, Charles Denby, said that when he returned to work at Ford in 1943 the atmosphere had changed. Though he was a critic of the UAW's racial practices, he admitted that the union's 1941 victory had led to a marked change in race relations. "It was altogether different," he noted in *Indignant Heart*. "Many whites were inviting Negroes to their homes for social outings," and many workers of both races testified to the existence of "closer relations" based on the experience of industrial work and industrial unionism. Still, as Philip Foner concludes in *Organized Labor and the Black Worker*, few "CIO unions were prepared to take great risks for the principle of racial equality." The purge of the left unions after the war eliminated the CIO's best interracial organizers and made the industrial unions even less inclined to fight for solidarity. The CIO's attempt to organize Southern industry in 1947—"Operation Dixie"—failed in part because its leaders refused to employ leftist or black organizers who would fight racism directly.

Vast social changes had occurred during the war. The altered composition of the working class seems striking in retrospect: more women workers than ever before, especially in the service and clerical sectors, and more black workingmen than ever before, especially in basic industry. But union leaders either failed or refused to see the significance of these changes. They were, of course, preoccupied with other concerns, the massive 1945–46 strike wave, the outbreak of the Cold War, a renewed anti-union offensive by employers and the state, and the issue of Communism in the CIO.

Frustrated by nearly four years of speedup, stretchout, cramped living conditions, and price inflation, millions of workers struck across the nation in 1945 and 1946. After Japan surrendered, the dam broke. Strikers simply ignored labor leaders who wanted to maintain the wartime no-strike, maintenance-of-membership pact with government and industry. By the end of 1945, 3.5 million workers had engaged in 4,750 work stoppages, costing employers 38 million work days. In January 1946, 174,000 United Electrical Workers and 800,000 Steelworkers joined the 225,000 G.M. auto workers already on strike, creating the greatest work stoppage in United States history. More was to come. In total, four industries experienced general strikes, and a total of 4.6 million people engaged in nearly 5,000 work stoppages, costing employers a staggering 116 million work days. This great strike wave involved more people than the 1919 post-war strikes, which had set the previous record.

The UAW's walkout against General Motors was a pivotal strike in 1946. Walter Reuther, the ambitious head of the union's G.M. division, hoped to emerge as a political leader of the post-war militancy. The UAW demanded a 30 percent wage increase (with no corresponding rise in car prices) and even challenged management prerogatives by demanding that G.M. ''open the books'' to prove that it could not afford to meet union demands. After a bitter 113-day strike, G.M. workers accepted a disappointing 18.5 percent pay increase, a rate previously agreed to by the UAW's Ford and Chrysler divisions and by the United Electrical Workers members employed by G.M.

During the great industrial conflicts of 1946, strikers again felt the force of government intervention on the side of employers. Harry Truman adopted a hard-line anti-strike policy, and sidetracked the regular collective-bargaining process in favor of settlements determined by a fact-finding committee. Using his wartime powers, the Chief Executive seized several industries, including coal, oil, meat-packing, and railroads, thus enhancing the authority of his fact-finding committee. Truman also abolished the wartime Office of Price Administration, and this resulted in a soaring cost of living. The President was using his authority to limit wage increases but not prices. The pro-labor era of the New Deal had ended. The Chief Executive even demanded the authority to draft strikers and to issue injunctions against labor leaders who incited members to strike. This second demand was a clear attack on the Norris–La Guardia Act, a key piece of New Deal labor legislation. Phil Murray of the CIO called these demands ''hysterical'' and Bill Green of the AFL said they would lead to a kind of ''slave labor under Fascism.'' A. F. Whitney of the Trainmen, whose role in the rail strike made him an object of Truman's wrath, pledged to raise millions against the President in the next election. A bill did pass the Senate giving the Chief Executive the right to seize an industry in any strike "affecting the public health, safety or security." Radical Congressman Vito Marcantonio, who led the opposition to this bill in the House, said that this attack on the right to strike would "make collective bargaining a mockery." Having impressed conservatives with his anti-labor ardor, Truman did an about-face and vetoed the bill. Marcantonio helped muster the votes in the House to sustain the veto. A. Philip Randolph and others who had called for a third party to help defeat Truman now drew back and returned to the Democratic fold.

Other unionists actually took action and formed third parties. In Akron, still a center of CIO militancy, a lively labor party was organized which fielded candidates for the 1946 elections. After the Congressional elections that year, in which New Deal Democrats were swamped by conservatives, a group called the Progressive Citizens of America arose to push for a national third party. By this time, the labor-union support for such a move had evaporated entirely, and the Communists, despite their hatred for Truman, opposed a third party because they did not want to alienate their center allies in the CIO. This was hardly the time for a new leftist movement to form. The Cold War was heating up, and conservatism was on the rise at home. In the CIO, anti-Communism became more overt, as was evidenced by Walter Reuther's successful red-baiting campaign for the UAW presidency. A right-wing opposition formed within the left-led United Electrical Workers. It was headed by former UE president James Carey, who had been defeated by Albert Fitzgerald, a left-wing candidate, in 1941. Like Reuther, Carey worked with the Association of Catholic Trade Unionists, a growing anti-Communist force. At the 1946 CIO convention, President Phil Murray stemmed the anti-Communist tide with a resolution that stopped short of expelling the CP and instead settled for condemnation of the party. The handwriting was on the wall. But the Communists continued to depend on Murray and their coalition with the center, even though the center-left coalition was already being subverted by Cold War hysteria.

This internal wrangling in the CIO weakened the industrial unions at a time when the ranks were demanding militant action and the employers were mounting a counterattack. Clearly, the political situation and the balance of class forces was shifting against the labor movement. Even the great 1946 strikes were largely defensive in nature. There were few important victories. The United Steelworkers did win a contractual clause protecting work rules and limiting management's ability to speed up and eliminate jobs. The United Mine Workers, at the peak of their power and prestige, under Lewis, won an unprecedented health- and pension-fund financed by the operators. Otherwise, the strikes won little more than wage increases, which failed to meet the rising cost of living.

Despite the increased earnings that came with overtime during the war, and wage settlements after the war, industrial workers found themselves on a treadmill. Inflation and changing consumption habits required greater incomes. The big unions responded with collective-bargaining strategies that emphasized wage increments and fringe benefits. Except for the steelworkers, few unions took a stand on working conditions, which had been the chief cause of strikes during the war. In 1944, just over 43 percent of the strikes centered on wages and hours, while just over 40 percent centered on "other issues," ranging from speedup to unsafe working conditions. In 1946, the percentage of strikes concerned with wages and hours climbed to 45 percent, and those concerned with "other issues" dropped to 23 percent. These figures implied that rank-and-file workers had abandoned control issues, like speedup and safety, in favor of wage increases that added to purchasing power and fringe benefits that added to security. Union officials, faced with a new management drive to regain control at the point of production, were happy to interpret the post-war strikes this way. Perhaps many rank-and-filers were willing to postpone the struggle for better working conditions. A new era of mass consumption and suburbanization had dawned. And industrial workers wanted to use their new bargaining power to enjoy some of the fruits that era promised. But the struggle for control would not be postponed for long.

By 1948, C. Wright Mills stated, the main drift in post-war industrial relations was clear. Big corporations in the monopoly sector were willing to concede wage increases and fringe benefits to the most powerful unions, because increased labor costs could be spread throughout the industry, thus hurting smaller competitors. The larger corporations could then reduce competition among themselves by leveling out costs and prices, so that no one firm enjoyed a competitive advantage. And then, Mills noted, in *The New Men of Power,* "all the corporations in the industry, along with the industry-wide union, can pass on to the consumers (in the end, mainly workers in other industries) the higher costs involved, and thus maintain high profits and high wages."

Labor leaders, aware of the new pattern in collective bargaining, pushed harder for wage increases which corporations were willing to grant. The big industrial capitalists were not willing to give the unions too much at the bargaining table, however, even in wages. A new attack on unions surfaced in the late 1940's, and it was utilized by business, government, and the press: union wage demands were the main cause of price inflation. This rhetoric became important in the postwar strikes because the corporations could no longer rely on government coercion to freeze wage settlements. As a result, employers took a much harder line. General Electric, for example, had adopted a liberal approach to industrial unionism at first. Gerard Swope argued that the United Electrical Workers should be recognized to reduce shopfloor conflict. A wage settlement with the UE would also make life more difficult for General Electric's smaller competitors. During the war, G.E. made some significant concessions to the UE, and it even sacrificed some shop-floor control to shop committees. The union attacked management's manipulation of the labor market by striking at regional wage differentials and demanding equal pay for women. Many management experts were concerned about the concessions granted to maintain war production and profits (which rose by 250 percent during the war). In *The Union Challenge to Management Control,* Neil W. Chamberlain noted that in the decade following the Wagner Act and the growth of the CIO, unions gained influence in many ways, not only in the determination of wages and hours. They also challenged management control over discipline, staffing and allocating labor power, hiring and firing, and promotions. Ignoring the ways in which the unions served to discipline the work force, Chamberlain emphasized the revolutionary aspects of collective bargaining as a "mechanism by which organized workers may achieve control and exercise it jointly with management." Some serious limits had to be placed on the new industrial unions. At first, corporations like G.E. responded with a hard-line strategy in strike situations. The corporation, now headed by conservative C. E. Wilson, abandoned corporate liberalism during the massive 1946 strike and adopted the aggressive anti-union policies advocated by Lemuel Boulware. "Boulwarism" became popular during the late 1940's, just as the "Mohawk Valley formula" had been in the late 1930's. Both strategies were aimed at turning strike situations against the unions by undermining support within the community and within the workers' own families. In the South, corporations used these and more violent tactics to beat back a CIO organizing drive in 1947. But in the rest of the country the big corporations were forced to deal with the industrial unions, and with their militant leaders. With wartime restraints ended, employers looked to the new conservative Congress to check the power of organized labor. They were especially anxious to remove radical labor leaders and to limit the right to strike in every way possible. They gained an immediate and most gratifying victory in Congress in 1947.

The Taft-Hartley Act passed through both houses that year wiped out many of the rights and protections unionists had won in the New Deal and war years. Taft-Hartley undermined the Clayton Act by making the unions subject to damage suits by employers and subverted further the Norris–La Guardia Act by making unions more vulnerable to injunctions. It outlawed the closed shop, thus striking at the traditional control strong unions exerted on hiring. The law reinforced management's right to hire freely in an open labor market, by invalidating joint agreements that forced employers to hire only union members. This was the kind of contract the militant West Coast dockers and warehousemen had won when they gained union-controlled hiring halls after the general strike of 1934. Besides reasserting management power over hiring and firing, the law prohibited union membership for foremen, thus maintaining an important form of control on shop-floor discipline, which had been seriously threatened during the war when a foremen's union at Ford expanded to other industries.

The Taft-Hartley Act also dramatically restricted the workers' right to strike. It permitted employers to sue unions for breach of contract in strikes taking place during the term of a collective-bargaining agreement. By making union officers vulnerable to fines and imprisonment for refusing to oppose wildcat strikes, the Congress penalized elected union officials for not acting as disciplinarians. The Act also outlawed secondary boycotts, thus restricting sympathy actions by unions, and it prohibited jurisdictional strikes and strikes by federal employees. It empowered the President to create a fact-finding board to inquire into any strike affecting the national health and safety and to act on the board's request to seek federal court injunctions and restraining orders that would make a strike "illegal" for a 90-day cooling-off period. The Act also expanded the National Labor Relations Board and added a general counsel who could bring unions to court for various violations, including a whole series of "unfair labor practices."

Thus, the NLRB, the product of labor's Magna Carta in 1936, could now be used against unions as well as against employers. Administrative law, like judicial law, reflects the alignment of class forces, and in 1947 the pendulum of forces was swinging against organized workers. Employers had benefited from the suspension of the right to strike during the war, when a system of arbitration was created to replace collective bargaining through strike action. Clearly, the greatest breakthroughs for the labor movement, from the first successful auto strike in 1933 to the victory over Ford's empire in 1941, had come through mass strikes with sympathetic support from various quarters. If the state could restrict that power, management would have an enormous advantage. Taft-Hartley gave management the advantage it sought. It would be extended during the next two decades by a series of NLRB and court decisions which further restricted the right to strike and required, instead, a solution to grievances through a cumbersome and costly process of arbitration.

Finally, the Taft-Hartley Act struck at the civil rights of union members, restricting freedom of speech and the freedom to control their own organizations. The Act prevented unions from contributing to campaign funds of any candidate running for federal election. It required unions to file annual financial statements and election reports with the Secretary of Labor. And most important, it demanded that officers of federal, local, and international unions file an affidavit swearing that they were not Communist Party members and that they did not support any organization advocating the overthrow of the government by force or by any "unconstitutional" means. These loyalty oaths were required in order for a union to obtain NLRB collective-bargaining rights. The legal net that was being thrown over the labor movement helped make the NLRB a "new master" that restricted workers' freedoms, as well as an agency that protected certain collective-bargaining rights.

President Truman had already demanded many of these anti-union measures, but he decided to veto the Taft-Hartley Act in order to maintain his labor-union support. Since a majority of the Democrats in both houses had already joined the Republicans in voting for the bill, Truman's veto was easily overridden. Congressional Democrats had supported the Act, so several AFL and CIO leaders called for a labor party. But again this threat came to nothing. Organized labor was now firmly tied to the Democratic Party at all levels. Even blatantly anti-labor acts by Congressional Democrats failed to break the ties. A number of labor leaders, including of course the leftist CIO leaders, joined CIO president Phil Murray in refusing to comply with the compulsory "loyalty oath." John L. Lewis, who had taken his UMW back into the AFL, single-handedly prevented the Federation's conservative Executive Board from endorsing the pledge for a time. But the AFL leaders, notably David Dubinsky of the ILGWU, soon caved in and signed the anti-Communist affidavits. Lewis condemned them for failing to fight the "first ugly savage thrust of Fascism in America." The Miners then voted to disaffiliate with the AFL. Opposition to the affidavits rapidly faded in the CIO as well. The new UAW president, Walter Reuther, who was moving to consolidate his power against the Thomas-Addes faction and its Communist allies, led the movement to sign the loyalty oaths, and helped to give the Taft-Hartley credibility.

Reuther's success in using anti-Communism to take full control of his union in 1947 encouraged other CIO leaders to exploit the tactic.

Anti-Communist hysteria was sweeping the whole nation by this time, and the unions were influenced by the craze. In 1947, Truman established the Federal Employee Loyalty Program, which gave the Attorney General and the FBI unchecked power to investigate and seek the dismissal of "disloyal" employees. This gross violation of federal workers' constitutional rights came in the same year as Taft-Hartley and Reuther's anti-Communist campaign in the UAW. It was also the year when the Truman Doctrine, the Marshall Plan, and the President's truculent stand against Russia involved the United States more deeply in the Cold War. Foreign-policy issues widened the breach in the CIO as Phil Murray and the center forces joined with the overtly anti-Communist forces to isolate the left. The split was further widened by the emergence of a third-party campaign for the 1948 elections which the Communist Party decided to support. A new Progressive Party was formed, and nominated as its Presidential candidate Henry Wallace, who had been Vice-President in F.D.R.'s third term. Wallace sought to prolong the New Deal reforms at home and prevent the Cold War from worsening.

A progressive third-party challenge to the Democrats might have gained some CIO support in 1946, because even AFL leaders were threatening to split with Truman over his strikebreaking actions. But by 1948, with anti-Communism at flood tide, there was no hope of winning labor-union support to a third party supported by the Communists. In any case, the CP failed to win significant CIO support for Wallace. Even the UE leaders refused to risk their shaky position in the CIO by pressing the issue. Nonetheless, the Wallace campaign was used against the Communists by their enemies in the CIO.

Truman won a surprising victory in the 1948 election against Thomas E. Dewey. He retained his labor support by vetoing the Taft-Hartley Act and exploiting the loyalty issue. He was even pressured by Randolph and other black activists to accept a civil-rights plank; it was liberal enough to drive the Dixiecrats out of the Democratic Party and into the racist States Rights Party headed by Strom Thurmond. Wallace ran a poor but courageous race, defending free speech for Communists, criticizing Cold War chauvinism, and speaking, at some risk, before integrated audiences in the South. He polled only a little over a million votes, as compared to La Follette's 4.8 million in 1924. Both Progressive Party campaigns marked the end rather than the beginning of third-party movements. Anti-Communist hysteria negated the efforts made by Wallace and his supporters to revive New Deal foreign and domestic policies. The Popular Front was dead.

When the CIO's 1949 convention assembled, the anti-Communists used the Wallace campaign and the CP's opposition to the Marshall Plan as the basis for a purge. The convention adopted a resolution that no CIO officer or board member could belong to the CP or any Fascist or totalitarian organization. The UE, the largest of the left-led unions, had already withdrawn from the CIO, but the convention still voted to expel its third-largest affiliate without an investigation. In the next two years, eleven unions with leftist leaders were purged, costing the CIO a total of 900,000 members. Most of these unions then died because they were fair game for employers. Harry Bridges's exceptional International Longshoremen's and Warehousemen's Union survived on the West Coast, and even expanded into Hawaii. The United Electrical Workers fought bitter battles against the anti-Communist dual union, chartered by the CIO. The International Union of Electrical Workers (IUE), headed by James Carey, raided UE shops and invited employers to sign sweetheart contracts; they needed little encouragement. The Association of Catholic Trade Unionists and the Church itself joined the fight against the UE, along with Senator Joseph McCarthy and the House Un-American Activities Committee. The UE leaders persevered, however, and kept their union alive in a drastically weakened form. The attack on the UE, one of the nation's most progressive unions, seriously hurt unionism in the electrical-manufacturing industry. In 1947, the UE represented 70 percent of General Electric's production workers, but by 1962 the UE and the IUE together represented only 40 percent. In the process, union members sustained significant losses in collective bargaining.

Clearly, the CP and the left in the CIO could not have survived this coordinated onslaught under any circumstances, but it is important to note that the Communists had not prepared themselves to meet the purge. The party's reputation as a militant fighter for the rank-and-file and for blacks suffered during the war. Its radical change from militant anti-Fascism in 1938 to anti-war activism in 1939 and then to a 100 percent pro-war position in 1941 hurt the party's trade-union cadre. Communists found it difficult to present themselves as defenders of trade-union democracy when they had to follow radical changes in line dictated in Moscow. After the war, the party's preoccupation with foreign policy again hurt efforts to develop union support. Instead of concentrating on pressing issues of concern to union members, party activists were compelled to fight against the Marshall Plan, and to engage anti-Communists on Cold War issues. Under these circumstances, it was more difficult than ever for the party to build political support for socialist politics on a local level. In fact, since the late 1930's, the CP had concentrated increasingly on high-level maneuvering to win support among progressives and to build a center-left coalition in the CIO. James Matles of the UE, who parted company with the party after the war, later said that the importance of the left-center coalition was highly overrated. Center allies like Murray used the coalition just as long as they needed it. But the left rode along on this strategy after 1939, "enshrining it as an immutable historic development," while it failed to organize vigorously or to expand its base. In Matles's opinion, "the Left pretty much wasted those ten years" 1939–49.

The Communists certainly made mistakes, but they had kept alive the practice of militant industrial unionism during the dark years of the twenties and early 1930's. And they performed much of the hard, dangerous work of building the key CIO unions. They were leading activists in the fight for black rights within the union movement. Though they compromised their position in some unions during the war, their absence from the House of Labor made it much harder for the civil-rights movement to find allies later on. Despite other compromises dictated from Moscow, the party tried to preserve the social unionism of the 1930's and extend it into the 1940's. And naturally, they tried to stem the tide of anti-Communism that helped many labor leaders reconcile themselves to conservative domestic policies and pro-business foreign policies. But the Cold War issue, which the Communists sought to defuse with an appeal to the old Popular Front, was the very issue that was used to destroy them.

In 1949, top Communist Party officials were tried and convicted of sedition under the Smith Act, and Foster ordered the party cadre to go underground. In 1950, when the Korean War broke out and worker militancy reappeared in many plants, the party was nearly driven out of existence by a new wave of hysteria which reached a fever pitch during the Rosenbergs' trial for allegedly passing atomic-bomb secrets to the Russians. Coming on the heels of Taft-Hartley and federal-government loyalty oaths, the CIO purge and the persecutions of McCarthy, these attacks removed the party as a force in political life. By the time McCarthyism reached its peak in the early 1950's, the anti-Communist craze had become so widespread that any form of dissent was branded as Communist and thereby discredited or repressed. By denying basic rights to free speech, the federal government had created a totalitarian political atmosphere in which all forms of genuine radicalism were suppressed. The implications of this development for the industrial unions has already been noted. Father Charles Rice, who helped turn Catholic trade unionists against the UE, later regretted his active role in the purge. "The CIO became part of the McCarthy hysteria. It was tragic that the Left was crushed. The CIO needed opposition and criticism. An ideal union requires strong opposition."

As a result of the left purges and the counterattack launched by employers, CIO membership dropped from a wartime peak of 5.2 million to only 3.7 million in 1950. At this point, the old AFL claimed 8.5 million. Discussions had already resumed about a return of the purified CIO to the original House of Labor. Indeed, the rebel unions began to resemble those in the parent body more and more after they expelled the left and embraced the Cold War. Many had also retreated from aggressive, interracial unionism and from socially concerned unionism generally. Commenting on the changed mood, Samuel Lubell noted in *The Future of American Politics* that the CIO dynamo had slowed down from a roar to a quiet hum. "The dynamic, near-revolutionary surge, which doubled union membership between 1935 and 1938 . . ." had nearly ebbed by the late 1940's. Returning in 1948 to a class-conscious UAW local he had visited eleven years before, Lubell found a much more pacific mood. "The going wage in the auto industry was three times the depression low." Almost half of the local UAW members owned their own homes, and most of the houses were freshly painted. "With their new stake in the political system, many workers had become wary of political radicalism," showing increased hostility to the Communists and Henry Wallace. Lubell was right. Unionized workers had increased their incomes during the 1940's, and by 1948 union militancy and labor radicalism were on the wane. But the causal link between the two developments was not as direct as Lubell implied.

During the war, real income had increased by 53 percent. After the war, earnings increased much more slowly, as inflation ate away at the gains made in the big 1945–46 strikes. Still, workers did dispose of more of their income than ever on refrigerators, cars, and new homes, often financed on the G.I. Bill. It was a time when the good life seemed attainable for millions of industrial workers who had suffered through the Depression and the war, and labor leaders emphasized this when they focused on winning wage concessions from employers. Many of these leaders used the demand for more pay to justify their support for the Korean War and for increased military spending to fight the Cold War around the world. Certain skilled workers and employees of major corporations, the vast majority of them white males, did benefit significantly from the growth of the military-industrial complex. Workers in the building trades and other sectors also gained from the economic growth generated by government subsidies and expenditures. But the great majority of working people did not benefit from the creation of a permanent war economy. By 1950 unemployment had risen to 12 percent and skilled workers still found it difficult to maintain year-round employment. In 1951, when mass layoffs hit the auto and other industries, the Truman Administration set forth a new base for the cost-of-living index which attempted to conceal a 100 percent rise in living costs over the previous decade. Early in the same year, a War Stabilization Board announced a new wage-freeze formula for the duration of the Korean War. At the same time, the government reported that corporate profits, before taxes, had shot up from just over $27 billion to $50 billion in one year. Small wonder, then, that prosperity seemed to fade before it reached the unionized worker. Nor was it surprising that the distribution of wealth became more slanted in favor of the upper classes. In 1915, the poorest 40 percent of the population received 19.8 percent of the national income; in 1934, it received 17.4 percent; and in 1950, just 12.0 percent. A minority resolution put before the UAW's 1951 convention expressed anger at this state of affairs and received one quarter of the votes in its call for a labor party, in spite of strong opposition from the Reuther organization. The resolution denounced Truman's Fair Deal as a raw deal that only gave lip service to social legislation. "The fight for a real Fair Deal now depends upon labor and the party it must and will create." But the chances for a labor party had been killed by the Cold War and the defeat of Henry Wallace's campaign. With the left removed from the unions, rank-and-file workers had no organized vehicle for protest.

Industrial workers pressed their grievances by striking. After falling to a post-war low in 1949, the number of recorded strikes escalated with the outbreak of the Korean War in 1950. Strike actions reached the highest level ever recorded during the last two years of the war, in 1952 and 1953, when more than 5,000 work stoppages took place each year. Like the 1945–46 strike wave, this wartime surge of labor militancy was largely defensive in nature. And unlike the smaller but more effective outburst of militancy between 1934 and 1937, little was accomplished in terms of increased organization or added power in the workplace. The Taft-Hartley Act and other actions taken to contain worker militancy did not actually prevent working people from organizing walkouts. But they did shorten the length of those strikes and limit the support strikers received. Furthermore, without the old cadre of radical leaders who built the CIO, the strikers lacked aggressive leadership at all levels. Containment policies adopted by the state and by the employers limited workers' capacity to strike, and had more to do with taming the CIO than the lure of suburban tract housing and other goods offered to workers in the brief period of post-war prosperity.

There were internal reasons for the containment of worker militancy and the pacification of the CIO. The obvious effects of the anti-Communist purge have already been noted. There were other forces at work during the 1940's that were not so obvious. As we have seen, the informal work groups that persisted through the 1920's became the basis of the new unions during the 1930's. And after union recognition these groups were the real loci of power in the struggle to battle speedup and management coercion. Stan Weir, a former seaman, auto worker, and docker, has studied these groups extensively and believes that they were seriously disrupted by the war. The draft and the high mobility of the labor force broke up many of the militant CIO cadre in the early years of the war. The composition of these groups changed radically as new workers entered the factories—black and white men from the South, white married women, and young men from the street corners who were deferred from the draft. These newly composed groups developed solidarities of their own. But they generally did not attain the cohesiveness and political consciousness of the earlier groups. "Educated militants who remained on the jobs they had helped to organize found it difficult to sustain struggles against their employers and for internal democracy," notes Weir. In any case, these wartime work allies were then dispersed by reconversion after the war.

With the shift of the social base of the new unions, the leadership became more removed from the rank-and-file. Some local militants were fired for leading wildcat strikes during the war. Others were taken out of their locals and assigned to other organizing tasks. This was a conscious policy in the new steelworkers' union, whose leaders thought it was time to co-opt or remove the militants and radicals, in order to build a more stable, responsible organization. After the Communist purges in 1949, international officers were able to exercise even more power over local affairs. Opponents of the top leaders could easily be branded as Communists. Finally, the routinization of grievance procedure and the bureaucratization of the union structure further extended the gap between elected officials and members on the shop floor. For example, the UAW's 1946 contracts created a new official, the union committeeman. Unlike the shop steward, who worked on the line, the committeeman worked full-time for the union, often in a special office off the factory floor, and was charged with policing the contract. The union committeeman, often ambitious for higher office, was clearly under more pressure from the top officials in the union than from the hundred or more workers he was supposed to serve. During wildcat strikes, committeemen usually had the difficult job of trying to get their department back to work. Even the shop stewards, who had once been organically connected to work groups, depended more on the higher union officials. The loss of the right to strike during the war and the weight of the grievance procedure prevented the stewards from negotiating on-the-spot settlements with foremen as easily as they once had.

The decline of CIO militancy must be seen, then, in the larger context of World War II and the Cold War, when many conservative forces closed in on the labor movement. C. Wright Mills concluded in *The New Men of Power* that a particularly important force was the employers' use of binding no-strike contracts to enlist the labor-union bureaucracy in disciplining rank-and-file workers. The union actually took over "much of the companies' personnel work, becoming the disciplining agent within the rules" established for contract bargaining and contract maintenance. Therefore, Mills added:

> The union bureaucracy stands between the company bureaucracy and the rank and file of the workers, operating as a shock absorber for both. The more responsible the union is, the more this is so. Responsibility is held for the contract signed with the company; to uphold this contract the union must often exert pressure upon the workers. . . . Unauthorized leaders of the union, the shop stewards, operating as whips within the plant, become rank-and-file bureaucrats of the labor leadership. As foremen are responsible to the company hierarchy, so shop stewards are primarily answerable to the labor union hierarchy, rather than to the rank and file who elect them.

Naturally, these changes affected the quality of the top labor leadership. These "new men of power" who emerged at the head of unions in the late 1940's were not necessarily arch-conservatives, Mills pointed out. In fact, some of them had been militants or even radicals in the 1930's. Then, "the labor leader spoke the language and acted the part of the rebel" because he had to fight the power of business and the laws of private property that protected business. If the CIO leader demanded the closed shop, he had to argue against "freedom of contract." If he demanded "an improvement in shop conditions" or a change in the "ways of managing the shop," he encroached "upon the received prerogatives of the managers of property.'' The radical union leader of the Depression who expressed the workers' demands for civil and human rights and for more control could play a different role when the context changed. In the war years he might have to hold back rebellion by opposing wildcat strikes, Mills observed, and after the war he might become a "manager of discontent" by using a contract strike to defuse rank-and-file militancy. Walter Reuther of the UAW seemed to typify this new kind of labor leader. Walter Reuther and his brothers, Roy and Vic, inherited a socialist belief in self-education and self-improvement from their father, a German brewery worker who was active among the numerous Debsian socialists in Ohio River Valley industrial towns. Walter, who was "contentious and pugnacious" in his youth, got a job as a skilled tool-and-die worker at Ford's River Rouge plant in the late 1920's. When he began to drift from his youthful commitment to socialism, his brother Victor came to Detroit and restored his faith in time for Norman Thomas's Presidential campaign in 1932. When Walter was fired at Ford's for his outspoken views on unionism, the two brothers departed for Europe, where they learned about Hitler's menacing drive for power and worked for fifteen months at a new Ford *autostroy* in the Soviet Union. The Reuthers, like many leftists and liberals of the time, were impressed by Russian economic planning; they returned to the United States in 1935 and Walter started work under a false name at a G.M. plant on Detroit's West Side. By 1937, the Reuther brothers were in control of a large UAW local there. Like Sidney Hillman, A. Philip Randolph, and other prominent union leaders, Walter Reuther's commitment and determination had been nurtured by socialist beliefs. During the late 1930's he worked closely with the Communists, and one party official even claimed he took out a secret membership. By 1940, however, Reuther had abandoned his Communist allies and his old comrades in the Socialist Party. In 1941, he led the movement in the UAW to bar the Communists from office, and seized on an issue that would propel him to the UAW presidency five years later. During the war, Reuther jockeyed for position within the UAW. After he was rebuffed by the rank-and-file for a proposal to sacrifice premium pay for overtime, the feisty redhead allied with the Rank and File Caucus. Though he refused to condemn the no-strike pledge, he gave voice to growing discontent with the incumbent administration and its Communist allies. Reuther's militant rhetoric during the 1946 G.M. strike increased his popularity within the ranks, even though the long walkout resulted in disappointing gains. He won the presidential race narrowly that year and then used the anti-Communist issue to consolidate power, though it meant accepting the Taft-Hartley Act, so that the loyalty oaths could be used to root out party members.

Without significant opposition within the union, Reuther negotiated a series of contracts which included some dramatic gains in wages and fringe benefits, but failed to address working conditions. In 1948, the UAW won an unprecedented cost-of-living escalator clause from G.M. and in 1949 a pension supplement to social security. But while these gains were achieved, speedup accelerated and working conditions deteriorated in many auto plants, while the UAW grievance procedure continued to frustrate many rank-and-filers. Wildcat strikes again became a problem for the UAW officials.

In 1950, Reuther negotiated a pathbreaking settlement with G.M. An unprecedented five-year contract pledged the UAW to refrain from strikes in return for a continuation of the cost-of-living escalator, improvements in pension, welfare, and insurance plans, plus the addition of a controversial clause that gave added pay for increased productivity. General Motors hailed the 1950 contract as the start of a new era of peaceful industrial relations. But auto workers were no more willing to sacrifice the right to strike against speedup than they had been during the war, and during the five-year peace pact UAW members became more alienated from their leaders.

Walter Reuther played a leading role in forging a modern form of industrial unionism which accepted management control of production in return for concessions in wages, pensions, and other fringe benefits. His approach was premised on the ability of giant corporations in a noncompetitive industry like auto to pass on increased labor costs in the form of higher prices. His collective-bargaining strategy was also keyed to the growing aspirations of auto workers as homeowners and consumers and the lingering fears of the Depression generation over layoffs and old-age insecurity. But Reuther and the other UAW leaders knew also that the auto workers would not accept these concessions without protesting the consequent surrender on the fight over speedup. Reuther's organization, which established one-party control over the UAW in 1947, made it difficult for dissent to coalesce, but it faced constant rebellions in the form of wildcat strikes to protest local working conditions and poor contract settlements. These were brushfires that could not be extinguished.

The UAW leadership was not openly contemptuous of the rank-and-file, as many oligarchical unions were in the post-war years. Indeed, Walter Reuther attempted to maintain his reputation as a progressive labor leader and social planner by demanding a guaranteed annual wage and speaking out on issues like unemployment and racial segregation. Many businessmen still regarded him as a socialist. He played the part of a liberal throughout the fifties and sixties by holding out the hope of industrial democracy and expressing the workers' hostility to corporate capitalism and class privilege. More than any of the other new men of power, Walter Reuther continued to speak the language of the socially conscious unionism that arose during the late 1930's but failed to survive World War II and the harrowing Cold War years.

Like the other new men of power in the unions, Reuther accommodated to the post-war context in which the hopes of the 1930's became little more than rhetoric. By 1950, the world of the worker had begun to change significantly. It was the dawn of another era in which even the new unionism of the CIO seemed obsolete. The labor movement entered the 1950's on the defensive. The workers' rights secured in the epic battles of the Depression had been drastically restricted. Management had again seized the initiative in the struggle for control and prepared a new drive for productivity in which it planned to use technology to eliminate thousands of jobs. No longer intent on destroying existing unions, employers hoped to use contract unionism as another form of control over rebellious workers.

7

The Workers' Changing World, 1950-80

The shape of the workers' world in the twentieth century can now be seen with some clarity. Its contours have changed significantly in the past three decades, and so our view must remain somewhat impressionistic. We do not lack factual information about recent workers' history. The study of industrial relations has become a profession unto itself. We have scores of detailed studies by social scientists concerning everything from workers' attitudes toward political candidates to the effects of fluorescent lighting on productivity. These studies are not, however, written from the workers' point of view. We also have a good deal of labor journalism, though it lacks the texture of the early-twentieth-century reportage. And we have many autobiographies and oral histories in which workers, largely organizers and officials, tell their own stories. This literature gives us a feel for recent working-class experience the survey research fails to provide. For example, during the great coal miners' strike of 1977 and 1978, reams of material appeared on the economics of the industry and the politics of the union, but it was very difficult to know what was happening among the rank-and-file at the local level, where the strike was sustained for over a hundred days, in spite of a Taft-Hartley injunction order.

Paradoxically, the volume of information on post-war industrial relations has not produced a clear picture of the changing world in which wage earners lived and worked. Perhaps a more comprehensive view will emerge as social and labor historians dig more deeply into the period since 1950. We can, however, focus on the major changes affecting working-class life during those perplexing years. We can examine the effects of changes on organized labor; we can look at the lives of workers, notably women and blacks, who remained unorganized. We can discuss how workers in the late 1960's and 1970's began to assert a new range of democratic and human rights.

In 1980, workers still lived and worked in a world that had been shaped during the 1940's: they were still struggling against the same corporations, now more powerful than ever; they were still striving to beat inflation, make mortgage payments, acquire new commodities, and save for their children's future and their own retirement; they still had to contend with unions over issues of autonomy, democracy, and authority; and they still lacked a sense of control in their work.

Organized workers have made great economic and social advances in this century. The conditions under which New York City clothing workers and Pennsylvania steelworkers lived and toiled at the turn of the century have changed significantly. Industrial unions have been responsible not only for better wages and working conditions but for the expansion and protection of workers' rights. For example, after reorganizing during the early 1930's, the International Ladies' Garment Workers' Union negotiated a thirty-five-hour, five-day work week—a radical change from the old days of endless piecework in the sweatshops—and won employer-financed vacation and retirement funds. Interviewed in 1975, Abe Kawer, a seventy-year-old immigrant from Warsaw, explained that he started on the Lower East Side as a $15-a-week errand boy and retired as a $200-a-week embroidery-machine operator. "We were the pioneers of the present generation of workers," he declared. "They get the benefits we fought for." The benefits are tangible. A 1979 survey by the Bureau of Labor Statistics showed that unionized workers earned an average of $262 a week, $41 more than non-union labor. Of course, they also enjoyed rights as well as benefits, the human rights and freedoms the union movement won in a half century of struggle.

For new immigrant clothing workers from Puerto Rico and Asia, freedom is still a hard-won thing. Retired needle-trades workers benefited from union gains, but in an age when manufacturing jobs are being exported, some unions are reluctant to press for higher wages, because employers threaten to close up shop. Many workers who now enter the needle trades enjoy only a few of the benefits attained by union workers in less competitive sectors of heavy industry.

In response to the very advances made by industrial unions during and after World War II, large corporations have reduced high-paying jobs and brought in more low-paying workers from the secondary labor market. Technology has become a powerful weapon in the struggle for more control, but no more powerful than the threat to close plants as a result of high labor costs or low productivity. In 1977, the multinational Lykes Corporation shut down the newly acquired Campbell Works, once owned by Youngstown Sheet and Tube. When over 5,000 workers lost their jobs in the heartland of CIO industrial unionism, the threat of plant closings took on new meaning. The next year, U.S. Steel, complaining of productivity problems, announced plans to close its plant in Youngstown, as well as its Homestead Works near Pittsburgh, where so many crucial battles had been fought over the years. By the late seventies these plant closings have jeopardized the movement to secure steelworkers' job rights.

In addition to outright closings, thousands of workers continue to lose jobs through plant migration, as corporations move their facilities in search of cheaper labor, lower taxes, and fewer regulations. In the decade after 1966, the Northeastern states lost over a million manufacturing jobs. The Southern states gained 860,000 factory jobs, partly because right-to-work laws still inhibited unions and employers still paid 20 percent less in wages. Manufacturing jobs have also been exported abroad at an increased rate. Between 1945 and 1970, United States companies established over 8,000 subsidiaries overseas, including many in underdeveloped countries, where reactionary rulers helped to ensure low wages and high levels of exploitation. And so, for the union steelworker faced with a plant shutdown, or the union clothing worker whose plant has moved to South Carolina or South Korea, the many gains of the past eighty years have been negated. The brutal social and economic conditions in steel towns like Homestead and immigrant ghettos like the Lower East Side no longer prevail. But in both places, where new immigrants have replaced the Slavic Catholics and Russian Jews, the world of the worker is still a very uncertain place.

The threat of plant closings and "runaway shops" has brought a new sense of crisis to the industrial worker, added to the long-standing threat of technological unemployment. Mechanization had always threatened skilled workers, but by the 1950's a new kind of assembly-line automation threatened the jobs of unskilled factory operatives as well. Congressional hearings on automation and technological change in 1955 yielded many examples of job loss, including these: two workers using automatic machinery could assemble a thousand radios a day, a task that once required two hundred workers; one worker in a

Ford plant could run a transfer machine performing the five hundred operations once done by thirty-five to seventy workers.

During the fifties, employers used mechanization to bring two of the nation's most militant union leaders to heel. During the thirties and forties, John L. Lewis of the United Mine Workers and Harry Bridges of the International Longshoremen's and Warehousemen's Union (ILWU) led their unions in militant strikes that increased their members' incomes and job security and challenged many management prerogatives. Both union leaders and their members defied the Taft-Hartley Act and refused to sign its anti-Communist affidavits. And both men were threatened by federal authorities, Bridges with deportation and Lewis with imprisonment. Lewis and the UMW had been especially bold in defying President Truman during major strikes in the late 1940's, strikes which gave the miners unprecedented gains, especially in health care and pensions. During the 1950's, however, the switch to petroleum fuels and competition from non-union mines eroded the UMW's bargaining power. Lewis accepted mechanization in the union mines and the UMW lost thousands of members in Appalachia. Faced with isolation from the AFL and CIO, and with competition from non-union ports, Bridges and the ILWU signed a Mechanization and Modernization Agreement in 1960. Under this contract, "cargo doubled from over 19 million tons to nearly 40 million tons," according to a union report. Labor cost per ton dropped 30 percent and the total West Coast longshore labor force fell nearly 50 percent. New workers, including many blacks, were hired without full union protection. As speedup increased, so did the accident rate.

In the steel industry, corporations launched a determined drive for productivity after World War II. Using technological innovations, speedup, the threat of foreign competition, and federal government intervention, the employers attempted to regain the control lost between 1937 and 1947 when the United Steelworkers Union (USW) won a remarkable clause (section 2B) requiring the maintenance of "local working conditions." Unlike the leaders of the auto workers' union, who allowed management to control production through the speed of the assembly line, the USW's negotiators built on the traditions of job control in an industry where there was no assembly line. The struggle raged in several major industry-wide strikes, culminating in the 110-day 1959 walkout in which the strikers refused to back down on the work-rules issue. David McDonald, a career union official who succeeded Phil Murray as USW president, was willing to make concessions. Indeed, he sought a "mutual trusteeship" between the companies and the union, but rank-and-file militancy prevented the leadership from making major concessions. In 1957, a rank-and-file slate challenged McDonald's brand of "tuxedo unionism" and demanded more union democracy within the USW. In 1965, a union reformer, I. W. Abel, defeated McDonald after pledging to "restore rank-and-file control over basic policy" and to respond to the angry protests of black steelworkers, who charged the union with condoning the racist job structure in the industry.

Abel, however, continued the policies of accommodation and accepted the productivity deal the Eisenhower and Kennedy Administrations had demanded of the union. The Abel leadership, using the process of continuous behind-the-scenes bargaining, and the threat of foreign-made steel, made major concessions to the companies, including a pledge to increase productivity in 1971. Dissident USW members criticized the productivity clause as an excuse for speedup. A leaflet written by the Rank and File Team (RAFT), a national caucus based in Youngstown, Ohio, put it this way:

> Since August [1971], many plants have been closed and thousands of jobs have been combined or left unfilled in the plants. Is this what productivity really means?
> Does productivity to the steel industry really mean more steel will be produced to meet the great needs of our nation? If so, all the industry needs to do is to put more unused facilities to work again. Or does productivity really mean profitability? Has the steel industry, like the coal industry before it, decided to create a new Appalachia, throwing away towns and putting thousands of steel workers onto the streets and unemployment lines?

The Experimental Negotiating Agreement (ENA) of 1973 extended the productivity deal, prohibited industry-wide strikes, and called for binding arbitration of grievances. The ENA provoked another wave of protest for rank-and-file democracy and the right to strike. In 1977, an insurgent slate headed by Ed Sadlowski of south Chicago carried most of the basic steel locals, but lost to the more conservative slate in other locals. The election, according to A. H. Raskin of *The New York Times,* pitted "the current trend toward cooperative union management relations" against a "renewed accent on the worker-versus-boss slogans of the early New Deal years."

By 1977, 400,000 workers in basic steel produced twice as much as 600,000 workers had produced in 1947. Management's productivity drive had been highly successful, partly as a result of technological change and the reduction of the work force. While many steelworkers now operate machinery, a large number of mill hands still toil under conditions that prevailed at Homestead in the early

1900's. A steelworker named Mike Lefevre, interviewed by Studs Terkel for *Working,* said that the world of work had changed. As a "laborer," he felt like the last of a "dying breed." His testimony harked back to the words of the Slavic steelworkers who wrote to folks in the old country about doing the work of three men. But it is not the "muscle work" that troubled Lefevre. He was willing to work hard and "pull steel" for eight hours to pay his bills and send his kids to college. What bothered him was the lack of autonomy and dignity on the job, and this complaint was shared by many workers, not only those who used their muscles. "I would rather work my ass off for eight hours a day with nobody watching me than five minutes with a guy watching me," said Lefevre. He recalled a shop-floor fight in which he shouted at the foreman: "I came here to work, I didn't come to crawl." Having lost the fight with his foreman, he despaired over the nature of the larger conflict. "Who you gonna sock?" he asked Terkel. "You can't sock General Motors, you can't sock anybody in Washington, you can't sock a system."

By the end of the sixties, even those with steady union jobs had begun to wonder if the price they paid at work was worth the pay they received. In *Blue Collars and Hard Hats,* Patricia and Brendan Sexton noted that a city worker aged thirty-eight with a family of four had to earn close to $10,000 a year to live what the Bureau of Labor Statistics called a "modest but adequate standard of living." In other words, he had to put in a steady forty-hour week fifty-two weeks of the year, at about $4.80 an hour, to live in modest comfort, but "even the most highly paid industrial workers," as in the auto industry, earned only $7,280 a year without layoffs. Hence, the need for overtime and for added income from other family members. In 1967, the average worker took home $90.86 per week. By June 1979, this figure more than doubled, to $194.86 per week. When that weekly pay check was translated into its purchasing power in 1967 dollars, it meant a take-home pay of $89.84, or slightly less than twelve years earlier.

Even those working-class families who earned more than required for an adequate standard of living enjoyed the fruits of affluence in a tenuous way. "Many of the refrigerators, washing machines, and other household conveniences that casual observers mistake for affluence are financed by installment debt—and represent voluntary but pressing obligations rather than assets," the Sextons contended. "A majority of American families owe such debt and the proportion grows each year." By the end of 1968, the installment debt reached a staggering $89 billion. In 1975, this figure reached nearly $165 billion, and four years later it grew to over $307 billion. The cost of buying on time had escalated alarmingly. Mortgage rates on new homes shot from 6.5 percent in 1967 to over 11 percent in August 1979. For younger workers or those who rented, the acquisition of a home, the most important sign of affluence in post-war life, became very difficult.

In a relative sense, the standard of living for United States workers remained high, though it was no longer the best in the Western world. Compared to the poverty of the 1930's or of Third World countries or the urban ghettos at home, the unionized worker was affluent. During the fifties and sixties, some social analysts even believed that the class lines had blurred between unionized blue-collar workers and middle-class professionals and proprietors. After all, when asked, many workers put themselves in the vast American middle class rather than the lower class.

Even the best-paid blue-collar workingmen lacked the incomes and various forms of job security enjoyed by professionals and managers. For example, a union building tradesman in the late 1960's earned $13,000 a year *if* he worked full-time for fifty-two weeks, an unlikely possibility. Unemployment remained primarily a problem for the working class. Job insecurity was built into the economy, even in the unionized industries. The overall joblessness averaged only 3.5 percent in the 1960's for white males, but it jumped to an average of 5.0 in the 1970's. Rates were higher for women and black men. Post-war prosperity, then, was not shared equally. Affluence hardly eliminated the distinction between working-class people and the professional-managerial class. Wage earners and their families still live and work in a different world from corporate executives and lawyers, bankers and doctors. Affluence has not overcome the difference between those who have to sell their labor in the wage market and those who own stocks and other assets or can parlay professional and managerial credentials into high incomes.

Even those blue-collar workers who escaped to the suburbs remained in the world of the working class. As Bennett Berger indicates in *Working Class Suburb,* residence in housing tracts outside the industrial cities did not alter class consciousness or class relations. The West Coast auto workers studied by Berger did not believe that a move to the suburbs was a significant step up the social ladder. Most of these workingmen accepted industrial work as a life sentence and, at most, aspired to occupational mobility within the sphere of blue-collar work. Herbert Gans's study of the vast new suburban tract in Levittown, New Jersey, from 1958 to 1962, showed that urban working-class culture survived and took on new forms. Blue-collar workingmen still socialized within their own sphere, transforming the local Veterans of Foreign Wars chapter into a surrogate for the city's neighborhood tavern. Refugees who left the urban villages did not adopt middle-class life styles, Gans observed in *The Levittowners*. Family life did become more private, but working-class families remained distinct from "other-directed," "success-oriented," upper-middle-class families. The blue-collar families still valued security more than mobility. In a middle-class suburban community, the "people of working class culture stay close to home and make the house a haven against a hostile, outside world."

Working-class family life seemed to become more intense in the suburbs and added to the tensions wives and mothers had to absorb. Many suburban working-class women were deprived of family- and community-support networks when they left the urban villages. Women have experienced this loss most acutely and, as a result, have had to create new networks in the suburbs. The social and cultural losses sustained through residential mobility affected entire families, however. Marc Fried and his associates traced the ethnic working-class families relocated after the destruction of the old West End "urban village" in Boston. In *The World of the Urban Working Class*, they concluded that suburbanized workers grieved for their old neighborhood. They missed the "close mutual assistance" that had prevailed through kin-relationships and through various informal group networks.

In the mid-1950's, the radical writer Harvey Swados defied the conventional wisdom by emphasizing these contradictions and exposing "The Myth of the Happy Worker." Reflecting on his own experience on the assembly line, he concluded: "The worker's attitude toward his work is generally compounded of hatred, shame, and resignation." In order to make ends meet, the average factory operative had to put in overtime and depended on the income of other family members. Workers who toiled in degrading factory jobs knew they could not buy middle-class status. As workers became more exposed to "middle-class values" and life styles, they came to see production work as even more degrading. In *Automobile Workers and the American Dream*, Ely Chinoy stated that the people he interviewed were alienated from themselves and their work. Because of the "extensive division of labor" and mechanization, which removed the sense of craft, workers felt no tie to the product they made. Going into a large, mechanized plant meant that they "surrendered control" over their actions for the hours they were paid. During these hours, the tempo and rhythm of work was set by machines and the managers who controlled them. Workers still had to submit to managerial authority, with the union acting only as an indirect check on the abuse of power.

As we have already seen, during and after World War II auto workers responded to oppressive working conditions with wildcat strikes and contract rejections. The UAW's five-year no-strike pact with General Motors, negotiated in 1950, offered workers increased wages in return for higher productivity. But the intensification of work resulted in frequent work stoppages throughout the life of the contract. The institutionalization of collective bargaining on a national level created a bureaucracy unresponsive to the local grievances that caused wildcat strikes. As the shop stewards' position weakened, the UAW's multi-step grievance procedure became a source of frustration. In previous years, shop stewards, backed by well-organized work groups, could negotiate grievances on the shop floor. By the 1950's, grievances were tied up in the bureaucratic process and left unresolved for long periods. The institutionalization of the CIO unions flowed from the need to gain bargaining power against huge national corporations, explains former auto worker Stan Weir in his analysis of rank-and-file labor revolts during the fifties and sixties. In negotiating nationwide contracts covering wages, hours, and benefits, union officials postponed the struggle to humanize working conditions. As the locals lost much of their original autonomy, the Reuther organization concentrated more power in the national office, and rank-and-filers became more distanced from their own leaders. The Reuther leadership adapted to the rebelliousness of the ranks during the early 1950's. In 1955, it shortened contracts to three years, authorized local bargaining, and occasionally supported local strikes over working conditions. During the early sixties, auto workers' real wages continued to rise, but UAW members remained frustrated with working conditions. In 1964, Detroit auto workers launched a campaign to "humanize working conditions." These workers, said Weir, "served notice on a now case-hardened bureaucracy that the ranks intended to resume the fight to win dignity at work."

The rank-and-file insurgencies that erupted in several major labor unions during the late sixties resulted essentially from the degradation of work and from the unions' insistence on making wages the central issue in collective bargaining. Wildcat strikes, contract rejections, and sabotage all increased during this period as industrial workers protested against dangerous, degrading working conditions and authoritarian management tactics. During the late sixties, another generation of workers entered the plants. The young people had absorbed many of their parents' values, but they were not as disciplined by the fear of poverty and insecurity. They were also more educated and less easily intimidated by arbitrary authority. Many young production workers, whites as well as ghetto blacks, shared the anti-authoritarian values of their college-educated peers who were active in the radical student movement. Often, these younger workers, especially the blacks and women, had no tradition of loyalty to the union. The white men who dominated the union leadership seemed to be just another group of bureaucrats who gave orders. To many young militants in the plants, the drift toward accommodation between unions and management made labor officials seem like company men.

Deep-seated discontent with shop conditions led to a climactic strike in 1972 at the new General Motors assembly plant in Lordstown, Ohio. The young workers in this plant not only acted against many of the chief causes of alienation (Taylorism, automation, authoritarianism, and a dehumanizing division of labor), they articulated with unusual clarity the workers' complaints against the modern labor process. In the largest sense, the rebellion at Lordstown resulted from a crisis in United States monopoly capitalism, a crisis reflected in the growing threat of foreign products. To compete with imported small cars, Chevrolet began producing its own economy-sized car (the Vega) at its Lordstown plant. In 1966, the Lordstown line produced roughly sixty Vegas per hour, but in 1971 a new cadre of managers from the General Motors Assembly Division (GMAD) introduced a series of changes to increase productivity. GMAD adopted "get-tough" tactics to reduce absenteeism (the most widespread response to alienating working conditions), which had been blamed in part for the drop in GM's profit margin in the late 1960's. The new regime also introduced high technology to the line (including the "unimate" welding robot) and cranked up the speed of the line to the staggering rate of a hundred cars per hour. Furthermore, GMAD ordered compulsory overtime; laid off "unproductive" workers; employed time-and-motion studies to set new production standards; "buried" hundreds of grievances filed by union reps; and attacked the informal agreements work groups had made with foremen.

When over a thousand unsettled grievances piled up, the workers waged a slowdown strike, refusing to produce at the new levels. More individualized forms of sabotage had been common on most auto-assembly lines, especially during speedup, but this organized slowdown represented a new kind of collective work resistance, the sort the Wobblies had in mind when they preached sabotage. In the spring of 1972, the Lordstown workers struck the newest, most productive plant in the country, and drew national attention to the issue of alienation.

Auto workers had been at war with the assembly line and the speedup since Ford built the first mass-production plants before World War I, but in the seventies the public began to discover alienation. President Richard M. Nixon declared in his 1971 Labor Day address that the "work ethic" was alive and well in America, but after the Lordstown strike government openly expressed doubts about the willingness of wage earners to work happily and productively under conditions imposed by the capitalist labor process. In Studs Terkel's 1972 book, *Working,* scores of articulate workers spoke about alienation. Gary Bryner, the young president of the Lordstown UAW local, best captured the alienated mood and angry feelings of the seventies, when he spoke about G.M.'s use of time-and-motion studies:

Our argument has always been: That's mechanical; that's not human.
   The workers said, We perspire, we sweat, we have hangovers, we have upset stomachs, we have feelings and emotions, and we're not about to be placed in the category of a machine. When you talk about that watch, you talk about . . . a minute. We talk about a lifetime. We're gonna do what's normal and we're gonna tell you what's normal. We'll negotiate from there.

The Lordstown strike was more than a response to the productivity drive that increased speedup and threatened safety. Like many of the other strikes that swept industry in the late sixties and early seventies, it was a rebellion against what labor lawyer Staughton Lynd called "arbitrary authority and the lack of respect for human rights in the capitalist workplace." Lynd was not the only New Left, anti-war activist who saw a parallel between the student revolt of the sixties and the young worker revolt of the seventies. A convergence of sorts took place in the anti-war movement that mobilized working-class soldiers against the military. Vietnam vets who returned to industry did not abandon their hostility to arbitrary authority. At Lordstown, these vets took the lead in refusing to "take bullshit from foremen." This strike involved a predominantly young and noticeably long-haired work force that seemed to reflect the new sensibility of the sixties. Gary Bryner, the strike leader, told Terkel that young workers were reluctant to submit to the degradation and alienation to which their Depression-era parents had been subjected. Unlike their parents, they were not satisfied with what Bryner called the pursuit of the "almighty dollar." Young people were increasingly concerned with the "social aspects" of their jobs and with the assertion of their "human rights." They derived satisfaction from "standing up" for their "rights" against "giants" like G.M.

In 1973, a Special Task Force of the Department of Health, Education and Welfare published a report called *Work in America* which concluded that "significant numbers of American workers" were "dissatisfied with their working lives."

> Dull, repetitive, seemingly meaningless tasks, offering little challenge or autonomy, are causing discontent among workers at all occupational levels. This is not so much because work itself has greatly changed; indeed, one of the main problems is that work has not changed fast enough to keep up with the rapid and widespread changes in worker attitudes, aspirations and values. A general increase in their educational and economic status has placed many American workers in a position where having an interesting job is now as important as having a job that pays well.

Alienation from work, according to the report, often resulted in declining physical and mental health, growing family and community instability, "unbalanced" political views reflecting disillusionment with democracy, increased drug and alcohol addiction, and violent forms of aggression.

Aggressiveness also appeared on the shop floor in the form of insubordination and sabotage. Employers worried about alarmingly high rates of absenteeism. All these results of alienation cut down on productivity and profitability. One response was to introduce automation to trouble spots on the assembly line, though these innovations actually increased resistance in plants like Lordstown. By the seventies, corporations were investing heavily in computerized technology that would allow them to gain a new level of control over the labor process. The machinists who had been a thorn in the side of management since the days of Frederick Taylor's experiments had been affected by technological unemployment and shop migration. Their numbers dropped from 535,000 in 1950 to 390,000 in 1970. Now machinists in auto and other monopoly industries are faced with the specter of computerized "numerical control" which threatens to remove all mental work from the shop floor.

As the corporate productivity drive gained force in the 1970's, some firms attempted to increase worker loyalty and efficiency by redesigning jobs so that the worker felt a greater sense of involvement in decision-making. A whole range of job-enrichment schemes were proposed, to combat the effects of alienation. Unions continued to oppose most forms of worker participation as a subtle form of speedup. On the other hand, employers often opposed job-enrichment schemes that opened the door to demands for increased worker control. Even if greater worker participation increased productivity—as all the experiments show—it also set a dangerous precedent. The Director of Employee Research and Training at General Motors stated in the *Harvard Business Review* that once workers began participating, they would not necessarily want to limit themselves to "those few matters that management considers to be of direct, personal interest to employees." Once workers demonstrated competence in one area, "and after participation has become a conscious, officially sponsored activity, participators may very well want to go on to topics of job assignment, the allocation of rewards or even the selection of leadership." In other words, increased participation could make "management's present monopoly" of control an issue of contention.

The cynicism of union leaders toward worker participation is easy to understand. Nonetheless, the general lack of concern about control has increased tension between union officials and the rank-and-file, who are more concerned with issues of freedom and authority. The HEW report *Work in America* concluded that by the end of the sixties large numbers of workers had become profoundly discontented with the limits of collective bargaining. Contracts covering wages, hours, and benefits were not sufficient. "Young workers who are rebelling against the drudgery of routine jobs are also rebelling against what they feel is 'unresponsive' and 'irrelevant' union leadership," the report concluded.

By the end of the seventies, the House of Labor was in profound crisis. The optimism surrounding the merger of the AFL and CIO in 1955 proved to be ill-founded, as the combined forces of labor declined thereafter and retreated more than ever into conservative business unionism. By 1956, industrial union membership seemed to have reached its limit, as most labor organizations withdrew from efforts to organize the unorganized. Ambitious Congressmen used charges of union corruption to turn public opinion against the unions and against labor leaders like Jimmy Hoffa of the Teamsters, who had connections with organized crime. A result was the Landrum-Griffin Act of 1959. Ostensibly designed to prevent union racketeering and protect internal democracy, the Act gratuitously incorporated a number of serious restrictions on picketing rights and outlawed secondary boycotts entirely. Congressional investigators blamed union corruption on a few dishonest men, but racketeering had been built into certain industries for decades. Employers were anxious to corrupt union leaders when a payoff could assure quick movement of cargo or prevent a strike in a competitive industry. There was little overt corruption in big industrial unions, because payoffs were not really as necessary as they were in industries like trucking and longshoring.

Industry-wide collective bargaining worked better all-around in the less competitive industries like auto, steel, and rubber, where labor costs could be passed along to consumers in the form of higher prices. In industries like coal mining and clothing manufacture, union contracts tended to encourage monopoly conditions by accepting large-scale mechanization, wage increases, and fringe benefits smaller firms could not afford. The needle-trades unions continued to demand fixed prices for various grades of clothing, so that smaller manufacturers could not break into the business and create harmful competition. In addition to policing the industry, unions like the ILGWU also engaged in joint promotional campaigns with employers to stimulate demands for their products. They also lobbied aggressively for trade restrictions on garments manufactured abroad. The ILGWU's "Buy American" campaign resulted in jingoist attacks on foreign labor that harked back to the primitive days of the labor movement. Ironically, the protectionist strategy to save United States jobs from foreign competition led to criticisms of the very countries whose anti-Communist regimes were supported by Cold War leaders of the ILGWU and other unions. The "my industry first" attitude seemed to coincide with the "my country first" attitude of the fifties. The whole strategy of protectionism was undermined by U.S. imperialism, however. By supporting American expansionism abroad, labor leaders helped to support reactionary regimes in places like Taiwan, South Korea, and the Philippines, to which U.S. manufacturers exported domestic jobs.

After expelling the left-led unions in 1949, the CIO joined the International Confederation of Free Trade Unions, formed largely through the efforts of the State Department and the Central Intelligence Agency. Later, various unions cooperated with the Inter-American Regional Organization of Workers (ORIT), whose agents attempted to subvert leftist unions and to create conservative labor organizations in Latin America. These agents not only undermined aggressive unions abroad; they worked hand-in-glove with corporations, including U.S.-owned firms, to foster peaceful industrial relations. When the ORIT endorsed the overthrow of a popularly elected leftist government in Guatemala, Emil Mazey of the UAW and a few other CIO leaders questioned the decision to make conditions more favorable to U.S. corporate expansion abroad. But most AFL and CIO leaders seemed, like the U.S. Marines, to be dedicated to making the world safe for the United Fruit Company and other corporations. Support for Cold War expansionism did not, however, increase organized labor's political clout in Washington. Jobs continued to flow out of this country, often to underdeveloped countries, and foreign-made goods continued to undercut U.S.-made products, despite AFL and CIO attempts to lobby for protective legislation.

Led by George Meany, a New York building-trades lobbyist who was elected president of the newly amalgamated AFL-CIO in 1955, most top labor leaders combined Cold War chauvinism with domestic conservatism. The expulsion and repression of the leftist unions not only removed critics of the Cold War, it eliminated critics of the drift toward accommodation in industrial relations. The decline of the "social unionism" that originated in the 1930's made way for revived business unionism. AFL and CIO leaders generally surrendered to market forces and the power of the giant corporations. Principles of solidarity seemed antiquated. The job security of newer workers could be sacrificed to protect workers with seniority. American jobs had to be protected at all cost, even if it meant support for policies that suppressed militant trade unionism abroad and weakened "social unionism" at home.

By the end of the seventies, the House of Labor was in a serious crisis. The tensions between leadership and membership increased over control issues. The character of the union leadership was itself an issue. George Meany, who held the AFL-CIO presidency from the 1955 merger until 1979, retired at the age of eighty-five. Like many union bosses, he clung to power and refused to open the door to younger leaders with new ideas. Meany and his allies, who dominated the AFL-CIO after 1955, clung to conservative business-union practices and Cold War policies long after they had proven ineffective. The conservative labor establishment's support for the unpopular Vietnam War began to create serious dissent in the late 1960's. When Walter Reuther took the UAW out of the AFL-CIO in 1968, he criticized the Meany leadership for its lack of "social vision, the dynamic thrust and crusading spirit that should characterize the progressive, modern labor movement." It appeared that the spirit of the early industrial unions might be revived. Reuther failed in his attempts to join with the Teamsters and other independents to form a powerful new labor federation. The UAW and the Teamsters were themselves tied too closely to the old order. When Reuther died in a 1970 plane crash, no one in the labor movement could challenge Meany's leadership.

Organized labor's internal problems were magnified by external threats. New technology and plant migration cut into union strength in industrialized areas. The economic crisis of the 1970's allowed both public and private employers to take the initiative against unionized workers, to the extent that the unions actually lost membership. Before we examine the effects of the recent crisis, we should look beyond the realm of organized labor to the wider world of work. For modern developments in corporate capitalism have led to major changes in the structure and composition of the work force.

Within the monopoly corporations, management has increased the division of labor. As Harry Braverman noted in *Labor and Monopoly Capital*, it has removed "all possible work" from the shop floor to the office, so that conception of a task is separated entirely from its execution. The growth of the office creates a "shadow replica of the entire production process in paper form" and "brings into being large technical and office staffs." The ratio of nonproduction employees to production workers in manufacturing increased from 19.5 per 100 in 1947 to 40.6 per 100 in 1975. In addition to a growing number of supervisors, engineers, technicians, and personnel experts, vast numbers of clerical workers engaged in what Braverman called a "ghostly form of production" as management "functions of control" increased dramatically and became production processes in themselves. In the modern corporation, paperwork has become essential to production, just as it is to administration and marketing. It is not surprising, then, that clerical work increased faster than any other occupation. While production workers lost jobs in manufacturing during the fifties and sixties, the number of stenographers and typists in the total work force more than doubled, from 1.6 to 3.9 million. Because they had become so important to the operation of the modern corporations, these office workers were subjected to the same scientific management imposed on factory operatives. Once regarded as relatively privileged white-collar workers, they now labor in large "pools," under close supervision. As early as 1951, C. Wright Mills explained in *White Collar* that office and sales work had been extensively mechanized. With an increasing division of labor, the level of skill required in white-collar jobs had been reduced. While differences among personnel were evened out, bureaucratic control increased through the creation of an office hierarchy, based, as Mills observed, "upon the power and authority held by the managerial cadre, rather than upon levels of skills."

Most office workers were drawn from what economists call the secondary or subordinate labor market. Workers who sold their labor power in this market were largely women and nonwhite men, who had fewer skills and less education than most of the workers in the primary labor market, who were predominantly white males. The first group rarely enjoyed union protection, whereas those who labored in the primary sector usually did belong to industrial or craft unions. This segmentation of the labor market is not new. Industrialists exploited the secondary labor market when they first started hiring women in textile mills and black or immigrant workingmen in steel mills. The classic "casual" labor market was characterized by low job security, poor wages, lack of opportunity for advancement, and a high degree of transiency. In modern days, casual labor still faced these conditions in the agricultural industry and in the competitive manufacturing industry, where high labor costs cut directly into profits. But the nature of the secondary labor market has changed drastically in the twentieth century. It is now dominated by clerical and service workers, most of them female. Offices, hospitals, computer companies, restaurants, and other service industries draw labor power from what is essentially a low-wage female labor market. Overall, the number of service workers increased nine times since 1900, and doubled from 4.5 to 9.0 million between 1950 and 1970. To these millions we should add some 3 million workers who in 1970 worked for wages in retail sales and performed similar service roles.

Employment in retail trade has boomed as a result of increased installment buying, the growth of suburban shopping malls, and the permeation of the media with advertising. Service employment has grown for other reasons as well. The decline of community and the rise of individual consumption first noticed by the Lynds in the 1920's reached new levels in the post-war years. In fact, Braverman contended, a kind of "universal market" now enveloped society, so that workers, alienated from their jobs, depend more and more on the market in their leisure and personal lives. Corporations have invaded this realm with profit-making enterprises producing everything from televised sports to drugs. The market invades personal and social life, just when people are more and more dependent on services once provided by family, community, and charity. As family members work more and more outside the home, Braverman observed, they "become less and less able to care for each other in times of need, and as the ties of neighborhood, community, and friendship are reinterpreted on a narrower scale . . . the care of humans . . . becomes more institutionalized."

Ironically, affluence has not created independence. On the contrary, more and more people, especially the physically and mentally ill, now depend on service workers. While most of the service employment remains in the public sector, there has been an enormous growth in the private, profit-making service sector, not only in health care, but in private security, recreation, entertainment, repair and scores of other "unproductive" enterprises. During the 1970's, the fiscal crisis of the cities and states has led to the closing of many public facilities, or to the "deinstitutionalization" of many services, so that the profit-making sector has expanded at the expense of the public sector.

In order to understand the relative positions of the unionized worker in the primary labor market and the unorganized, unskilled worker in the subordinate or secondary labor market, we must see how and why the composition of the working class changed. The table below shows that the clerical and service sectors have increased much faster than the industrial sectors. Operatives and laborers declined from about half the working class in 1900 to about one third in 1970. Skilled craftsmen also decreased in proportion to the rest of the proletariat. Clerical workers jumped from 5 to 26 percent of the wage-earning work force. As the number of farmers declined, the overall size of the proletariat grew from roughly half of the labor force to nearly 70 percent in seventy years.

WORKERS IN MILLIONS, 1910–1970

	1900	1910	1920	1930	1940	1950	1960	1970
Operatives and Laborers	7.3	9.9	11.5	13.0	14.4	15.5	16.4	18.1
Craftsmen	2.9	4.0	5.0	5.7	5.6	7.3	8.0	9.5
Clericals	.9	2.0	3.4	4.3	5.0	7.1	9.6	14.3
Service and Sales Workers	3.6	4.9	4.9	7.3	8.8	8.7	10.6	13.4
Total	14.7	20.8	24.8	30.3	33.8	38.6	44.6	55.3
Workers as a *percentage* of total labor force	50.7	55.8	58.8	62.2	65.4	66.7	69.1	69.1

The wage-labor market, on which more and more people became dependent, was highly segmented. Some of the old divisions based on skill and nationality had been eliminated. For example, the distinction between skilled, native-born steelworkers and unskilled, immigrant laborers diminished with changes in the steel industry and the unity created by CIO organizing. By the 1970's, white working-class "ethnics," as they were called, seemed to have many things in common. As a result of labor struggles, many enjoyed the benefits and protec-

tions characteristic of the primary labor market. This traditional proletariat differed from the growing mass of unskilled, low-wage workers
in the secondary labor market, where jobs offered less security and opportunity for advancement.

This subordinate labor market has expanded since World War II as
millions of new workers entered the labor force without skills, job
training, or union protection. The secondary labor market consisted of
a variety of people. Young men and women increased as a proportion
of the labor force, even though more and more of them attended
college in the fifties and sixties. Blacks continued to leave the South
after the collapse of the cotton-plantation system in the 1940's. The
black population in the South dropped from 5.4 million to 4.8 million
in the fifties, and increased by 2.7 million in the North and West.
Overall, this population grew by 6.5 million between 1950 and 1966,
with 98 percent of the growth occurring in urban areas. During the sixties black birthrates remained much higher than white rates, so that the
black population increased twice as fast as the white population. With
the liberalization of immigration laws in 1965, people from foreign
countries added new millions to the subordinate labor market. In addition to thousands of new immigrants from Mexico (including many
super-exploited illegal aliens), immigration from the Caribbean, Asia,
and Europe doubled between 1965 and 1970. The yearly average of
migrants from Puerto Rico to the United States multiplied six times
between the 1950's and the 1960's.

Women comprised the largest group in the secondary labor market.
In 1950, 18.4 million women worked for wages; by 1976, their
numbers had swelled to 38.4 million, or 40 percent of the work force.
By 1974, more than half of the mothers with school-aged children
worked outside the home. While unprecedented numbers of married
women went to work, the demands placed on them as wives and
mothers had not diminished. Even with more household appliances,
convenience foods, and ready-to-wear clothing, women spent a bit
more time on housework in the 1960's than they had in the 1920's,
because standards of cleanliness and efficiency rose and new tasks
were added to the household routine. Studies of family time schedules
in the 1970's show that a typical working woman devoted at least
thirty hours a week to housework, extending her work week to as
much as seventy-five hours. Women are said to have come "a long
way," especially in the professions, but even college-educated women
still had a long way to go. Although 70 percent of college-educated
women in the seventies worked, 20 percent labored in clerical, sales,
or factory jobs, and, overall, they earned only 51 percent of what men

with degrees earned. In any case, the vast majority of working women remained secondary wage earners in traditional "women's jobs," holding down 55 percent of the positions in retail trade, 79 percent in office work, and 80 percent in medical services. Some racial differences remained. More black women worked and headed their own families than white women, but a significant convergence began to occur in both respects as labor-force participation rates of Anglo, Mexican, and Afro-American women fell between 44 and 50 percent in 1976.

During the 1940's and 1950's, the new domestic ideology advocated by baby doctors, child psychologists, and others placed extraordinary new demands on mothers. This ideology had not disappeared by the seventies, even though women were limiting the size of their families and depended more on child care outside the home. A "supermom" could work full-time in the office or factory and still meet all of her children's demands. Employers, public and private, contended that working mothers were still primarily responsible for child care, and refused to meet the widespread demand for adequate, inexpensive day care. Working women depended largely on family and community networks for affordable child care, though the breakup of urban working-class neighborhoods disrupted such networks. For single women with children—whose numbers doubled between 1950 and 1976—the cost of child care became an all-consuming emotional and financial preoccupation. Filmmakers sensitive to the plight of the single working woman even made a few of them heroines in films like *Alice Doesn't Live Here Anymore* and *Norma Rae.*

Married women who worked found it more difficult to find satisfaction in a dual role which made them primarily wives and mothers and secondarily wage earners. Betty Friedan exposed the contradictions in *The Feminine Mystique.* In the next decade, working-class women themselves expressed anger at the oppressiveness of women's sphere at home and at work. And their complaints sounded remarkably similar to those of their middle-class feminist sisters. During the mid-seventies, Lillian Breslow Rubin interviewed fifty white working-class couples and reported her findings in *Worlds of Pain: Life in the Working-Class Family.* In general, these people felt that the "good life" had eluded them, even though they had worked hard. Consumer goods brought burdens as well as pleasures. The bills kept coming in faster than the money. "Wages were increasing, but never quite as fast as prices," Rubin observed. "There was little free time in which to enjoy the prized possessions since it took the combined income of husband and wife plus every hour of overtime pay they could get just to stay even.'' As a result of the recession of 1974, median income actually dropped 5 percent when adjusted for the effect of inflation. Rubin's interviews reflected the tensions arising in working-class family life at the end of a period of income growth. The tensions she found were also of long-term social origins.

Changing expectations of married life produced new strains in the homes of blue-collar workers. As more women entered the work force in response to the increasing demand for their labor, fewer depended solely on marriage for economic support. Rising separation rates in the 1970's correlated directly with increased labor-force participation. According to Rubin's findings, many working-class women saw marriage not so much as an "economic arrangement" but more as a relationship in which "emotional needs" were "attended to and met." As this aspect of marriage became paramount, and as women contributed more than ever to the family income, the traditional segregation of roles became less acceptable. Segregation was most profound in working-class families. Tensions were strongest among blue-collar wives who stepped out of their traditional roles, and whose husbands were asked to step out of their singular role as providers. As Rubin explains, expectations are changing. "Suddenly, new dreams are stirring," she writes. *"Intimacy, companionship, sharing*—these are now the words working-class women speak to their men, words that turn *both* their worlds upside down!''

A number of forces brought more women into the secondary labor market during the past three decades: smaller families, made easier by contraception and legalized abortion; the rising cost of living for working-class families; the desire of isolated suburban housewives for companionship; and the expansion of jobs in the clerical and service sectors. Women did not generally enter the labor market to compete for men's jobs. Rather, they competed for work in a distinctly female labor market. Women's increased participation in the labor force did not alter the sex segregation of occupations. Racial segregation of jobs decreased after 1950, but statisticians showed that male and female workers remained as segregated as they were in 1900. Sex segregation appeared most clearly in office work. In 1975, 97 percent of all typists and 99 percent of all secretaries were women. Service jobs were almost as feminized. And women still dominated certain professions, such as nursing and elementary-school teaching. Sex-typing of jobs often resulted from employers' efforts to exploit female sexuality. Attractiveness remained the most important criterion for hiring waitresses, receptionists, and airline stewardesses. Other occupations were restricted to women because they were extensions of the work women had always done in the home—cleaning, cooking, serving food, caring for children, and so on. Employers also believed that women's socialization prepared them for certain jobs that required patience and politeness. As a result, certain service jobs that involve dealing with the public—selling goods and operating a telephone switchboard, for example—became more feminized than ever.

One effect of women's massive participation in the labor market was that sexual segregation and wage discrimination became much more obvious. Feminist groups like the National Organization of Women exposed the effects of sexism in the 1960's. In 1960, over 40 percent of all women worked in jobs requiring an education, but still earned less than men with the same level of education. Sex segregation allowed employers to disregard women's education and training and set wages according to sex. Equal-pay legislation in 1963 allowed women to bring discrimination suits if they received less than men for the same work, but job segregation was so pervasive that few suits could be won. Working women, even those with education, found it difficult to break out of the job ghetto because they were still saddled with traditional homemaking responsibilities. By the fifties, over one third of all wage-earning women had to care for school-age children. This double duty forced many women to work in part-time jobs and made it more difficult for them to compete with men for higher-paying jobs. By the 1970's, the gap between average male and female earnings was actually widening, due partly to the economic crisis, which hit the secondary labor market hardest. In 1955, women earned 64 percent of what men earned, but by 1974, a recession year, this proportion had dropped to 57 percent. These figures led the Department of Labor to state: "Despite the fact that increasing numbers of women are securing high-level better-paying positions, there is still a predominance of women in lower-status occupations of a traditional nature which provide limited opportunity for advancement." "In sum," notes historian Mary Ryan, "the quantum leap in women's participation occasioned a more multifaceted and widespread pattern of sexual inequality. It welcomed females into secondary jobs outside the home, where they contributed immeasurably to the expansion of the economy and enhanced the profit margin of their employers, without offering equivalent rewards to the women themselves."

Jobs in the secondary labor market are not only low-paying, dead-end jobs. They are also subjected to an extreme division of labor and a high degree of mechanization. Thus, women's work tends to be particularly alienating. For example, journalist Elinor Langer showed in 1971 that women in the New York Telephone Company were under constant supervision while performing highly "programmed" and highly subdivided communications tasks. The system aimed at nothing less than turning human workers into machines. In addition to the constant observation, in which there was a ratio of three supervisors for every job, the system aimed at "keeping intelligence suppressed and channeling it into idiotic paths" through the "scientific" division of jobs into "banal components." Women in the telephone company found their union of little value in battling alienation, and resorted to work stoppages and work sharing when they were desperate.

Besides the alienating effects of bureaucratic and scientific management, workers in the secondary labor market suffer from unemployment. Black men, who are still restricted mainly to the casual or subordinate labor market, have consistently experienced double the joblessness of white men. Unemployment for black and other nonwhite men averaged 10.6 percent between 1955 and 1959, as compared to 4.3 percent among whites; this differential held during the sixties as the first group experienced 8.4 percent joblessness as compared to 3.8 percent for the second group. The rate of joblessness for nonwhite women was higher than for men, but the racial differential was not as great. Racial minorities fared even worse in the prosperous years of the fifties and sixties if under-employment is taken into account. The "under-employed" include part-time workers looking for full-time work, full-time employees earning less than $3,000 a year, and those who dropped out of the labor force entirely. The 1968 report of the U.S. Commission on Civil Disorders pointed to joblessness as a key cause of ghetto poverty and frustration and indicated that in addition to the 318,000 blacks unemployed in the central cities, another 716,000 were under-employed. The civil-rights movement that emerged from the South in the 1950's was primarily a protest against segregation in schools and other public facilities and against the disenfranchisement of black voters. But since the freedom movement directly confronted racist institutions and values, it struck at the main forces of segregation in the South and the North that kept black workers restricted to the subordinate labor market. The Civil Rights Act of 1964 established a Fair Employment Opportunity Commission and prohibited racial discrimination by employers as well as unions. During the late sixties, the growth of the economy, stimulated by military spending for the Vietnam War, reduced unemployment and created increased demand for black labor. These developments, combined with the pressure of the civil-rights movement, allowed more black workers to move into government jobs and into unionized industrial jobs. As a result, some improvement occurred in the relative distribution of income between the races, but the deprivation of black people still remained glaringly obvious. Overall, 40.6 percent of the nation's blacks lived in poverty, according to the Social Security definition, as compared to 11.9 percent of all whites.

Racial discrimination, then, prevailed throughout the labor market. In examining the "political economy of racism," Harold M. Baron indicated that a "dual labor market" functioned to "create an urban-based industrial reserve army," providing a ready supply of workers in a period of labor shortage like the 1960's. This labor market existed as part of a larger "complex of institutional control" constituting what Baron calls "the web of urban racism." The highly profitable dual labor market coexisted with a segregated housing market, educational system, and political apparatus, over which black people themselves had little control.

The civil-rights movement, the ghetto strife of the mid-sixties, and the demands for black power indicated that a major portion of the industrial reserve could not be controlled. The state, especially at the federal level, was forced to create many costly programs to quell black discontent. In some cases, however, the existence of these programs only fostered more turmoil. Black welfare mothers, for example, created a militant movement to demand the full compensation to which they were entitled by law. These women, previously regarded as the most dependent group in the labor force, became surprisingly independent and well organized. By adopting the tactics of disruption and disobedience, "welfare mothers" increased the "social wage" paid by the state to keep them off the labor market.

The welfare-rights movement indicated that women in the subordinate labor market could organize themselves very effectively, even without significant financial resources. While "welfare mothers" made increasing demands on the state for a greater social wage, black women in low-paying service jobs were also making more militant demands. In 1969, a bitter strike of black hospital workers erupted in Charleston, South Carolina. The walkout was organized by Local 1199 of the Drug and Hospital Workers, whose progressive leaders had unionized many health-care workers in New York. The Charleston hospital workers' struggle combined the spirit of the civil-rights movement with the old-fashioned militancy of the 1930's labor movement.

Like white women in clerical and health jobs, black women in the private service sector found it difficult to obtain union protection. Most of the gains women and blacks made through unions came in the public sector, which expanded enormously in the post-war era as the state assumed more and more social and economic responsibilities.

The percentage of federal jobs held by blacks rose from 7 percent in 1944 to 16 percent in 1975. Though most nonwhites held lower-paid, lower-grade civil-service positions, they did benefit from union protection. In 1962, President John F. Kennedy signed Executive Order 10988 allowing for collective bargaining by federal employees. During the next two decades, government workers joined unions in large numbers. The membership of the American Federation of Government Employees jumped from 196,000 in 1967 to 482,000 in 1969. All public employees felt the effects of inflation and found that their wages compared poorly with those of union workers in the private sector. They also demanded more respect from the public bureaucracies they served.

By the mid-sixties, the image of the docile public worker had been shattered. Municipal employees were particularly hard-pressed and increasingly militant. During the fifties, strikes by government employees were rare, but in the following decade 119 walkouts occurred in the public sector, involving 70,000 workers. The strikers ranged from professionals, especially teachers and nurses, to blue-collar workers such as garbage collectors and fire fighters. Violating laws that prohibited public employees from striking, the American Federation of Teachers adopted militant tactics and gained thousands of new members. The American Federation of State, County, and Municipal Employees (AFSCME) also used the strike effectively, increasing its membership from 182,000 in 1960 to 350,000 in 1967. Since AFSCME organized large numbers of blue-collar workers, service employees in hospitals, and clerical workers, it included many black members and a number of outstanding black leaders like Lillian Roberts and William Lucy. In 1968, the predominantly black sanitation workers of Memphis, who were represented by AFSCME, struck against the city. The strikers demanded higher wages but also wanted an end to the bureaucratic oppression that violated their human rights. They carried signs that read: "I AM A MAN." Martin Luther King, the greatest human-rights leader of the post-war era, immediately came to Memphis to support the strikers, and it was there that he was assassinated. King was still trying to build an alliance between the unions and the civil-rights movement when he died. The victory of the Memphis sanitation men was of course the result of that alliance.

The black workers in Memphis were striking for dignity as well as higher wages. City workers faced increasing job pressures during the sixties, whether they were bus drivers wrestling with poor equipment, teachers contending with growing classroom violence, or mental-health workers dealing with the large numbers of people who could not cope with the urban "rat race." While public employees absorbed the human and social effects of urban disintegration, they also faced increased demands for productivity and efficiency. As public-sector bureaucrats adopted strategies for control used in the private sector, government workers rebelled. Public-school teachers, who had enjoyed a good deal of control on their jobs, fought to remain in charge of their classrooms and to reduce the power of administrators. By the end of the sixties, public employee unions had become powerful, especially in large cities, where they wielded significant political clout. Some analysts of public administration worried that strong public employee unions had won contractual concessions that gave workers too much control over working conditions and prevented administrators from increasing productivity. A few unions did exert significant control over public bureaucracies and could resist the intensification of work that continued in the private sector. As a result, demands for productivity in the public sector increased as recession hit during the Nixon Administration in the early 1970's. As wage inflation in the state sector grew, politicians, businessmen, and many taxpayers blamed the public-service unions for the fiscal crisis of the state in the 1970's, even though wage increases for public workers lagged behind those of unionized industrial workers.

After a decade of relative improvement in wages and working conditions, government workers were thrown on the defensive in the seventies as the state clamped down on wage demands, cut services, and reduced payrolls, while implementing a variety of schemes to increase productivity. In New York, where the fiscal crisis assumed its most alarming proportions during the mid-seventies, public workers engaged in militant wildcat strikes to prevent massive layoffs. These strikes, which tied up New York City in 1975, could not prevent layoffs, however, nor did they prevent a three-year wage freeze declared by the anti-labor Financial Control Board. By 1976, the largest public-sector unions in New York invested their own pension funds in the city notes and bonds that had been dumped by the same banks who precipitated the fiscal crisis. The unions accepted the wage freeze and productivity deals in order to save the city from bankruptcy. By the end of the decade, real wages for public-sector employees were falling, and once-militant union leaders were calling for moderation because they feared that strike actions would lead to further cuts.

The gains black working people made during the sixties ended with the crisis of the seventies, a time when many losses were sustained. Welfare recipients suffered from the effects of inflation and from actual cuts in vital services. Layoffs hit major industries like steel and auto which employed black workers, and despite complaints of favoritism toward minorities, these workers were the first to be fired. It was not a surprise, therefore, when the Department of Labor announced in 1977 that the gap between black and white earnings had actually widened. In 1969, black families earned 61 percent of the income earned by whites; eight years later, this figure had dropped to 57 percent.

As James O'Connor noted in *The Fiscal Crisis of the State,* government policies that had ensured post-war capitalist growth began to create serious problems for the whole political and economic system during the late sixties. Corporate capitalism depended on labor stability and productivity in the monopoly sector, U.S. world hegemony and overseas economic expansion, and the growth of a state sector that would socialize various costs of production for the monopoly sector such as welfare, social security, transportation, research and development, and education. These activities caused inflation, especially during the war in Southeast Asia, when military spending absorbed additional billions of dollars. Since political leaders were afraid to pay for increased costs through a proportionate increase in taxes, a fiscal crisis emerged as government expenses exceeded revenues. At the same time, the United States suffered major defeats in Asia and lost some of its power to police the world. The balance of trade continued to shift in favor of rival capitalist countries. The Nixon Administration responded to this first phase of the crisis by engineering a recession in 1969–70 to check inflation. In 1971, Nixon declared a New Economic Policy based on wage and price control to limit the incomes of unionized workers. The Republican Administration then created a National Commission on Productivity to promote new labor-saving technology and to eliminate union-contract provisions that restricted productivity in any way. More welfare recipients were required to work in order to receive payments, thus increasing the size of the secondary labor market at a time when unemployment rates reached nearly 5 percent. These policies enhanced employers' ability to manipulate the subordinate labor market and to threaten unionized workers in the primary labor market.

The recession of 1974–75 threw millions of people out of work. Official unemployment figures reached 9 percent early in 1975, but the actual rate was probably one and a half to two times as high. The Administration actually encouraged the recession by cutting federal spending. A deep recession, it was believed, would cut inflation. In the aftermath, inflation did fall from 7.0 percent in 1975 to 4.8 percent in 1976. But by the time Jimmy Carter's Democratic Administration took power in early 1977, inflation was back up to 6.8 percent. During the first seven months of 1979, it averaged 13 percent, and by the decade's end, the crisis of the seventies threatened to become even worse in the 1980's.

During the 1970's, the House of Labor began to reflect the general crisis that prevailed within the world of the worker. Labor-union membership rose gradually from 17.5 million in 1956 to 19.4 million in 1970, largely as a result of public-service union organizing. This growth in unions did not keep pace, however, with the expansion of the work force, so that the percentage of organized non-agricultural laborers dropped from 33 to 27 percent during the same period. As a result of the economic crisis of the 1970's, unions suffered many losses. Layoffs, plant migrations, shop closings, all undermined union strength. In addition, corporations spent an estimated $100 million annually to defeat unions in NLRB elections and to prevent elections. Corporations like J. P. Stevens also hired high-priced lawyers to tie up the NLRB procedure so that they did not have to actually bargain with unions. As a result, unions lost 346,000 members between 1974 and 1976, and the percentage of the industrial work force belonging to unions dropped to the lowest point since the late 1930's.

Organized labor also seemed to lose its clout in government. AFL-CIO lobbyists failed to achieve much-needed labor reforms during the late 1970's, despite the fact that the Democrats controlled the White House and had an overwhelming majority in Congress. As a result of the deepening crisis, a number of liberal labor leaders, notably William Winpisinger of the Machinists and Douglas Fraser of the Auto Workers, called for a new progressive alliance to push the Democrats to the left. In one sense, the call for a politically revived labor movement was a defensive response to the rise of the anti-union "new right" and the decline of the unions' clout in government. In another sense, it was an attempt to bring the unions' outmoded policy demands in line with more advanced programs of European trade unions which had gained many reforms, from socialized medicine to effective mine-safety regulations, through social-democratic and Communist parties. Winpisinger, who joined Michael Harrington, the socialist intellectual, Victor Reuther, and other union reformers, as a leader of the Democratic Socialist Organizing Committee, even challenged organized labor's Cold War accommodation to the military-industrial complex. Though his own members' jobs were at stake, the IAM president questioned the social value of billion-dollar defense budgets and the safety of nuclear-power plants. These views, which no labor leader would have expressed in the sixties, reflected the new concerns of rank-and-file workers, especially younger men and women who had been sympathetic to the anti-war and environmental movements. However, Winpisinger, Fraser, and the other social democrats opposed militant insurgents within their own ranks, and made no effort to include rank-and-file leaders in their progressive coalition.

Many forces converged on the workers' world in the seventies, calling forth a defensive response. The highest rates of unemployment since the Depression, cutbacks in welfare and other social services, and double-digit inflation focused workers' concerns on survival. The fear of layoffs and plant closings increased the concerns of many workers. An elderly labor hierarchy, troubled by economic threats and lack of power in government, provided little aggressive leadership. Even the dynamic sectors of the union movement, the public-service unions and the United Farm Workers, found it difficult to move forward in the seventies. A series of troubling social issues—affirmative action, abortion, tax cuts, and school desegregation—seemed to heighten divisions among workers. As political leadership moved to the right, it seemed as though workers were becoming much more conservative.

A look at the economic, social, and political events of the 1970's makes it difficult to understand the high incidence of workers' rights campaigns that occurred in those years. From the unprecedented health and safety movement begun by the coal miners to the revived women's-rights struggle on the job, movements seemed to take on lives of their own. Like the great workers'-rights movements of the early 1930's, the various expressions of struggle in the 1970's ran against the economic grain. The notable aspect of workers' activity in the past decade is that it ran against the political grain as well. Millions of new workers entered the workplace with different hopes, fears, and ideas from those of their parents. They found life frightening in the 1970's. Workers worried about industrial pollutants and accidents, fuel crises and nuclear-power accidents, as well as perennial problems such as layoffs and plant closings. The world seemed out of control. Some responded by reasserting old rights and demanding new freedoms in an attempt to regain some control over a world that seemed bent on its own destruction.

The black struggle for equality has had a significant effect on the labor movement in the post-war period. A. Philip Randolph and the NAACP scored some victories within the AFL-CIO during the peak of the civil-rights movement from 1959 to 1963, when the federal government began to pressure the unions on discrimination issues. The Civil Rights Act of 1964 promised a new era for black workers, but it has not been used to guarantee real equality of opportunity for all races. Martin Luther King, Jr., sought to forge an alliance between the civil-rights movement and liberal labor leaders such as Walter Reuther, but the ghetto rebellions, the black power movement, and King's assassination prevented that alliance from developing. Indeed, Reuther faced a black power rebellion in his own union. A new generation of black production workers was angered by the racism they experienced in their union and especially in the auto "plantations." Radicalized by the black power movement and the brutal suppression of the Detroit ghetto uprising of 1967, militants formed the Dodge Revolutionary Union Movement (DRUM) after a wildcat strike at the Dodge Main Plant in May 1968. Several groups later came together with DRUM to form the League of Revolutionary Black Workers. Like the Black Panthers, who were active in the inner cities at the time, the League combined black nationalism and Marxism in condemning racism as well as capitalism. The UAW, whose leaders had supported the civil-rights movement, was attacked as part of the white power structure. In other cities, black workers also fought for autonomy by forming all-black caucuses within their unions or creating their own unions to break into industries controlled by white unions. While some white labor leaders used these militant demands to press for an extension of the civil-rights movement, others joined the white backlash against minority demands. During the seventies, black leaders have become more prominent in a few industrial unions like the Packinghouse Workers and especially in public-service unions like AFSCME. In 1972, these leaders gathered in Washington and formed the Coalition of Black Trade Unionists, to "enhance black power and influence in the labor movement."

The economic crisis and the decline of the civil-rights and black power movement made it difficult to increase black influence in the unions, however. Black workers in some unions still turned to the federal government instead of union leaders in an effort to gain equal rights and equal opportunities. In 1971, black workers at the Sparrows Point plant of Bethlehem Steel brought suit against the company and their own union (the United Steelworkers) for racial discrimination. This suit led the Labor Department to issue orders prohibiting separate white and black seniority lists that kept blacks out of better-paying skilled jobs. At the end of the decade, black workers, with or without union protection, continued to suffer widespread discrimination. And blacks still enjoyed much less influence in the unions than their numbers warranted. However, the equal-rights movement had made an impact. Some unions supported affirmative-action programs, even though white workers often objected to measures that threatened their positions, pay scales, or seniority rights. In 1979, the Supreme Court upheld the constitutionality of affirmative-action plans in the crucial Webber case. The Court accepted the legality of an affirmative-action job-training plan sponsored by the Kaiser Aluminum Company and the United Steel Workers Union to correct past discrimination. The decision was hailed by civil-rights groups.

The most important change in workers' rights of the decade resulted from the impact of the women's liberation movement. Like the civil-rights movement, which did not focus on the special needs of black women, the women's movement raised the hopes of oppressed workers in low-level jobs. It did so by opening up educational opportunities and by pressuring the government to ensure more equal job opportunities and to act against wage discrimination. Women organized themselves on the job and extended the traditional struggle for equal rights. In the seventies, feminists led campaigns for previously unrecognized women's rights such as paid pregnancy leaves, legalized abortions, and freedom from sexual harassment by male supervisors and co-workers. The feminist movement in the late sixties was led by college-educated professional women who had been active in civil-rights and anti-war movements. Within a few years, feminists were active in many workplaces. The women's movement stimulated more organizing among clerical workers than the unions had. Secretaries protested against mechanized, dehumanized working conditions, but they also organized against the male-dominated office hierarchy.

In *Not Servants, Not Machines: Office Workers Speak Out,* Jean Tepperman reviewed incidents of resistance and concluded that they "signify a growing trend" toward a "movement of office workers." "Starting slowly in the late sixties, office rebellions have become more and more frequent" and management publications have commented on the "increasing restiveness" of white-collar workers. Several groups of women clericals have formed in major cities, and some, like "9 to 5" in Boston, have become labor unions, but the vast majority still remain unorganized. The principal organizations serving these women workers are not unions but feminist groups. As the clerical workers' movement spread to major cities, several women's organizations formed to demand "rights and respect" for secretaries. Karen Nussbaum, one of the organizers of "9 to 5," went on to the national group called Working Women. She favors unionization among clericals but she also emphasizes the importance of feminist consciousness among working women. "Many women who come to us say 'I'm no women's libber' or 'I'm no joiner,' but . . . ," she said in 1979.

"The ideas of equality for women have seeped down and affected the lives of working women who were not involved in the women's movement."

The women's movement has had some impact within the House of Labor as more female workers have become unionized and have protested against sexism. The percentage of women in unions expanded from 18.5 percent in 1956 to 22.2 percent in 1976, during which time females accounted for about half of all new members. Despite this change, only 11 percent of all women workers belonged to unions. Women served in the top leadership of only nine unions. Frustrated with these limited gains, but hopeful that a new working women's movement could be fostered, labor unionists formed the Coalition of Labor Union Women (CLUW) in 1974. The leaders of unions officially supporting CLUW became alarmed at the radical demands of feminists and socialists, and therefore drew in the reins. Though the Coalition was less closely connected to the women's movement in the late seventies, its leaders did promote a feminist approach to workers' rights. In 1972, a new consciousness of women's rights spread to the unions when the AFL-CIO abandoned its traditional defense of protective legislation and endorsed the ratification of the Equal Rights Amendment.

Like the civil-rights movement, the women's rights movement attempted to take advantage of the 1964 Civil Rights Act. Activists centered their demands on Title VII, which prohibited discrimination on the basis of sex, color, race, religion, or national origin and which called for affirmative efforts by employers to provide equal opportunities for women and minorities. Title VII offered a strong legal mechanism for eliminating old protective legislation which had been used to keep women out of men's jobs. The Equal Employment Opportunity Commission, charged with enforcing Title VII, did win suits against some large corporations, like American Telephone and Telegraph, that resulted in settlements correcting past discrimination against women. A series of court cases based on Title VII also forced employers to hire women in jobs once restricted to men. Women plaintiffs had somewhat less success in challenging employment laws that discriminated against them for pregnancy. The women's movement has affected the law, government, and union policy, and most important, it has affected the consciousness of women workers and some of their male co-workers. However, the movement has not significantly altered the sex segregation in the labor market that restricts women to secondary status as wage earners, citizens, and human beings. More women are joining the labor movement as a way of protecting and extending their rights, but with nearly 90 percent of all working women still unorganized, other strategies are required. During the late seventies, as the economic crisis continued and unions declined, it became apparent that women would have to fight to defend their gains against the conservative, anti-feminist forces of the "new right." Unlike earlier defenders of the nuclear family, these reactionaries have not attacked women's entry into the labor force. Women in the wage market had become an irreversible necessity by 1980, but the "new right" has attacked the freedom of working mothers to make their own choices about wage earning and childbearing. Recent challenges to women's reproductive freedom take many forms, according to feminist historian Rosalind Petchesky—"the cutbacks in publicly supported child care; the abolition of publicly funded abortions . . . ; the nonreimbursement of abortion in many work-related health plans; the full coverage, on the other hand, of maternity costs; and even the policy of offering sterilization as the *only* alternative to losing one's job." These attacks, says Petchesky, are not intended primarily to make women full-time mothers, but rather to "make it impossible for women to control the conditions of their sexuality or to risk raising children without male support, outside the traditional family forms."

The fight to extend working women's reproductive rights emerged as part of the struggle for health and safety in the workplace. Traditionally, women trade unionists had advocated special protective legislation, but during the seventies they adopted the feminist argument for equal rights. Protective laws had traditionally been used to maintain sex segregation. In order to advance women's equal opportunity to job rights, groups like CLUW advocated equal protection for the health and safety of all workers, male and female. Otherwise, women could be excluded from certain jobs because they are pregnant or even for being of childbearing age. Some employers have even demanded that women be sterilized in order to retain high-paying jobs in dangerous jobs previously restricted to men. Olga Madar of the UAW, a founder of CLUW, put it this way in 1979:

> Industry prefers excluding a group with a problem rather than dealing with it. After the fertile women are removed, who will be next? Blacks who carry the sickle-cell anemia trait in their blood? Older male workers who have the highest probability of heart problems?

Predominantly male unions, like the United Steelworkers, are now supporting some feminist demands for reproductive rights. They are concerned about the violation of seniority rights involved in removing workers for health reasons, but they are also supporting the idea that men as well as women face job-related dangers to their reproductive organs. By rejecting paternalistic protective legislation, women have made the fight for health and safety rights into a much broader movement for workers' rights.

Workingmen and their unions have traditionally placed health and safety reforms low on their list of priorities. They have remained suspicious of industry-initiated laws, which never seem to be enforced. They have also objected to safety laws that might inhibit earnings on piecework jobs. Nineteenth-century values also inhibited workers' consciousness about health and safety. The ethos of manliness dictated courage in the face of danger. Protective laws were only required for women and children. Men would take their chances. The unions' voluntaristic philosophy, combined with a sense of fatalism, further reduced interest in state laws to protect health. The extension of industrial unionism and the effects of New Deal labor laws reduced work accident rates from the appalling level of the 1920's. Nonetheless, American industry remained far more dangerous than Eastern or Western European industry in the post-war years.

The movement for health and safety began during the late sixties among the coal miners, who continued to suffer most from hazardous working conditions. The movement became intimately involved with a struggle for rank-and-file members' democratic rights. In 1969, hundreds of coal miners, many of them organized into the Black Lung Association, marched on the state capitol in West Virginia to demand compensation for the disease. This demonstration stimulated a remarkable strike for a black-lung law as workers closed the state's coal mines. United Mine Workers' leaders, who were unresponsive to the safety issue, opposed this unprecedented wildcat. In the same year, Consolidation Coal Company's No. 9 mine near Farmington, West Virginia, exploded, killing seventy-eight workers; this disaster provoked further action, including lobbying for a national mine-safety act by the UMW's leaders, who played down rank-and-file pressure. The federal Coal Mine Health and Safety Act of 1969 included compensation for black lung, though miners would find it difficult to obtain compensation. The agitation for health rights in the UMW led to a campaign against the corrupt, dictatorial administration of W. A. "Tony" Boyle, who had succeeded John L. Lewis as president. Under Boyle's conservative leadership the UMW abandoned its militant tradition entirely. Needless to say, the union's officials showed little interest in health and safety.

The Black Lung Association actively supported the insurgent presidential candidacy of UMW reformer "Jock" Yablonski, who charged that Boyle was "in bed with the operators." Yablonski won wide-spread rank-and-file support for his campaign to democratize the UMW and improve health and safety conditions in the mines, but he lost the election to the incumbent, amid charges of vote fraud. On New Year's Eve 1969, Yablonski, his wife, and his daughter were murdered by gunmen, who, it was later discovered, acted on Boyle's orders. After the Yablonski funeral, the Miners for Democracy was organized by his sons and various union reformers. The MFD brought together a coalition composed of opposition elements from the Lewis years, young miners who had been active in many of the wildcat strikes over safety concerns and other issues, the Black Lung Association, and the Disabled Miners and Widows Group formed after a 1970 wildcat strike protesting lack of compensation for these two groups. When the Department of Labor ordered a new election of officers in 1972, Arnold Miller, a West Virginia miner with black lung, defeated Boyle with the support of the MFD. After Miller's victory, substantial democratic reforms swept aside the oligarchical policies and procedures introduced during Lewis's forty-year reign. With Miller's victory, the MFD and the Black Lung Association disbanded, and the rank-and-file movement relaxed. The UMW relied on lobbying to press for more protective laws from the state and federal governments.

In 1970, shortly after the miners' black-lung strike, the Nixon Administration, still courting blue-collar votes, created the Occupational Safety and Health Administration (OSHA). This kind of agency had been proposed by a few progressive labor leaders, by medical people in occupational health, and by Ralph Nader, the consumer advocate who had turned his attention to workers' rights issues. The existence of OSHA stimulated the health and safety movement in several unions and among worker groups in various industrial cities. The movement for occupational health and safety has been on the defensive as the government and courts have systematically weakened OSHA regulations. The Carolina Brown Lung Association, for example, failed in its efforts to gain safe cotton-dust standards in textile plants. Though the rank-and-file health-rights movement has declined, some unions have taken up the issue more actively. The Oil, Chemical and Atomic Workers Union struck Shell Oil in 1973 over safety issues, and supported the case of Karen Silkwood, a union activist and nuclear-plant technician who was killed en route to a meeting with a union official and a reporter in which she planned to reveal lack of safety in a Kerr-McGee nuclear-energy plant near Oklahoma City. In 1979, the courts found Kerr-McGee guilty of contaminating Silkwood's apartment and awarded a substantial settlement that established corporate liability for contamination from nuclear radiation. The Silkwood case has revived the struggle for health rights on the job and has helped to create more concern about the dangers of nuclear radiation. The health and safety movement expanded significantly during the 1970's to attack the traditional dangers faced by the coal miner and steelworker, and also newer issues like job stress on office workers and the reproductive rights of women workers.

During the past two decades, much of the impetus to extend workers' rights has come from outside the House of Labor, principally from the civil-rights and women's rights movements and from the more radical demands of black power advocates and feminists. Within the unions, workers' rights activity has usually begun at the base by rank-and-filers and their political allies. As a result, the old tension between leaders and members has reappeared, especially over the question of union democracy. In the case of the United Mine Workers, the health and safety movement helped the Miners for Democracy overthrow the old leadership. Arnold Miller's reform administration soon found itself in conflict with rank-and-file militants, however, as they continued to engage in wildcat strikes over safety issues and other grievances. In 1974, thousands of miners struck in opposition to the contract agreement. Wildcat strikes continued at a high level as young miners, including many Vietnam veterans, rebelled against authoritarian foremen and the breakdown of the grievance system. When the courts fined wildcatting miners in Kanawha County, West Virginia, a national walkout took place, and continued, despite Miller's opposition, until the courts withdrew their fines. Rank-and-file opposition to the Miller administration reached a new level during the long strike of 1977–78 as members rejected several contract proposals that would have dismantled the free medical care won after the great strike of 1946. They also objected to the willingness of union negotiators to sacrifice the right to strike during the term of the contract, a right rank-and-file miners frequently exercised to protect their safety. In fact, as the leadership showed its willingness to concede miners' basic rights to the owners, the rank-and-filers virtually took control of their own strike and held on for more than a hundred days. The 1977–78 miners' strike was a dramatic example of ordinary union members taking matters into their own hands.

The success of the Miners for Democracy in 1972 set off rank-and-file reform movements in other major unions. We have seen how the presidential campaign of Ed Sadlowski raised the issues of union democracy and workplace safety within the United Steelworkers Union in 1977. Sadlowski's Steelworkers Fight Back movement also raised the old demands for the right to vote on contract ratification, the improvement of grievance procedures and of contractual provisions for minority hiring. Like the rank-and-file miners, the insurgent steelworkers also oppose productivity deals written into no-strike contracts. Membership-rights movements have also emerged in other big unions, notably the International Brotherhood of Teamsters, in which the TDU (Teamsters for a Democratic Union) has gained widespread rank-and-file support in its efforts to topple corrupt, dictatorial officials in the union hierarchy.

Rank-and-file movements have found it difficult to dislodge the powerful political machines that control the international unions. Even in the UMW, where substantial democratization took place, rank-and-file militants complain about the excessive power of union bureaucrats. Nonetheless, the various insurgencies from below have greatly expanded workers' rights consciousness. And in some unions, top officials have responded to the increasing pressures from below, especially as the economic crisis heightens the need for new strategies and new policies.

The leaders of the steelworkers, auto workers, and other large industrial unions have slowly responded to members' concern over plant closings and shop migration. When the Campbell Works in Youngstown was shut down, a coalition of threatened steelworkers, community groups, and a few radical allies organized to reopen the works under worker-community ownership. The wave of plant closings throughout the industrial North has raised serious questions about the unions' ability to defend members' job rights. Some also criticized the courts' willingness to defend private property rights of corporations whose owners are concerned only with profitability and not with the economic security of the communities in which they have been located for years. Once again, union officials who accept the primacy of private-property rights have had to question their own assumptions, out of sheer necessity. In 1978, when the Heat Transfer Division of American Standard threatened to close down in Buffalo, the city AFL-CIO council voted to take over the plant and, if necessary, operate it under union direction. The crisis of the seventies has literally forced some workers to expand the frontier of control struggles to include ownership. Several plants in the Northeast have been kept open when the workers assumed ownership. The Steelworkers Union gave little support to the Youngstown plan to reopen the Campbell Works, but officials later showed more concern. When U.S. Steel announced the closing of several plants, including the Homestead Works, and the construction of a massive new facility in Conneaut, Ohio, several USW locals joined environmental groups and lodged a suit to stop the move. According to the newspaper of the Homestead local, the plaintiffs questioned the environmental and human impact of the new plant, and made a case for the modernization of mills in older steel communities. Implicitly, they asserted their own job rights and human rights against corporate property rights. Other industrial unions, influenced by their social democratic counterparts in Europe, have proposed legislation that would require companies to notify workers at least six months before a plant closing and to defend their decision before government agencies. In some versions of this legislation, the company must offer to sell the plant to workers or community groups. The crisis caused by plant migration has also raised serious questions about the Cold War policies of United States unions and about the viability of protectionist strategies. Auto companies, which have taken the lead in exporting jobs throughout the world, are now closing major plants in Detroit and other cities. There developments led Martin Gerber, the UAW's vice-president, to sound this note of alarm for the 1980's: "The real threat is the international mobility of capital. In the coming years we are going to have to move from an industrial union perspective to an international perspective," just as the labor movement once moved from craft to industrial unionism.

If a new strategy is required on an international level, equally radical changes must take place on the home front. Just as more workers, especially women and minorities, demand more protection from unions, labor organizations are reeling from one defeat to another. Old organizers look at the House of Labor in despair. The unions seem to be the prime victims of political apathy, economic dependency, and bureaucratic rigidity that has characterized the post-war era. The writings and musings of old militants who created the industrial unions call for a return to the rank-and-file creativity and militancy that increased workers' power in earlier times. Interviewed in 1976, Enrico Porente, an Italian-born pioneer of industrial unionism, reflected on his own work in the IWW, the Amalgamated Clothing Workers, and the CIO. He then called on ordinary workers to reassert themselves actively, and not to shrink from conflict.

The labor movement in this country is not the same labor movement it was. There was class struggle; now everything is agreement. The labor movement needs a third renaissance, a third "risorgimento." The first was in 1905 with the birth of the IWW; the second was the birth of the CIO in 1936. Now we need a third. The majority of our people still do not have power.

The obstacles to a new movement for workers' power are formidable. The unrestricted mobility of capital keeps workers on the defensive, but there are subjective as well as material obstacles to the rebirth of a militant workers' movement. The tradition of struggle and self-help which engaged the life of Enrico Porente and thousands of other militants cannot be allowed to die if ordinary workers are to assert themselves and to make their own history. The seeds of a new labor movement lie in the assertions of workers' rights by rank-and-file groups throughout the country. The civil-rights movement, the women's movement, the health and safety struggle, the campaigns to defend the democratic rights of union members, have all vastly expanded our notion of what the labor movement could be.

Bibliographical Essay

This bibliography is a selective listing of the sources I relied on most in writing this book. I hope these references will adequately substitute for footnotes by referring the reader to my sources and also by indicating my enormous debt to other scholars and writers.

GENERAL WORKS

Several studies, which span most of the decades of this century, have proven useful in more than one chapter. In tracing the struggle for control at the workplace, I have relied a great deal on Harry Braverman, *Labor and Monopoly Capital: The Degradation of Work in the Twentieth Century* (1974); Richard Edwards, *Contested Terrain: The Transformation of the Workplace in the Twentieth Century* (1979); and, especially, David Montgomery, *Workers' Control in America* (1979). Most of my statistics come from U.S. Department of Commerce, Bureau of the Census, *Historical Statistics of the United States, from Colonial Times to 1970* (1975), 2 vols. Few surveys cover the entire period since 1900, but Thomas R. Brooks, *Toil and Trouble* (1964, rev. ed. 1971) comes the closest and proved a useful reference. Melvyn Dubofsky, *Industrialism and the American Worker, 1865–1920* (1975) offers a helpful synthesis of the Progressive Era. Jerold S. Auerbach, ed., *American Labor* (1969) provides an excellent range of documentary sources. I have also depended heavily on Rosalyn Baxandall, Linda Gordon, and Susan Reverby, eds., *America's Working Women: A Documentary History* (1976); and on two interpretive surveys of women's history: William H. Chafe, *The American Woman* (1972), and Mary P. Ryan's excellent *Womanhood in America* (1975). Philip S. Foner, *Organized Labor and the Black Worker, 1919–1973* (1974) is the best work on the subject. In interpreting the effects of race and sex

249

segregation on the workers' world, I have benefited from reading Harold M. Baron, "The Demand for Black Labor: Historical Notes on the Political Economy of Racism," *Radical America* V (March–April 1971); and Alice Kessler-Harris, "Stratifying by Sex: Understanding the History of Working Women," in Berenice Carroll, ed., *Liberating Women's History* (1975).

CHAPTER 1

I have learned much about the world of the worker, especially the immigrant worker, from reading Herbert G. Gutman, *Work, Culture and Society in Industrializing America* (1976). The following works helped place immigration in a larger context: Gabriel Kolko, *Main Currents in American History* (1976); Michael J. Piore, *Birds of Passage: Migrant Labor and Industrial Societies* (1979); and Frank Thistlewaite, "Migration from Europe Overseas in the 19th and 20th Centuries," in Herbert Moller, ed., *Population Movements in Modern European History* (1964). C. Vann Woodward, *Origins of the New South, 1877–1913* (1951) is a pivotal study of class, race, and industrialization in the South. For firsthand information on the Pennsylvania steel towns, I used three volumes of the Pittsburgh Survey: Margaret F. Byington, *Homestead: Households of a Mill Town* (1910); Crystal Eastman, *Work Accidents and the Law* (1910); and John A. Fitch, *The Steelworkers* (1911). I also relied on John Bodnar, *Immigration and Industrialization: Ethnicity in an American Mill Town, 1870–1940* (1977); John Bodnar, Michael Weber, and Roger Simon, "Migration, Kinship, and Urban Adjustment: Blacks and Poles in Pittsburgh, 1900–1930," *Journal of American History,* 66 (December 1979); David Montgomery, "Workers and Machine Control in the 19th Century," *Labor History* XVII (Fall, 1971); Daniel Nelson, *Managers and Workers: The Origins of the Factory System in the United States, 1880–1920* (1975); and Katherine Stone, "The Origins of Job Structures in the Steel Industry," *Radical America* VII (November–December 1976). Thomas Bell's novel *Out of This Furnace* (1950) is very evocative in re-creating the immigrant experience in steel towns like Homestead. I am most indebted to the fine work by David Brody, *Steelworkers in America: The Nonunion Era* (1960). Contemporary works relevant to the Lower East Side study were: Robert Hunter, *Poverty* (1904); Jacob Riis, *How the Other Half Lives* (1890); Mary K. Simkhovitch, *The City Workers' World in America* (1917); and John Spargo, *The Bitter Cry of the Children* (1906). Three Jewish novelists offered special insights into life in the Lower East Side: Abraham Cahan, *The Rise of David Levinsky* (1917); Mike Gold, *Jews without Money* (1931); and Anzia Yezierska, *Bread Givers* (1925). Hutchins Hapgood, *The Spirit of the Ghetto* (1905); Mary White Ovington, *Half a Man: The Status of the Negro in New York* (1911); and Allon Schoner's documentary collection, *Portal to America: The Lower East Side, 1870–1925* (1967), include valuable descriptions. I am most indebted, however, to two historical studies: Moses Rischin, *The Promised City: New York's Jews, 1870–1914* (1962); and Irving Howe, *World of Our Fathers* (1976). Alan Trachtenberg's essay on Lewis Hine in *America &*

Lewis Hine (1977) helped me understand Hine's child-labor photos. Several studies by social historians increased my understanding of women's work in the early twentieth century and the role of the family economy: Mary Bular-zik, "Sexual Harassment at the Workplace," *Radical America* XII (July–August 1978); Herbert G. Gutman, *The Black Family in Slavery and Free-dom, 1750–1925* (1976); David M. Katzman, *Seven Days a Week: Women and Domestic Service in Industrializing America* (1978); Susan J. Kleinberg, "Technology and Women's Work; The Lives of the Working-Class Women in Pittsburgh, 1820–1900," *Labor History* XVII (Winter, 1976); Elizabeth H. Pleck, "A Mother's Wages: Income Earning among Married Italian and Black Women, 1896–1911," in Michael Gordon, ed., *The American Family in Social-Historical Perspective* (1978); Judith Smith, "Our Own Kind: Family and Community in Providence," *Radical History Review* XVII (Spring, 1978); Robert W. Smuts, *Women and Work in America* (1959).

CHAPTER 2

The best critical account of labor history in this period is Philip S. Foner, *The Policies and Practices of the American Federation of Labor, 1900–1909*, Vol. III of *History of the Labor Movement in the United States* (1964). Sam-uel Gompers's autobiography, *Seventy Years of Life and Labor* (1925) is a classic defense of "pure and simple unionism." Other relevant biographical material includes: Bernard Mandel, *Samuel Gompers: A Biography* (1963); John Brophy, *A Miner's Life* (1964); James O. Morris, "The Acquisitive Spirit of John Mitchell," *Labor History* XX (Winter, 1979); Mary Harris Jones, *The Autobiography of Mother Jones* (1925); Priscilla Long, *Mother Jones, Woman Organizer* (1976); William D. Haywood, *The Autobiography of Big Bill Haywood* (1929); and Ray Ginger, *Eugene V. Debs: A Biography* (1949). Several studies of nineteenth-century labor history contributed to this chapter, notably: Mary H. Blewett, "The Union of Sex and Craft in the Haverhill Shoe Strike of 1895," and Martin H. Dodd, "Marlboro, Mas-sachusetts, and the Shoemakers' Strike of 1898–1899," *Labor History* XX (Summer, 1979); Alan Dawley, *Class and Community: The Industrial Revolu-tion in Lynn* (1976); Alexander Saxton, *The Indispensable Enemy: Labor and the Anti-Chinese Movement* (1971); Gerald N. Grob, *Workers and Utopia: A Study of Ideological Conflict in the American Labor Movement, 1865–1900* (1961); Victor Greene, *The Slavic Community on Strike: Immigrant Labor in Pennsylvania Anthracite* (1968); Jon Amsden and Stephen Brier, "Coal Miners on Strike: The Transformation of Strike Demands and the Formation of a National Union," *Journal of Inter-Disciplinary History* VII (1977); and Her-bert Gutman, "The Worker's Search for Power", in H. Wayne Morgan, ed., *The Gilded Age: A Reappraisal* (1963). Robert Christie, *Empire in Wood: A History of the Carpenters Union* (1956), was helpful to understand one group of skilled workers and their trade union. I also relied on several articles in David Brody, ed., *The American Labor Movement* (1971), notably, Melyvn Dubofsky, "The Origins of Western Working-Class Radicalism"; Michael

Rogin, "Voluntarism: The Origins of a Political Doctrine"; David Brody, "The Expansion of the American Labor Movement." Andrew Dawson, "The Paradox of Dynamic Technological Change and the Aristocracy of Labor in the U.S., 1880–1914," *Labor History* XX (Summer, 1979), presents an analysis of skilled workers. Bruno Ramirez, *When Workers Organize: The Politics of Industrial Relations in the Progressive Era, 1898–1916* (1978), was an influential study that set labor unionism in the larger political and economic context. Paul B. Worthman and James R. Green, "Black Workers in the New South, 1865–1915," in Nathan I. Huggins, Martin Kilson, and Daniel M. Fox, eds., *Key Issues in the Afro-American Experience,* Vol. II (1971), and Juan Gómez-Quiñones, "First Step: Chicano Labor Conflict and Organizing, 1900–1920," *Aztlán* III (1972), provide information about minority workers and unions. Robin Miller Jacoby, "The Women's Trade Union League and American Feminism," and Elizabeth Jameson, "Imperfect Unions: Class and Gender in Cripple Creek, 1894–1904," in Milton Cantor and Bruce Laurie, eds., *Class, Sex, and the Woman Worker* (1977), offered insights into women's attitudes toward unions. Material on the Industrial Workers of the World was drawn from Joyce Kornbluh, ed., *Rebel Voices: An IWW Anthology* (1964). The definitive account of the IWW's origins and development is Melvyn Dubofksy, *We Shall Be All: A History of the IWW* (1967). Rhodri Jefferys-Jones, *Violence and Reform in American History* (1978), seeks, unconvincingly, to minimize the extent of class violence in this period, but helps explain the nature of anti-union repression. Robert Hoxie, *Trade Unionism in the United States* (1912), is a classic study. John T. Cumbler, "Accommodation and Conflict: Shoe Workers in Twentieth Century Lynn," in *Essex Institute Historical Collections,* CXV (1979); Seymour Martin Lipset, Martin Trow, and James Coleman, *Union Democracy: The Internal Politics of the International Typographical Union* (1956); and Milton Derber, "The Idea of Industrial Democracy in America," *Labor History* VIII (Winter, 1967), were helpful in understanding the workers' struggle for democratic rights.

CHAPTER 3

My interpretation of this period has been strongly influenced by David Montgomery, "The 'New Unionism' and the Transformation of Workers' Consciousness in America, 1909–1922," *Journal of Social History* VII (Summer, 1974), notwithstanding my critical comments, published along with the article. The literature on labor and progressivism is rich, though it rarely puts workers' struggle in the kind of central focus provided by Montgomery. Useful studies include: Graham Adams, Jr., *The Age of Industrial Violence: The Activities and Findings of the United States Commission on Industrial Relations* (1966); Raymond Callahan, *Education and the Cult of Efficiency* (1962); Melvyn Dubofsky, *When Workers Organize: New York City in the Progressive Era* (1968); Arthur Goren, *New York Jews and the Quest for Community: The Kehillah Experiment, 1908–1922* (1970); William Graebner, *Coal Mining Safety in the Progressive Period* (1976); Samuel P. Hays, "The Politics of

Reform in Municipal Government in the Progressive Era," *Pacific Northwest Quarterly* LV (October 1964); Haggai Hurvitz, "Ideology, and Industrial Conflict: President Wilson's First Industrial Conference of October, 1919," *Labor History* XVIII (Fall, 1977); J. Joseph Hutchmacher, "Urban Liberalism and the Age of Reform," *Mississippi Valley Historical Review* XLIX (September, 1962); Michael B. Katz, *Class, Bureaucracy and Schools* (1971); Stanley I. Kutler, "Labor, the Clayton Act, and the Supreme Court," *Labor History* III (Winter, 1962); Marvin Lazerson, *Origins of the Urban School: Public Education in Massachusetts, 1870–1915* (1971); David Thelen, "Social Tensions in the Origins of Progressivism," *Journal of American History* LVI (September 1969); James Weinstein, *The Corporate Ideal and the Liberal State, 1900–1918* (1968); and Robert Wesser, "Conflict and Compromise: The Workmen's Compensation Movement in New York," *Labor History* XI (Summer, 1971). My account of the women clothing workers' struggles relies heavily on Barbara Meyer Wertheimer, *We Were There: The Story of Working Women in America* (1977). Also helpful were Rose Schneiderman, with Lucy Goldthwaite, *All for One* (1967); Alice Kessler-Harris, "Organizing the Unorganizable: Three Jewish Women and Their Union," *Labor History* XVII (Winter 1976); Nancy Schrom Dye, "Creating a Feminist Alliance: Sisterhood and Class Conflict in the New York Women's Trade Union League," *Feminist Studies* II (Nos. 2–3, 1975); and Leon Stein, *The Triangle Fire* (1962). On socialism and the labor movement, I have consulted: Henry F. Bedford, *Socialism and the Workers in Massachusetts, 1886–1912* (1966); Paul Buhle, "Debsian Socialism and the 'New Immigrant' Worker," in William L. O'Neill, ed., *Insights and Parallels* (1973); James R. Green, *Grass-Roots Socialism: Radical Movements in the Southwest, 1895–1943* (1978); Robert Hoxie, "The Rising Tide of Socialism," *Journal of Political Economy* XIX (October 1911); John Laslett, *Labor and the Left: A Study of Socialist and Radical Influences in the American Labor Movement, 1881–1924* (1970); Charles Leinenweber, "Socialists in the Streets: The New York City Socialist Party in Working Class Neighborhoods, 1908–1918," *Science & Society* XLI (Fall, 1977); Bruce M. Stave, ed., *Socialism and the Cities* (1975); and James Weinstein, *The Decline of Socialism in America, 1912–1925* (1967). In addition to Dubofsky, *We Shall Be All*, and Kornbluh, *Rebel Voices*, citied earlier, I used these works on the Industrial Workers of the World: Joseph R. Conlin, *Big Bill Haywood and the Radical Union Movement* (1969); Mike Davis, "The Stop Watch and the Wooden Shoe: Scientific Management and the Industrial Workers of the World," *Radical America* IX (January–February 1975); Philip S. Foner, *The Industrial Workers of the World, 1905–1917*, Vol. IV of *History of the Labor Movement in the United States* (1965); Elizabeth Gurley Flynn, *The Rebel Girl: An Autobiography* (1955); and William Z. Foster, *Pages from a Worker's Life* (1939); James R. Green, "The Brotherhood of Timber Workers, 1910–1913," *Past & Present*, No. 60 (August 1973). Two works on the machine proletariat by IWW theorists were also very helpful: Austin Lewis, *The Militant Proletariat* (1911); and Louis Fraina, *Revolutionary Socialism* (1918). Most of the material on the Lawrence strike was drawn from the sources just listed. John T. Cumbler, *Working-Class Community in Industrial America: Work, Leisure and Struggle in Two Industrial Cities, 1880–1930* (1979); Tamara K. Haraven, "The Laborers of Manchester, New Hampshire, 1912–1922: The Role of Family and Ethnicity in Adjustment to Industrial Life," *Labor History* XVI (Spring, 1975); and Milton A. McLaurin, *Paternalism and Protest: Southern Cotton Mill Workers and Organized Labor, 1875–1905* (1971), provide different perspectives on textile-mill workers. James R. Green and Hugh Carter Donahue, *Boston's Workers: A Labor History* (1979); Frances Russell, *A City in Terror: 1919, The Boston Police Strike* (1975); and Stephan Thernstrom, *The Other Bostonians: Poverty and Progress in the American Metropolis, 1880–1970* (1973), were informative on Boston's workers and politicians. Maurine Greenwald, "Women Workers and World War I: The American Railroad Industry," *Journal of Social History* IX (Winter, 1975), is a revealing case study. The crisis in race relations during the war years is described in Elliot M. Rudwick, *Race Riot in East St. Louis, July 2, 1917* (1964), and William M. Tuttle, Jr., *Race Riot: Chicago in the Red Summer of 1919* (1970). On the problem of race and labor during the Progressive Era, two essays proved valuable: August Meier and Elliott Rudwick, "Attitudes of Negro Leaders Toward the American Labor Movement from the Civil War to World War I," and Marc Karson and Ronald Radosh, "The American Federation of Labor and the Negro Worker, 1894–1949," in Julius Jacobson, ed., *The Negro and the American Labor Movement* (1968). Post-war strikes are well accounted for in David Brody, *Labor in Crisis: The Steel Strike of 1919* (1965), and Harvey O'Connor, *Revolution in Seattle* (1964). H. C. Peterson and Gilbert C. Fite, *Opponents of War, 1917–1918* (1957), and Robert K. Murray, *Red Scare: A Study in National Hysteria, 1919–1920* (1955), are the key studies of anti-radical repression during and after World War II. Ronald Radosh, *American Labor and United States Foreign Policy* (1969), explains how AFL leaders supported President Wilson's wartime military and foreign policy.

CHAPTER 4

Irving Bernstein, *The Lean Years: A History of the American Worker, 1920–1933* (1960), is the definitive work on organized labor in the 1920's, though it does not address broader questions about working-class culture in this period. Several contemporary accounts useful for understanding worker activity in the twenties are: Louis Adamic, *Dynamite!* (1931); J. B. S. Hardman, ed., *American Labor Dynamics* (1928); Sylvia Kopald, *Rebellion in the Unions* (1924); Harold Seidman, *Labor Czars: A History of Labor Racketeering* (1938); and Tom Tippett, *When Southern Labor Stirs* (1931). R. H. Tawney's comments on labor-union bosses are from J. M. Winter, ed., *Essays on History and Society by R. H. Tawney* (1977). On Ford and Fordism, I consulted Antonio Gramsci, "Americanism and Fordism," in *Prison Notebooks* (1971); Jack Russell, "The Coming of the Line: The Ford Highland Park Plant, 1910–1914," *Radical America* XII (May–June 1978); Charles Reitell,

"Machinery and Its Effect upon Workers in the Automobile Industry," in Alfred D. Chandler, ed., *Giant Enterprise: Ford, General Motors, and the Automobile Industry* (1964). On Taylorism, I referred to Lee Galloway, *Office Management* (1918); Jean T. McKelvey, *AFL Attitudes Toward Production, 1900–1932* (1952); and Milton J. Nadworny, *Scientific Management and the Unions, 1900–1932* (1955). Other studies of welfare capitalism are: Stuart Brandes, *American Welfare Capitalism, 1880–1940* (1976); Gerd Korman, *Industrialization, Immigrants and Americanizers* (1967); and Robert Ozanne, *A Century of Labor-Management Relations at International Harvester* (1967). Information on the Hawthorne experiments is drawn from a thoughtful book by Paul Blumberg, *Industrial Democracy* (1968). David F. Noble, *America by Design: Science, Technology, and the Rise of Corporate Capitalism* (1977), is an important study of corporate reform which includes a discussion of the "human engineering" projects of the twenties. Two indispensable studies that show how workers formed groups to resist management control are Susan Porter Benson, "The Clerking Sisterhood: Rationalization and the Work Culture of Saleswomen," *Radical America* XII (March–April 1978), and Stanley B. Mathewson, *Restriction of Output among Unorganized Workers* (1931). Daniel T. Rodgers, *The Work Ethic in Industrial America, 1850–1920* (1978), interprets ideas about work in an earlier period, but his remarks seem appropriate to the twenties. Margery Davies, "A Woman's Place Is at the Typewriter: The Feminization of the Clerical Labor Force," *Radical America* VIII (July–August 1974), examines an important change in women's work that emerged more clearly during the decade. Two valuable community studies of working-class life in the period can be found in the classic study by Robert and Helen Lynd, *Middletown* (1929), and in the more recent study by Sam Bass Warner, Jr., *The Private City: Philadelphia in Three Periods of Its Growth* (1968). Stuart Ewen, *Captains of Consciousness: Advertising and the Social Roots of Consumer Culture* (1976), contains some fascinating suggestions about the effects of consumerism on working-class families. Humbert S. Nelli, *Italians in Chicago, 1880–1930: A Study in Ethnic Mobility* (1970), explains the contradictory effects of Americanization and nationalism on an ethnic group. Felix Frankfurter, *The Case of Sacco and Vanzetti* (1927), and Marion D. Frankfurter and Gardner Jackson, eds., *The Letters of Sacco and Vanzetti* (1928), are excellent contemporary sources. Roberta Strauss Feuerlicht, *Justice Crucified: The Story of Sacco and Vanzetti* (1977), is the best recent history of the case, though it ignores the political importance of anarchism. The third novel in the John Dos Passos trilogy *U.S.A., The Big Money* (1937), offers a profound comment on the Sacco–Vanzetti execution and its meaning for America. John Higham, *Strangers in the Land: Patterns of American Nativism, 1860–1925* (1963), puts the immigration-restriction movement in the context of chauvinistic "tribalism" in the 1920's. Kenneth T. Jackson, *The Ku Klux Klan in the City, 1915–1930* (1967), describes the rise and fall of the K.K.K. and how a middle-class movement won working-class support. A highly important study by Sterling D. Spero and Abram L. Harris, *The Black Worker* (1931), accounts for critical developments in race relations within labor and the working-class generally. Edward Greer, "Racism and U.S. Steel, 1907–1974," *Radical America* X (September–October 1976), analyzes racist use of the job structure. Ricardo Romo, "Responses to Mexican Immigration, 1910–1930," *Aztlán* VI (Summer, 1975), and Paul S. Taylor, *Mexican Labor in the United States* (1932), describe Chicano workers' problems. Activities of the Communist Party are carefully examined in one industry by Roger R. Keeran, "Communist Influence in the Automobile Industry, 1920–1933," *Labor History* XX (Spring, 1979). The party's changing approach to trade-union work is defended in William Z. Foster, *American Trade Unionism: Principles, Organization, Strategy and Tactics* (1947), criticized in James Weinstein, *Ambiguous Legacy: The Left in American Politics* (1975), and set in context by Theodore Draper in two comprehensive volumes, *The Roots of American Communism* (1957) and *American Communism and Soviet Russia* (1960). Foster's own life is partially described in William Z. Foster, *Pages from a Worker's Life* (1939). Frank Marquart, *An Autoworker's Journal: The UAW from Crusade to One-Party Union* (1975), gives a socialist perspective on the early organizing efforts in auto and explains much about the development of the auto workers' union. Fred E. Beal, *Proletarian Journey* (1937), is the revealing autobiography of a tough Communist textile organizer active in the major mass strikes from Lawrence to Gastonia. Liston Pope, *Millhands and Preachers: A Study of Gastonia* (1942), gives insight into the power of class and religion in a mill town torn by a major strike in 1929. Several industrial studies written by Communist Party researchers in the 1920's are still informative, notably, Robert W. Dunn, *Labor and Automobiles* (1929), and Robert W. Dunn and Jack Hardy, *Labor and Textiles* (1931). From the other side of the fence, Selig Perlman's influential *Theory of the Labor Movement* (1928) presents an intelligent defense of mainstream AFL "pure-and-simple unionism."

CHAPTER 5

Irving Bernstein, *The Turbulent Years: A History of the American Worker, 1933–1941* (1970), is the definitive account of unionism in the 1930's, though it generally raises different questions than the ones posed in this account. The author's criticism of Bernstein's work and other interpretations of the period can be found in James Green, "Working-Class Militancy in the Depression," *Radical America* VI (November–December 1972). An important interpretation focusing on the new unions is David Brody, "The Emergence of Mass Production Unionism," in John A. Braeman et al., *Change and Continuity in Twentieth Century America—the 1930's* (1964). Christopher L. Tomlins, "AFL Unions in the 1930's: Their Performance in Historical Perspective," *Journal of American History* LXV (March 1979), accounts for the old unions' revival. Two essays which emphasize the importance of rank-and-file militancy are George Rawick, "Working-Class Self-Activity," *Radical America* III (1968), and Frances Fox Piven and Richard A. Cloward, "The Industrial Workers' Movement," in their *Poor People's*

Movements (1977). Studs Terkel, *Hard Times: An Oral History of the Great Depression* (1970), is an invaluable source. Mary Heaton Vorse, *Labor's New Millions* (1938), gives an exciting firsthand account of CIO organizing drives. Two classic community studies of the Depression's impact are E. Wight Bakke, *Citizens without Work* (1940), and Robert and Helen Lynd, *Middletown in Transition* (1937). On the unemployed workers' movement, I consulted: Daniel J. Leab, " 'United We Eat': The Creation and Organization of the Unemployed Councils in 1930," *Labor History* VIII (Fall, 1967); Roy Rosensweig, "Radicals and the Jobless: The Musteites and the Unemployed Leagues, 1932–1936," *Labor History* XVI (Winter 1975); and "Organizing the Unemployed: The Early Years of the Great Depression, 1929–1933," *Radical America* X (July–August 1976). Frances Fox Piven and Richard A. Cloward, *Regulating the Poor: The Functions of Public Welfare* (1971), offers a convincing interpretation of how the unemployed movement influenced the federal relief program. Firsthand accounts of the important 1934 strikes can be found in Farrell Dobbs, *Teamster Rebellion* (1972), and Mike Quin, *The Big Strike* (1949), on the Minneapolis and San Francisco general strikes, respectively. There is a wealth of autobiographical information on 1930's labor organizers, most of them radicals. Personal histories of Communists include: Len DeCaux, *Labor Radical* (1970); Wyndham Mortimer, *Organize!* (1971); Al Richmond, *A Long View from the Left* (1972). H. L. Mitchell, *Mean Things Happening in This Land* (1979), is the colorful story of the socialist who co-founded and led the Southern Tenant Farmers Union. In addition, there are many valuable oral histories of leftist organizers, including: Alice and Staughton Lynd, eds., *Rank and File: Personal Histories of Working-Class Organizers* (1973); Nell Irvin Painter, *The Narrative of Hosea Hudson: His Life as a Negro Communist in the South* (1979); and Theodore Rosengarten, *All God's Dangers: The Life of Nate Shaw* (1974). "No More Moanin': Voices of Southern Struggle," *Southern Exposure* I, Nos. 3 & 4 (1974), also contains revealing oral histories of labor organizers. Ronald Schatz, "Union Pioneers: The Founders of Local Unions at General Electric and Westinghouse, 1933–1937," *Journal of American History* LXVI (1979), tells about the backgrounds of local union organizers. Saul Alinsky, *John L. Lewis, An Unauthorized Biography* (1949), offers a glowing view of the CIO leader. The book has now been superseded by the definitive study, Melvyn Dubofsky and Warren Van Tyne, *John L. Lewis, A Biography* (1977), which illuminates the whole period. The best study of the Communists' role in the new unions is Bert Cochran, *Labor and Communism: The Conflict That Shaped American Unions* (1977). Less critical, but also informative, is Charles P. Larrowe, *Harry Bridges, The Rise and Fall of Radical Labor in the U.S.* (1972). I have been influenced by Staughton Lynd's interpretation of CP activity in the 1930's: "The Possibility of Radicalism in the Early 1930's: The Case of Steel," *Radical America* VI (November–December 1972), and "The United Front in America: A Note," *Radical America* VII (July–August 1974). Sidney Fine, *Sit-Down: The General Motors Strike of 1936–1937* (1969); the documentary film "With Babies and Banners" (1979); and Ruth McKenney,

Industrial Valley (1939), provided information on the sit-down strikes, while Jeremy Brecher's compelling discussion in *Strike!* (1974) offered a generally persuasive interpretation. Horace R. Cayton and George S. Mitchell, *Black Workers and the New Unions* (1939), testifies to the CIO's importance to black workers and to race relations in union shops. Mark Naison, "Harlem Communists and the Politics of Black Protest," *Marxist Perspectives* I (Fall, 1978), gives a fine sense of the strengths and limitations of the new unionism and labor radicalism in the nation's largest urban black community. Alfred W. Jones, *Life, Liberty and Property* (1941), shows how the CIO helped to create a more liberal and sometimes more radical consciousness among Akron rubber workers. Of the many studies of the New Deal, I found William Leuchtenberg, *Franklin D. Roosevelt and the New Deal, 1932–1940* (1963), most helpful for placing the labor movement in context. Jerold S. Auerbach, *Labor and Liberty: The La Follette Committee and the New Deal* (1966), shows how anti-union repression by employers and local law officers hurt the CIO. Karl Klare, "Judicial Deradicalization of the Wagner Act and the Origins of Modern Legal Consciousness, 1937–1941," *Minnesota Law Review* LXII (March 1978) explains how the courts restricted workers' rights under the National Labor Relations Act. Peter Freidlander, *The Emergence of a UAW Local, 1936–1939* (1975), emphasizes how uneven was the consciousness of various ethnic and work groups in a CIO local. A careful reading of Clinton Golden and Harold Ruttenberg, *The Dynamics of Industrial Democracy* (1942), reveals how power was concentrated in the new CIO unions and how local militants were handled in order to pave the way for smoother collective bargaining. Warren I. Susman, "The Culture of the Thirties," in Stanley Coben and Lorman Ratner, eds., *The Development of American Culture* (1971), suggests how popular culture reflected and encouraged conservative reactions to the Depression.

CHAPTER 6

This chapter is based primarily on the following articles in "American Labor in the 1940's," *Radical America* IX, Nos. 4–5 (1975): Nelson Lichtenstein, "Defending the No-Strike Pledge: CIO Politics during World War II"; Ed Jennings, "Wildcat! The Wartime Strike Wave in Auto"; Martin Glaberman, "Epilogue"; Paddy Quick, "Rosie the Riveter: Myths and Realities"; Augusta Clawson, "Diary of a Woman Welder"; Stan Weir, "American Labor on the Defensive: The 1940's Odyssey,"; and Ronald Schatz, "The End of Corporate Liberalism: Class Struggle in the Electrical Manufacturing Industry." My own overview, "Fighting on Two Fronts: Working-Class Militancy in the 1940's," has been revised somewhat, based partly on unpublished comments and some of the criticisms contained in Joshua Freeman, "Delivering the Goods: Industrial Unionism during World War II," *Labor History* XIX (Fall, 1978), but the major interpretive points have not been changed. My account relies heavily on C. Wright Mills, *The New Men of Power: America's Labor Leaders* (1948), and Art Preis, *Labor's Giant Step: Twenty Years of the*

CIO (1964). My reservations about Preis's Trotskyist interpretation and Mills's top-down approach are presented, along with other critical comments, in James Green, "Working-Class History in the 1940's: A Bibliographical Essay," *Radical America* IX, Nos. 4–5 (1975). Recent work by Nelson Lichtenstein, "Ambiguous Legacy: The Union Security Problem during World War II," *Labor History* XVIII (Spring, 1976), and an unpublished paper on auto-worker militancy in the 1940's have been very informative. The standard scholarly work is Joel Seidman, *American Labor from Defense to Reconversion* (1953). Paul A. C. Koistinen, "The 'Industrial-Military Complex' in Historical Perspective," *Journal of American History* LVI (March 1970), shows how business dominated labor in domestic policy-making during wartime. Sumner Schlicter, *Union Policies and Industrial Management* (1941), and Neil W. Chamberlain, *The Union Challenge to Management Control* (1946), express concern about the new unions' encroachment on management prerogatives. Lawrence Lader, *Power on the Left: American Radical Movements Since 1946* (1979), gives an account of the left's demise in the late 1940's. Joseph Starobin, *American Communism in Crisis, 1943–1957* (1972), discusses party politics during the chaotic 1940's, but Cochran, *Labor and Communism,* cited earlier, is far more revealing as far as unions are concerned. James J. Matles and James Higgins, *Them and Us: Struggles of a Rank-and-File Union* (1974), defends leftist policies in the UE and examines the effects of the purge. K. B. Gilden, *Between the Hills and the Sea* (1954), and Harvey Swados, *Standing Fast* (1970), offer novelistic treatments of labor leftists in the harrowing days after World War II. James R. Prickett, "Communism and Factionalism in the UAW, 1939–1947," *Science & Society* (Summer, 1968), is more critical of the Communists while at the same time exposing the destructiveness of anti-Communism. A social-democratic view which defends the anti-Communist purge in the auto union is to be found in Irving Howe and B. J. Widick, *The UAW and Walter Reuther* (1949). The overall effects of the anti-Communist hysteria in the late 1940's are examined in Richard Freeland, *The Truman Doctrine and the Origins of McCarthyism, Foreign Policy, Domestic Politics, and Internal Security, 1946–1948* (1971), and Athan Theoharis, *Seeds of Repression: Harry S. Truman and the Origins of McCarthyism* (1971). Norman D. Markowitz, *The Rise and Fall of the People's Century: Henry Wallace and American Liberalism, 1941–1948* (1973), is the best account of the 1948 progressive campaign. Staughton Lynd, "A Chapter from History: The United Labor Party, 1946–1952," *Liberation* XVIII (December 1973), shows how CIO activists in Akron broke free of the Democratic Party. The CIO's entry into Democratic Party electoral politics in this period is discussed in Samuel Lubell, *The Future of American Politics* (1951), and J. David Greenstone, *Labor and American Politics* (1969). Victor G. Reuther, *The Brothers Reuther and the Story of the UAW, A Memoir* (1976), offers the inside story of the UAW leaders. It should be read with more critical accounts, including Marquart, *An Autoworkers' Journal,* cited earlier. James Boggs, *The American Revolution: Pages from a Negro Worker's Notebook* (1963), includes a bitter attack on the Reutherized UAW. Charles Denby (Matthew

Ward), *Indignant Heart* (1952, rev. ed. 1978), is an autobiography of another black revolutionary; he is also critical of the UAW, but has many more perceptive comments about race relations. A more general criticism of CIO policy on race is to be found in Sumner Rosen, "The CIO Era," in Julius Jacobson, ed., *The Negro and the American Labor Movement* (1968). Herbert Garfinkel, *When Negroes March: The March on Washington Movement in the Organizational Politics for FEPC* (1959), was informative, as was August Meier and Elliott Rudwick, *Black Detroit and the Rise of the UAW* (1979). The material on A. Philip Randolph is drawn from Jervis Anderson, *A. Philip Randolph: A Biographical Portrait* (1972); William L. Harris, *Keeping the Faith: A. Philip Randolph, Milton P. Webster, and the Brotherhood of Sleeping Car Porters* (1977); and Manning Marable, "A. Philip Randolph and the Foundations of Black American Socialism," *Radical America* XIV (March–April 1980). The following sources included important information on women and work during and after the war: Howard Dratch, "The Politics of Child Care in the 1940's," *Science & Society* XXXVIII (Summer, 1974); Betty Friedan, *The Feminine Mystique* (1966); Chester W. Gregory, *Women and Defense Work during World War II* (1974); Lelia J. Rupp, *Mobilizing Women for War: German and American Propaganda, 1939–1945* (1978); and Lyn Goldfarb, *Separated and Unequal: Discrimination Against Women Workers After World War II, the U.A.W. 1944–1954* (1976). Harriette Arnow, *The Dollmaker* (1954), is a profound fictional treatment of an Appalachian woman's confrontation with wartime Detroit and modern consumer culture.

CHAPTER 7

Howard Zinn, *Post-War America, 1945–1971* (1973), is a fine survey of the period covered in this chapter. There is no comprehensive history of workers since 1950, but two books offer important political perspectives on the labor movement and the workers' world: Stanley Arnowitz, *False Promises: The Making of American Working-Class Consciousness* (1973), and Gil Green, *What's Happening to Labor* (1976). The first expresses New Left pessimism about trade unionism; the second embodies Old Left optimism about the prospects for reform within the unions. Daniel Bell, "The Racket-Ridden Longshoremen" and the "Capitalism of the Proletariat," in *The End of Ideology: On the Exhaustion of Political Ideas in the 1950's* (1961), comment on the problems of corruption and the decline of "social unionism." The discussion of rank-and-file militancy and workers' rights in this chapter was most affected by: Richard Betheil, "The ENA in Perspective: The Transformation of Collective Bargaining in the Basic Steel Industry," *The Review of Radical Political Economics* X (Summer, 1978); Staughton Lynd, "Workers' Control in a Time of Diminished Workers' Rights," *Radical America* X (September–October 1976); Stan Weir, "Class Forces in the 1970's," *Radical America* VI (May–June 1972); and "Rank-and-File Labor Rebellions Break into the Open," in Staughton Lynd, ed., *American Labor Radicalism: Testimonies and Interpretations* (1973). William Serrin, *The Company and the Union: The 'Civilized*

Relationship' of the General Motors Corporation and the United Automobile Workers (1970), helps to explain why the "main drift" in industrial relations is toward accommodation. Dan Georgakas and Marvin Surkin, *Detroit: I Do Mind Dying: A Study in Urban Revolution* (1975), examines the effects of ghetto militancy and black nationalism among production workers. John C. Leggett, *Class, Race and Labor: Working-Class Consciousness in Detroit* (1968), and William Kornblum, *Blue Collar Community* (1974), offer more favorable views of industrial unions as the main integrated institutions in modern working-class life. Leon Stein, ed., *Out of the Sweatshop* (1977), includes moving documents, articles, and interviews from the history of the ILGWU, but should be read together with Herbert Hill's criticisms of the union's racial practices, in Burton H. Hall, ed., *Autocracy and Insurgency in Organized Labor* (1972). The excellent documentary film "The Inheritance" (1964) tells the story of the Amalgamated Clothing Workers' growth as an industrial union. Recent Amalgamated struggles are described in "Here Come a Wind! Labor on the Move," *Southern Exposure* IV (1976), and Mimi Conway, *Rise Gonna Rise: A Portrait of Southern Textile Workers* (1979). Sterling Spero and John M. Capozolla, *The Urban Community and Its Unionized Bureaucracies* (1973), explains the emergence of public-employee unionism, and James O'Connor, *The Fiscal Crisis of the State* (1973), examines the forces that led to expansion and later to crisis in the public sector. C. Wright Mills, *White Collar* (1951), helps us to understand the growth of the clerical sector and the degradation of office work. Jean Tepperman, *Not Servants, Not Machines: Office Workers Speak Out* (1976), shows why women office workers are rebelling. Louise Kapp Howe, *Pink Collar Workers: Inside the World of Women's Work* (1977), and Elinor Langer, "Inside the New York Telephone Company," in William O'Neill, ed., *Women at Work* (1972), explore other kinds of women's work. Ann Oakley, *Women's Work: The Housewife Past and Present* (1974), looks at women's unpaid labor and how it has changed. "Women and the Workplace, The Implications of Occupational Segregation," *Signs* I (1975); "Workers' Reproductive Hazards, and the Politics of Protection," *Feminist Studies* V (Summer, 1979); and Annemarie Troger, "Coalition of Labor Union Women: Strategic Hope, Tactical Despair," and Susan Reverby, "An Epilogue . . . or Prologue to CLUW?" in *Radical America* IX (November–December 1975), analyze crucial issues for modern working women and attest to the impact of women's liberation on the workplace and the unions. An important study, Heather A. Ross and Elizabeth V. Sawhill, *Time of Transition: The Growth of Families Headed by Women* (1975), evaluates some effects of women's increased participation in the labor force. There are many studies of post-war working-class family and community life. The findings of many such can be found in Arthur B. Shostak and William Gomberg, eds., *Blue Collar World* (1964), though they are rendered obsolete in many instances by more recent research. The most useful studies for this book were: Peter Binzen, *Whitetown USA* (1970); Bennett Berger, *Working Class Suburb: A Study of Autoworkers in Suburbia* (1960); Marc Fried, et al., *The World of the Urban Working Class* (1973); Herbert Gans, *The Urban Vil-*

lagers: Group and Class in the Life of Italian Americans (1962) and *The Levit-towners* (1967), and Patricia and Brendan Sexton, *Blue Collars and Hard Hats* (1971). Andrew Levison, *The Working-Class Majority* (1974), links politics and social problems and emphasizes the dignity of working people. None of these studies offers more insight into working-class family problems than Lillian Breslow Rubin, *Worlds of Pain: Life in the Working-Class Family* (1976). Elliott Liebow, *Talley's Corner: A Study of Negro Streetcorner Men* (1967), and Carol Stack, *All Our Kin* (1974), examine the lives of poor black working people, though the insights they provide are not nearly as profound as those derived from black autobiography and fiction since the 1960's. Harold M. Baron, "Racial Domination and Advanced Capitalism," in Richard C. Edwards, Michael Reich and David M. Gordon, eds., *Labor Market Segmentation* (1973), is a very helpful explanation of how racism is used in the modern economy. On work itself, Braverman, *Labor and Monopoly Capital*, cited at the outset, is the most important book. Several earlier studies are also useful: Robert Blauner, *Alienation and Freedom* (1964); Ely Chinoy, *Autoworkers and the American Dream* (1955); Alvin W. Gouldner, *Patterns of Industrial Bureaucracy* (1954) and *Wildcat Strike* (1954); and Harvey Swados, "The Myth of the Happy Worker," in Lynd, *American Labor Radicalism*, cited earlier. All are restricted to factory work, however. For a more varied discussion of work in the 1970's see Studs Terkel's remarkable interviews in *Working* (1972). Also illuminating is the Department of Health, Education and Welfare study, *Work in America* (1973). Daniel M. Berman, *Death on the Job: Occupational Health and Safety Struggles in the United States* (1978), is the best source of information on workers' rights activity in the area of health. The following articles influenced the interpretation of rank-and-file struggles within unions: Matt Rinaldi, "Dissent in the Brotherhood: Organizing in the Teamsters' Union," *Radical America* XI (July–August 1977); John Lippert, "Fleetwood Wildcat," *Radical America* XI (September–October 1977); Jim Green, "Holding the Line: Miners' Militancy and the Coal Strike of 1977–78," *Radical America* XII (May–June 1978); Frank Kashner, "A Rank-and-File Strike at G.E.," *Radical America* XII (November–December 1978); and Stan Weir, "Doug Fraser's Middle Class Coalition," *Radical America* XIII (January–February 1979). The quote from Enrico Porente on the need for a revived labor movement is from Sari Roboff, *Boston's Labor Movement: An Oral History of Work and Union Organizing* (1977). David Montgomery, "The Past and Future of Workers' Control," *Radical America* XIII (November–December 1979), raises important questions about the struggle for control.

Index

Abel, I. W., 214
Abramowitz, Bessie, 76
Adamic, Louis, 120
Adamson Act (1916), 83
Addams, Jane, 43, 44
AFL-CIO, 224, 237, 238, 241, 246
African Blood Brotherhood, 96, 118
Agricultural Adjustment Act (1933), 148, 149, 150
Agricultural Workers Organization (IWW), 91
Akron (Ohio), 87, 135, 151, 153, 159, 184, 195
Alinsky, Saul, quoted, 146
Amalgamated Association of Iron, Steel and Tin Workers, 9, 10, 11, 18, 32, 33, 68, 69, 88, 142, 147
Amalgamated Clothing Workers, 76, 78, 101, 120, 125, 126, 141, 172, 186
Amalgamated Meat Cutters and Butcher Workmen, 64, 120
Amalgamated Wood Workers, 42
American Anti-Boycott Association, 63
American Civil Liberties Union, 148
American Federation of Government Employees, 234
American Federation of Labor (AFL), xi, 32, 33, 34, 36, 41–49 *passim,* 58–69 *passim,* 71, 76, 77, 78, 79, 83, 84, 86, 87, 92, 93, 95, 96, 98, 99, 100–1, 119, 123–24, 127–32 *passim,* 199, 223, 224; Bryan endorsed by, 62–63, 77; craft

unions regain controlling interests in (1920's), 123; Executive Council of, 123, 146, 151, 199; during Great Depression, 141–47 *passim,* 151, 153, 154, 158, 165, 173; industrial unions formed within, 79; members lost by (1920's), 123; membership of (1950), 203; merges with CIO (1955), 222, 224; "new unionism" within, during Progressive Era, 68, 88; racism of (1920's), 125; socialist faction within, 78; Wilson endorsed by, 77, 78, 83, 84, 90; women denied access to internationals of, 126; during World War I, 91; during World War II, 186
American Federation of State, County, and Municipal Employees (AFSCME), 234, 239
American Federation of Teachers, 234
American Labor Party (ALP), 154, 171, 186
American Mining Congress, 82
American Newspaper Guild, 143
American Plan, 119, 120
American Railway Union (ARU), 79
American Telephone and Telegraph Company, 231–32, 241
American Woolen Company, 84, 85, 87
American Workers' Party, 128, 131, 138, 144
Americanization programs, 110, 115, 116, 118
Ameringer, Oscar, 42, 65

263

1946), 93, 94, 95, 194; injunctions against, 64, 89, 121, 198, 210; during Korean War, 204; munitions, in New England (1915), 90; and 90-day cooling-off period, 198; by public employees, 234, 235; Pullman (1894), 62, 79; railroad, 89, 101, 120–21; sit-down, 153, 155, 156, 157, 158, 163, 166, 167; slowdown, 219; in steel industry, 6, 18–19, 31, 32, 33, 67, 69, 94, 97–98, 129, 164, 165, 176, 177, 181, 194, 195, 213; sympathy, 39, 53, 54, 58, 63, 65, 90, 95, 145, 176; in textile industry, 84–86, 93; wildcat, 140, 172, 175, 183, 184, 185, 198, 205, 206, 208, 218, 244, 245; during World War II, 182–85, 196: after World War II (1945–46), 193–94, 195–96, 197, 203

strikebreaking, 46, 50, 61–62, 64, 89, 98, 124–25, 160

Supreme Court, U.S., 45, 63, 121, 126, 165, 240

Susman, Warren, 169

Swope, Gerard, 197

syndicalism, 88–89, 95, 96, 129, 130, 131

Taft, William Howard, 63, 78, 121

Taft-Hartley Act (1947), 150, 174, 198, 199, 200, 202, 204, 208, 210, 213

Taiwan, 223

Tammany Hall, 28, 81, 154

Tawney, R. H., 122

Taylor, Frederick Winslow, 70, 71, 104, 106, 127, 221

Taylor, Myron, 159

Teamsters for a Democratic Union (TDU), 246

Tepperman, Jean, 240

Terkel, Studs, 135, 215, 220

textile industry, 84–86, 93, 131, 132

Thernstrom, Stephen, 81

Thistlewaite, Frank, 7

Thomas, Norman, 171, 207

Thomas, R. J., 184, 185

Thompson, E. P., 21

Thurmond, Strom, 200

Tobin, Dan, 144, 146

Toledo (Ohio), 135, 144

Townsend, Francis, 147–48

Trachtenberg, Alan, 24

Trade Agreement Department of NCF, 88

trade agreements (no-strike contracts), 39, 54, 60, 64, 65, 68, 76

Trade Union Educational League (TUEL), 127, 128, 129, 130

Trade Union Unity League (TUUL), 130, 131, 137, 142, 146, 147

Trautman, William, 65

Travis, Bob, 155

Tresca, Carlo, 85

Triangle Shirtwaist Company, 71, 74, 75

Trotsky, Leon, 96

Trotskyists, 144, 165, 177

Truman, Harry S., 174, 189, 194, 195, 199, 200, 204, 213

Truman Doctrine, 200

Tulsa (Okla.), 119

Tuttle, William M., 99

Unemployed League (1930's), 138, 144

unemployment: during Great Depression, 135, 137, 138, 139, 140; rates of (1960's–1970's), 216; in secondary labor market, 232; technological, 221

United Auto Workers (UAW), 155–60 passim, 163, 165, 176, 177, 178, 180, 184, 185, 186, 188, 190, 193, 194, 195, 200, 203, 204, 205, 207, 208, 218, 220, 223, 224, 237, 239, 247

United Brewery Workers, 65, 78, 123, 146

United Brotherhood of Carpenters and Joiners, 35–42 passim, 61, 78, 88, 123

United Cloth Hat and Capmakers' Union, 29, 72, 93, 95

United Electrical Workers (UE), 163, 188, 190, 194, 195, 197, 200, 201, 202, 203

United Farm Workers, 238

United Fruit Company, 223

United Garment Workers (UGW), 76

United Hebrew Trades (UHT), 29, 30, 47, 72

United Mine Workers (UMW), 50, 51, 53, 56, 57, 58, 78, 82, 87, 93, 101, 104, 121, 122, 123, 127, 129, 130, 140, 141, 152, 160, 171, 181, 182, 195–96, 199, 213, 243, 244, 245, 246

United Rubber Workers (URW), 153, 184

United Shoe Workers (USW), 41

United States Commission on Civil Disorders, 232

United States Industrial Commission, 46, 51, 89, 90